D1169484

Political Ethics
and Public Office

Political Ethics
and Public Office

DENNIS F. THOMPSON

HARVARD UNIVERSITY PRESS

*Cambridge, Massachusetts
and London, England*

Copyright © 1987 by the President and Fellows of Harvard College
All rights reserved
Printed in the United States of America

Library of Congress Cataloging-in-Publication Data

Thompson, Dennis F. (Dennis Frank), 1940–
  Political ethics and public office.

  Bibliography: p.
  Includes index.
  1. Political ethics. I. Title.
JA79.T57 1987   172   86-29482
ISBN 0-674-68605-5 (alk. paper) (cloth)
ISBN 0-674-68606-3 (paper)

Acknowledgments

Most of the chapters of this book differ in substantial ways from the versions in which they originally appeared, and in this process of writing and revising, I have benefited from the help of many hands. Since those who have helped me could not have reasonably foreseen how I might abuse their advice, they escape any blame for what I have written here.

My thinking about political ethics has profited greatly from my collaboration with Amy Gutmann in teaching a course and editing a casebook on ethics and policy, and in writing an article on legislative ethics (from which parts of chapter 4 are drawn). She also suggested specific improvements in each of the other chapters. For general advice about some of the concepts and arguments that recur in the book, I am indebted to Sissela Bok, Joseph Carens, Joel Feinberg, Albert Hirschman, Stanley Kelley, T. M. Scanlon, and Michael Walzer.

Several former students, some already recognized scholars and others soon to be, aided my research and thinking: David Aladjem, Charles Beitz, Mike Comiskey, David Johnston, and Marion Smiley. I received valuable comments on my analysis of paternalism from Gerald Dworkin, and on my discussion of criminal responsibility from Jameson Doig and Christopher Stone. Douglas Arnold, Gary Jacobson, and Nancy Schwarz improved my understanding of legislative behavior, and Michael Doyle and Harold Feiveson corrected some of my mistakes about nuclear deterrence. Trina King prepared the index.

For opportunities to observe political ethics in action (and inaction), I am grateful to the staff of several legislative committees and governmental agencies, especially the Senate Select Committee on Ethics, the Office of Personnel Management, and the Department of Health, Education and Welfare (and later Health and Human Services). During the time in May 1980 that I served as a consultant to HEW on the termination of the DIME, several members of the staff of the department, especially Michael Barth, provided helpful information concerning the experiment. I also learned much from my fellow participants in several projects sponsored by the Hastings Center, especially those directed by Daniel Callahan and Bruce Jennings, in which politicians and academics came together to discuss and write about ethical issues of public life.

The Center for Advanced Study in the Behavioral Sciences in Stanford, the Institute for Advanced Study in Princeton, and the Woodrow Wilson School of Public and International Affairs at Princeton University generously provided intellectual and financial support during the time I was working on the problems that this book addresses. My wife, Carol, provided both kinds of support, and more.

Contents

Introduction

"Politics says: 'Be ye therefore clever as serpents'; but morals adds as a limiting condition: 'and innocent as doves'."[1] So says Kant, who believes that serpents and doves can coexist, and furthermore that the doves will prevail. A more wary philosopher would say: the serpents and the doves shall lie down together, but the doves will not get much sleep.[2] Political ethics—the practice of making ethical judgments about political action—proceeds in this spirit. Properly conceived, it joins ethics and politics without supposing that it can eliminate the conflict between them.

This conflict should not be understood in the conventional way: politics as a realm of pure power, governed by prudential prescriptions, and ethics as a realm of pure principle, ruled by moral imperatives. So described, the opposition makes it easier for the inhabitants of each realm to ignore those in the other. They can speak their own language and live their own lives, oblivious to the judgments of the other. Morality becomes irrelevant to the pursuit of power. Dean Acheson, secretary of state under President Truman, pointedly expresses this widely held view. Recalling discussions among key decision makers during the Cuban missile crisis, he writes that "judgment centered about the appraisal of dangers and risks, the weighing of the need for decisive and effective actions against considerations of prudence . . . Moral talk did not bear on the problem." Acheson told a "respected colleague" who raised moral objections that "on the Day of Judgment his view might be confirmed . . . [but] it was not a view which I could entertain as a public servant."[3]

Such stark opposition fails to capture the complexity of our common moral life in politics. Citizens criticize politicians for violating moral principles, and politicians criticize each other and defend themselves by appealing to the same principles. The criticisms may often be self-right-eous, and the defenses self-serving. But whatever its motives, moral talk makes a difference in politics. At least, many politicians evidently believe that some citizens powerful enough to cause them political trouble think that it makes a difference, and that is enough to assure it a prominent place in political life. More important, ethical judgments not only oppose but also support the claims of politics. Appeals to the public good and the duties of office are no less founded on moral principles than are appeals to individual rights or the obligations of persons. Even Acheson's claim implicitly depends on moral principles to determine what views a public servant may properly entertain.

The conflict between ethics and politics that engages political ethics is better conceived as a conflict between the different demands that ethics itself makes on politics. Ethical principles that apply in almost any context including politics confront those that apply typically in political contexts. In its most general form, ethics requires that persons act on principles that could be accepted universally, that is, by anyone who did not know his or her particular characteristics, such factors as social class, race, sex, and nationality. How this requirement should be interpreted, and whether it should itself be accepted and if so on what grounds, are difficult and unresolved questions in moral philosophy. But even this bare statement of it can produce conflicting imperatives for action in the circumstances of politics.

Politics in part involves action in cooperation with others for common ends. The kind of actions demanded by the principles that govern moral relations in politics may violate the principles that guide all moral relations, including those in politics. Ethics may tell political leaders, for example, not to harm the innocent, but it may also require them to sacrifice innocent lives for the good of the nation. Faced with the plight of the Americans held hostage in Iran, President Carter had to choose between mounting a rescue that posed grave risks to many innocent people (including the hostages and Iranian civilians), or continuing ne-gotiations that threatened the moral credibility of the United States in the future. Although similar conflicts arise in other activities, they are likely to be more intense or more frequent in politics. The scope and structure of modern politics multiply the occasions on which they arise, and magnify the consequences that they produce.

Those conflicts that arise in public office are the principal subject of this book. A political ethics of public office is necessary because so much of modern politics is a mediated politics. Most citizens spend most of their political time choosing and calling to account others who act on their behalf. Many of their political judgments refer to those who hold or hope to hold public office, and to the decisions and policies they make or would make while in office. Although we might wish to see citizens take a more direct part in making these decisions and policies, we cannot afford to ignore the more indirect participation that gives many citizens their only voice in the political process. Even in the small-scale democracies that many democrats would re-create if they could, citizens still delegate much authority to those who hold office and therefore still need principles to judge the exercise of that kind of authority. If political ethics is to play a constructive role in democratic politics, it must help inform these judgments.

A leading theme of this book is the mutual dependency of ethics and democracy. It is a more intimate relationship than moral philosophers or democratic theorists usually suggest. Although ethics and democracy pose serious problems for each other, they also provide each other with some resources for resolving those problems. Political ethics provides support for democratic politics in many ways. It supplies criteria with which citizens can better judge the actions of officials and ascribe responsibility to officials. It suggests the need for devices of democratic accountability, and helps overcome principled impediments to them.

Democratic politics, in turn, supports political ethics. Many of the disputes in political ethics, even about fundamental principles, must be resolved finally or at least partly through some form of the democratic process. This process should not be seen as merely majority rule, or any other set of procedures that reflect only the relative power of some (even all) citizens. Whatever its other elements, an adequate conception of democracy should include, as a necessary condition, collective deliberation on disputes about fundamental values. The democratic process thus must satisfy certain ethical constraints, such as the requirement of publicity, which demands that officials act on principles that can be made known to all citizens. But once these basic constraints are satisfied, the process itself can be the source of ethical judgments.

Problems of the Ethics of Office

The ethical conflicts that officials confront arise from two general characteristics of public office—its representational and its organizational nature. Officials act *for* us, and they act *with* others. The first characteristic generates conflicts between principles of action; the second, conflicts between principles of responsibility.

Because officials act for others, they assume rights and obligations that ordinary citizens do not have, or do not have to the same degree. As agents for citizens, officials are judged by different principles, or principles differently interpreted, than those applied to persons who act for themselves and for less inclusive groups. But officials are also persons, and they have rights and obligations that all citizens share. As persons, they are judged by the same principles that govern all moral relations.

In office, they act on both of these kinds of principles: they are expected to promote the general values we share as well as the distinctive values that inhere in the duties of their particular offices. For the sake of those for whom they act, officials may take their duties to permit or even require them to lie, break promises, and manipulate citizens. These and worse violations of our shared moral principles create what is known as the problem of dirty hands. The problem is familiar, but, as chapter 1 argues, its implications in democratic politics are not. Democracy protects officials from some of the old ways of dirtying their hands, but furnishes some new, perhaps even more pernicious, ways.

Although not strictly problems of dirty hands, most of the other conflicts discussed in the subsequent chapters have the same structure. They are conflicts between two kinds of principles that public offices impose on their occupants. Officials who break the law can sometimes claim immunity on ethical grounds, but other ethical principles deny them that immunity. The duty of legislators is to serve their constituents, but also to serve the public good. All officials have rights of privacy as citizens, but they must sometimes also sacrifice those rights for the good of democratic government. To promote the welfare of some citizens, officials may have to act paternalistically, violating the liberty of those same citizens. In carrying out social experiments in the pursuit of just social policies, officials may sometimes have to use citizens only as means.

The organizational nature of public office creates a different set of ethical problems. Here the difficulty is not which principles to apply, but which agents to apply them to. Like any kind of morality, political ethics assumes that the persons whom it judges can be responsible for the actions for which they are judged. But the structure of public office subverts this assumption. Because officials act together with many others in an organization, we may not be able to ascribe moral responsiblity to anyone for the decisions and policies of government. This is the problem of many hands, and it is the subject of the second chapter.

The problem returns in various guises in the other chapters. Many kinds of practices and policies of government, especially those that extend over time and produce unintended consequences, reveal no fingerprints of responsibility. When we look for officials to punish for the crimes of government, we may not discover any individuals who are sufficiently guilty. When legislators try to excuse their individual failings, they frequently (sometimes legitimately) point to the collective failings of the legislature. When the privacy of a public official is violated by prejudiced public reaction to his homosexual activities, often no identifiable individual, only an indeterminate public, seems to be culpable. When welfare workers encourage clients to change their habits of spending and personal care, they also cause the clients to conform to conventional styles of life. This kind of paternalism may contribute to the erosion of the independence and identity of cultural groups in society, but such harm does not seem fairly attributable to the welfare workers or to their superiors. When a governmental project harms some citizens, even when some official is at fault, we may not be able to decide who is responsible for compensating them.

Political ethics, as presented here, resists the growing tendency to deny responsibility to persons, and the complementary tendency to attribute it to collectivities of various kinds. The aim is to preserve the essentials of the traditional idea of personal responsibility against the pressures of organizational life. But our familiar notions of personal responsibility do not emerge unaltered from the encounter between ethics and politics. Political ethics calls for some changes in our usual ways of ascribing responsibility to agents as much as it suggests changes in our usual ways of understanding the principles on which they should act. We have to abandon some of the individualistic assumptions that guide the way we normally praise and blame persons. Officials should not be judged mainly by the sincerity of their motives or the integrity of their character. They should be held responsible for some decisions and policies that result from defective structures, not only those they could have corrected but also some of those that they could not have corrected. The judgments of political ethics are meant to provide a link between the actions of individuals and the structures of organizations.

Political ethics could in this way help us begin to recapture the sense that men and women make the decisions that constitute our common life. In the mediated and organized dramas of modern politics, persons are more and more often relegated to minor roles. Although this decline is partly the result of changing social conditions, it is reinforced by the way we think about those changes. Much of recent philosophy directs our thinking toward policy outcomes, basic structures, disciplinary networks, and other impersonal entities. This is no less true even of liberal theories that seek justice for individuals; they concern themselves with the persons who are the subjects of the justice, but not with those who exercise the power that impedes or promotes that justice.

No doubt it is important (no less so in political ethics) to understand the aspects of political life that these approaches emphasize. But the exclusive—almost obsessive—emphasis on these aspects impoverishes the language of political judgment. It leaves citizens without any way to connect their criticisms of the structures of government with the actions of some of the persons who ought to be most responsible for trying to change those structures. This connection is important whether one believes that the society is basically just, or that it must be radically transformed. Even if one doubts that public officials can be an instrument for radical change, it does not follow that what public officials decide may be neglected. Their decisions may not make so much difference to those whose social positions insulate them from the direct consequences of the mistakes that officials make. But to most citizens, the everyday actions of officials matter more than the possibilities of social transformation. Political ethics should not ignore such actions, even as it seeks to connect them to the larger structures in which they take place.

This book concentrates on officials of government because their role is more public: their dilemmas are known, and their duties owed, to more citizens. But the conflicts these officials face are not unique. A political ethics of public office reveals general characteristics of judgments about any persons who exercise collective power over citizens, be they corporate executives, medical and legal professionals, or revolutionary leaders. The theory of political leadership that Machiavelli inspired and Weber developed is in this respect a misleading guide to the problems of modern officials. Even the choices that most closely resemble those that preoccupied Machiavelli and Weber—the use of violent means for the public good—are not without their analogues outside of government. And the more typical moral choices of public officials are much less dramatic than this heroic tradition suggests. Just like their counterparts in private organizations, public officials spend most of their time making marginal choices among policies, most of which are likely to have mixed moral results, and most of which are likely to bring only incremental change. Officials compromise more than they agonize.

Because of the scale of modern government and its cumulative influence through time, these marginal choices are often no less morally significant than the more memorable decisions of national security or public safety. A political ethics of public office should bring out the moral significance of the routine in government. We should be concerned not only with large-scale conspiracies of corruption such as Watergate, but also with single-handed acts of negligence such as the failure to criticize the corruption of colleagues. We should scrutinize the actions not only of presidents and their associates, but also of personnel officers and city inspectors. Similarly, we should consider not only policies like nuclear deterrence that affect the fate of the world, but also practices like social experimentation that affect only a few people at a time. Through the multiplying effects of modern politics, the consequences that are significant for some citizens now may become significant for all citizens in the future.

Methods of the Ethics of Office

Political ethics consists of judgments or criteria for making judgments, not particular rules or general theories. It is not a mirror for princes— a handbook to tell officials what decisions to make and what policies to adopt. The criteria should be conceived as a set of factors that citizens as well as officials consider as they deliberate about decisions and policies. Citizens and officials who would use the criteria must work through the analysis from which they come. The analysis—guided by principles and informed by examples—is at least as important as any criteria it yields. Equally so at this stage of the development of political ethics is criticism of misleading assumptions, distinctions, and principles that stand in the way of making ethical judgments about political action.

Although guided by theory, especially moral and political philosophy, political ethics seeks neither to construct a theory of its own, nor even finally to determine the philosophical validity of existing theories. Instead of trying to decide between consequentialist and deontological moral theories, for example, it uses the dispute between them to demonstrate the need for some different, more political, ways of assessing officials and their decisions. Instead of choosing among various strategic doctrines of deterrence, for example, it shows why disagreements about such doctrines call into question our usual standards for judging what officials do.

In formulating the criteria for political judgment, we move back and forth between a proposed criterion and particular cases, modifying the criterion to fit our considered view of the cases, and changing our view of the cases to fit the considered criterion. This process goes on until we arrive at a coherent set of criteria that seems to yield consistent and reasonable judgments about cases. The process resembles what philosophers call the search for a "reflective equilibrium."[4] In political ethics, however, we do not try to trace the criteria back to their foundations in some philosophical theory. We operate with middle-level principles that may or may not be derivable from philosophical foundations. We assume that we can make reasonable judgments without being able to ground them in this way. In a polity marked by disagreement about fundamental values, citizens have to find ways to make reasoned collective judgments without presuming the truth of any single foundational theory. Even if the conflicts with which political ethics deals can be resolved at some fundamental level of philosophy, we still need some middle-level principles to guide our judgments at the level of political action.

The nature of judgment is still not well understood, but some of its characteristics are clear enough. Judgment relates the principles of our theories to the specific circumstances in which we act. It is not quite the union of theory and practice that modern political theorists long for, but it is a prerequisite for forging that union. One of the few philosophers to examine the nature of judgment carefully, Kant saw it as a kind of link between the general and the particular. It is the "faculty of thinking the particular."[5] Judgments about particulars do not always embody a single theoretical principle, and they may not be logically deducible even from a set of principles. But they do impart general significance to the particulars to which they refer: they give the particulars "exemplary validity."[6] Particulars, in turn, give judgments their content: "examples are the go-carts of judgment."[7]

Consequently, political ethics cannot proceed without examples. Through them, the general keeps in touch with the particular. Some of the examples therefore should be real, or at least should represent real situations better than the hypothetical examples that philosophers commonly devise. The reality is important to convey the complexity of the circumstances in which political judgment typically takes place. Examples draw our attention to one of the most difficult but least examined steps in political judgment—identifying the issues themselves. Issues do not usually come with labels announcing themselves as moral dilemmas. Examples also force us to come to terms with the difficulty of employing more than a single criterion or principle to judge political actions.

Most important, examples remind us that the judgments of political ethics must function in nonideal circumstances. Much of political ethics is about what officials should do when things go wrong, and when others do wrong. What may be required when most people do their duty, or when the society is nearly just, is often quite different from what is required when many neglect their duty, or the society is far from just. Also, under these circumstances, we must attend to topics that do not figure so prominently in ideal theory—such topics as excuse, negligence, punishment, disobedience, and compensation.

Because context is so important in political ethics, the examples cited in this book are drawn mostly from American public life of the past several decades. More readers are more likely to share an understanding of their context. Although political ethics certainly could profit by a comparative study of cases in other times and places, it must begin more modestly. The fuller social and historical descriptions that such a study calls for would overwhelm the task of clarifying the elements of the ethical judgments we make about public officials.

In both content and method, then, the political ethics of public office lies between politics and ethics as conventionally conceived. That is a precarious position. The judgments of political ethics are in persistent danger of collapsing into pure prudence on the one side or pure principle on the other. But it is possible to steer a course between them, and even to use the forces of each to help keep the course steady. That is the hope that motivates the theoretical analysis in this book.

It is also a hope acted upon sometimes by some public officials. The leaders of the Tennessee state senate several years ago combined both prudence and principle in their struggle to win passage of a code of ethics.[8] In the wake of political scandal, the leaders decided that the senate needed a tough code of ethics. Senators who did not want the code were reluctant to vote against it in the prevailing climate of reform, but when the code came to the floor, they thought they had found a way out. One senator proposed, as a substitute amendment, the Ten Commandments and the Golden Rule. The leaders knew that in Tennessee no legislator could vote against the Ten Commandments or the Golden Rule, and they scrambled to find a parliamentary compromise that would save the code. The substitute amendment became a regular amendment, and Tennessee became the only state to have a code of ethics that included, along with strong conflict-of-interest provisions, all ten of the Commandments. From Article IV with its detailed procedural rules, the document jumped immediately to Article V, which read in its entirety: "Thou shalt have no other gods before me."[9]

Exploiting the mundane prudence of their colleagues and the divine principles of the amendment at the same time, the senate leaders got their code. Political ethics cannot afford to scorn such tactics. The curious combination of high principle and low strategy deployed by the senate leaders may often turn out to be the best way to further the cause of political ethics in practice. But the content of this code—and that of virtually any code—does not represent the central concerns of political ethics. Those concerns dwell in a world of ethical judgment different from both the detailed regulations and the noble aspirations that constitute most codes and many conceptions of ethics. It is the logic of that world that this book explores.

1

Democratic Dirty Hands

Public officials commit immoral deeds out of greed, the desire for power, or loyalty to family and friends. But the most perplexing kind of immorality in public office displays a more noble countenance. It is that committed, not in the interest of personal goals, but in the service of the public good. The problem of dirty hands concerns the political leader who for the sake of public purposes violates moral principles.

The problem originates in the world of kings and princes, who for reasons of state transgressed the conventional morality of their time. It reappears in our time most dramatically in the dilemmas of revolutionaries. In Sartre's play that gives the problem its modern name, it is the leader of the revolutionary party who has "dirty hands right up to the elbow."[1] More recently, some political theorists have suggested that the leaders of established democratic states may have hands that are no less dirty. These seemingly conventional politicians also break the rules of conventional morality. They lie to protect national security, and they stand ready to order death and destruction in a nuclear exchange.

These theorists are right to see dirt on the hands of the officials of modern democracies, but the theorists fail to appreciate the difference that democracy makes. Because democratic officials are supposed to act with the consent of citizens, they face a further dilemma. If they gain that consent, they are not uniquely guilty in the way that the problem in its traditional form presumes. If they act without that consent, they not only commit a further wrong (a violation of the democratic process), but they also cast doubt on the justifiability of the decision itself. They undermine some of the conditions of moral discourse that are necessary to judge the morality of any decision in a democracy. In this way, the

---

11

traditional problem of dirty hands becomes a modern problem of democratic dirty hands. The transformation reveals some important implications for the decisions that officials make and the process by which they make them.

The Persistence of the Problem

In its classic formulation in the thought of Machiavelli, the problem of dirty hands poses a conflict between two moralities—one suited for ordinary life, the other for political life. On the question of whether this conflict can be resolved, Machiavelli is ambiguous in a way that foreshadows the subsequent dispute about the problem of dirty hands. Sometimes Machiavelli suggests that political morality not only differs from, but in its sphere completely replaces, ordinary morality. The good of the state (and the virtue of the prince) calls for "something resembling vice," while "something resembling virtue" may bring about its ruin.[2] On this view, political morality fully justifies the (apparent) immorality of the means necessary to secure the ends of the state. "When the act accuses, the result excuses."[3] When a politician faces a conflict between ordinary and political morality in any particular case, he can resolve it completely by applying the appropriate principles of political morality. In this mood, Machiavelli shares with many modern moral philosophers what may be called a coherency view of the problem. There is no ultimate conflict between principles. Either one coherent morality applies to both private and public life, or one applies exclusively to private and the other exclusively to public life.[4]

But Machiavelli also suggests a different, more disturbing, view. It implies a basic incoherency in political morality: the conflict between moral principles persists permanently in the political sphere. The politician cannot escape the conflict either by relegating principles to their proper spheres, or by appealing to some higher principle for final adjudication. On this view, the prince is caught between two moralities. He lies and murders for the good of the state, but he also knows that these actions are wrong, and that, though they may be excused, they are never justified. Cruelty, however necessary, is still an "evil in itself."[5] That is why Machiavelli admonishes the good prince to "learn how not to be good."[6] The paradox that Machiavelli leaves implicit becomes explicit in modern writers who take the problem of dirty hands most seriously.

In the best recent formulation, Michael Walzer argues that "a partic-ular act of government may be exactly the right thing to do in utilitarian terms and yet leave the man who does it guilty of a moral wrong."[7] The point is broader than the reference to utilitarianism suggests. The contrast is between consequentialism, which evaluates an action wholly from an impersonal perspective on the states of affairs the action produces, and deontology, which judges an action at least partly from the perspective of the agent who does it.[8] Walzer accepts the necessity of consequentialist action in politics, but resists the consequentialist assumption that what is necessary is justified.

Against the deontologist who holds that a politician should never violate moral rules even to achieve a better outcome, Walzer suggests that we should "not want to be governed by men who consistently adopted that position."[9] They would keep their hands clean at the expense of the good, perhaps even the survival, of the rest of us. If the stakes are high enough, the rules must be broken, and in such circumstances the con-sequentialist prescription for action is correct.

But against the consequentialist who holds that this prescription ex-hausts the content of moral judgment, Walzer insists that the politician remains guilty for breaking the rules. It is a "crucial feature of our moral life" that when we break a moral rule, we know we have "done something wrong even if what we have done was also the best thing to do on the whole in the circumstances."[10] That lingering sense of wrongness should be preserved in our moral judgment of the politician who violates moral principles. If the politician fails to feel guilty, we judge him more severely, and conclude that he should be punished. Even if he does feel guilty, we may still insist on punishment, Walzer suggests, since the guilt must be socially expressed so that we can know that the penalty fits the offense.[11] Since the paradox cannot be resolved, the critical problem is to discover some form of social acknowledgment for the necessary wrong that pol-iticians inevitably do.

The complete moral judgment we make of the politician thus combines consequentialist and deontological elements. The prescription for action is consequentialist; the evaluation of the motivation is deontological. It should not be surprising that this unstable mixture is in constant danger of dissolution, as each element seeks to expel the other. Neither deontologists nor consquentialists succeed in dissolving the paradox of dirty hands, but it must be understood differently from the way in which either usually presents it.

The deontological challenge to the paradox takes two different approaches—one denying the necessity of immoral means to achieve good ends; and the other the immorality of the means necessary to achieve them.[12] Those who take the first insist that the good that political leaders achieve does not require the wrongs they commit. The belief that good ends require evil means is the result of an historical illusion that comes from looking at the good through the evil that produced it, as Hegel did in justifying Napoleon's deeds, and from assuming (again with Hegel) that history could not have happened any way other than it did.[13] Once we expose the sources of this illusion, it is said, we can see that there might have been other, morally acceptable, ways to achieve the good results of history.

Exposing the causes of the illusion is easier than escaping the problem of dirty hands. To escape the problem we would have to assume that there are always moral means available to achieve good ends. This assumption, no less than Hegel's contrary assumption, relies on historical necessity: history *must* offer good alternatives to achieving any good end that agents achieved through immoral means. Quite apart from the implausibility of any doctrine of historical necessity, we cannot avoid the problem by any appeal to how history turned out. The problem confronts a political leader at a particular time, and he must choose means on the basis of the knowledge available at the time. Even if it turns out that there was a moral alternative that would have produced the good end, he cannot be expected to choose it unless it is also the alternative that appears at the time to have a reasonable chance of achieving that end.

Instead of hoping that history somehow rescues politicians from the clutches of dirty hands, some deontologists suggest that their morality itself dissolves the dilemma. They argue that deontological principles, properly understood, do not prevent politicians from using many of the means that consequentialism would prescribe. Defending deontological principles in the form of what he calls common morality, Alan Donagan argues that believers in the paradox of dirty hands oversimplify those principles.[14] The principles are not, or need not, be so absolutist as they are usually interpreted.

Donagan reconsiders Walzer's example of the honest politician who in order to win the election must make a corrupt deal with a ward boss to award a construction job to his favorite contractor. If the election is important enough and if the indirect effects of the deal are limited, Walzer suggests that we should approve of this politician's making the deal. Donagan agrees that we should accept the deal but denies that this approval contradicts common morality. In this case, a principle resembling that of self-defense warrants the bribe. It would be wrong to initiate corruption, but it is "not wrong to defend yourself by means of corruption against corruption already initiated by others."[15] The fundamental principle of common morality requires that we respect human beings as rational creatures, but that does not mean that we cannot defend our rights against those who do not respect ours.[16]

It is surely correct to look for principles that can accommodate the necessities of political life. No plausible political morality should leave a politician defenseless against the immoral actions of others. But the principle of self-defense is misapplied here. The honest politician can best defend himself against corruption in these circumstances by not running for office at all. If it is his career that is supposed to be the object of the protection, then we should want to know whether the promotion of his career is on balance good for society, taking into account the corruption that is required to promote it. But furthering his career, however desirable, is not a matter of defending his rights, or even of defending the rights of citizens who might wish to further his career. If the deal is worth making, it is because on balance it promotes the public good, including the general welfare as well as the system of rights. Our approval of it should ultimately rest on an estimate of the consequences for society as a whole.

Insofar as deontologists can give a plausible reason for approving of deals or similar morally suspect actions, the reason turns out to be consequentialist. The approval cannot eliminate the deontological wrong, and the paradox persists, at least for anyone who wishes to preserve a distinctive, independent basis for deontological principles. Notice, however, that the decision about whether the deal is justified is one that neither the politcian nor his supporters have the final right to make. Citizens, it must be assumed, would approve the deal, and if so they would seem to relinquish any right to punish the politician. The paradox begins to slip away, but (as we shall see in more detail later) for democratic, not deontological, reasons.[17]

15

Consequentialists are no more successful in dissolving the paradox, though their attempts are not so easily dismissed as is often assumed. Consequentialists recognize that sometimes public officials should feel guilty or suffer punishment for breaking a moral rule even if they act rightly on the whole. But consequentialists deny that there is any paradox since they believe that their theory can justify any guilt or punishment that is appropriate. It is socially useful for the officials to feel guilty and suffer punishment so that they and others will be reluctant to break the rule on the (more common) occasions when the consequences do not justify breaking it.

The objections that are usually raised against this consequentialist justification do not seem compelling. The guilt and punishment are not, as critics imply, unjustly imposed, as they would be if they were imposed on ordinary citizens. To accept public office is to accept, along with greater benefits, greater burdens than those of ordinary life. Among the burdens to which officials could be assumed to consent is the risk of punishment for actions that are in fact justified. Neither is the utility of the guilt necessarily destroyed if the guilt is in fact merely useful. It may be true that politicians who regard the guilt as merely useful are not likely to feel guilty.[18] But consequentialists could, and generally do, believe that politicians themselves should not be (pure) consequentialists. The moral beliefs that politicians hold could include deontological principles. If politicians do not themselves believe that consequentialism is true, then the guilt they feel and the punishment they endure are from their perspective more than merely useful.

The consequentialists' success in finding a place for guilt comes at a price, however. The success depends on creating a sharp separation between the reasons that motivate persons and the reasons that justify their actions. However justified politicians may be in breaking a moral rule, they continue to believe that they have done wrong because they are motivated to accept the rule. In itself, the separation between justification and motivation need not be objectionable. Consequentialists at least since Henry Sidgwick have recognized the need for such a separation. They have plausibly denied that the moral principles in which people believe must be the same as the principles on which consequentialism rests.[19]

But then the question arises: *who* should believe consequentialism? If the answer must be that only a few perceptive persons (notably, consequentialist philosophers), that does not necessarily embarrass consequentialism as a moral theory. But the answer disqualifies it as a political theory of democracy. For its point as such a theory should be not only to understand but to influence political practice. Even if consequentialists conclude that politics should not be practiced in consequentialist terms, they do not in a democracy have the authority to impose that conclusion on other citizens. They would have to persuade citizens of the rightness of that conclusion through the democratic process. That process, properly conducted, presupposes publicity: that participants acknowledge the principles they espouse—in this instance, the principles of consequentialism. Otherwise, the process could produce policies based on principles that most participants have no opportunity to challenge. The coercive power of the state would be enlisted to enforce principles to which most citizens could not consent or from which they could not dissent. But if consequentialists were publicly to acknowledge their principles, they would undermine the separation of justification and motivation on which their denial of the paradox of dirty hands depends.

The Limits of Democratic Distance

The paradox stands against both deontological and consequentialist efforts to dissolve it—but only when it is firmly rooted in a democratic politics. Its defense against the deontologist appeals to a judgment about the public good that citizens have a right to make, and its defense against the consequentialist invokes principles that politicians share with citizens. Both defenses thus assume that citizens participate in the political decisions that the paradox poses—at least that citizens have the opportunity to approve or disapprove, on principled grounds, the decisions or the officials who make them. Yet the way the paradox is presented obscures this democratic dimension.

It is true that in the democratic version of the paradox the politician, unlike Machiavelli's prince, stands accountable to citizens. But this accountability is understood in a way that preserves and even reinforces the moral isolation of the politician. More than a trace of the Machiavellian origins of the paradox remain in its image of a lonely leader making hard choices. It is he who dirties his hands, and it is he whom we would punish if we could. Walzer writes as if the difficulty of punishing the dirty-handed politician were mainly a problem of finding an authority to whom to entrust the task. If we could discover a way to enforce the

17

moral rules against the politician, then we should simply "honor the man who did bad in order to do good, and at the same time we would punish him. We would honor him for the good he has done, and we would punish him for the bad he has done."[20]

What this conception overlooks is that the bad that the official does, he does not only for us, but with our consent—not only in our name but on our principles. It is not clear, therefore, that as citizens we have any grounds for punishing him, or even for regarding him as particularly guilty. If he acts contrary to the fundamental principles of citizens, or if he acts beyond the legitimate scope of office, his action could be treated as a standard case of political misjudgment or official misconduct, and citizens could punish him accordingly. But it is essential to the paradox that the official decides correctly and legitimately, and citizens therefore cannot claim that he should have decided differently. How then can they criticize, let alone punish, him for deciding the way he did?

Perhaps citizens do not have to impose the punishment: politicians could punish themselves in some public way. The most familiar (though hardly the most frequent) social expression of such self-inflicted punishment is resignation from office. Like Weber's suffering servant, the dirty-handed politician courageously accepts the guilt himself but unlike that servant, he also steps down from public office. The resignation of Secretary of State Cyrus Vance exemplifies such an action. Vance announced his resignation in the spring of 1980 after the abortive raid to rescue the Iranian hostages. Before the mission began, he had told President Carter that whatever the outcome he would leave the government. He resigned not only because he disagreed with Carter's plan, but also—let us assume—because he had deceived our allies.[21] For nearly two months, while the U.S. military prepared for the raid, Vance supposedly told officials in the governments of the European allies that if they cooperated in imposing economic sanctions on Iran the United States would not undertake military action. U.S. officials hoped that the deception would encourage Iranian officials to believe that military action was not imminent, and thereby increase the chances of success of the raid.

Vance's conduct in some respects may serve as a model of how a dirty-handed politician should act. If we accept (for the sake of analysis) the decision to risk innocent lives to save the American hostages, the deception seems a justifiable part of the means of implementing the decision. Had Vance declined to dirty his own hands by refusing to deceive the allies, he would have sabotaged the strategy and increased the risk to American lives mainly for the purpose of keeping his own hands clean. It mattered, moreover, that it was Vance, a man with a high reputation for honesty, not just any official, who carried out the deception. Vance played his part, but as soon as he could without undermining the decision, he accepted his "punishment" by leaving office.

But the question remains: why should Vance suffer any punishment or guilt at all? There may have been good reasons for him to resign— his loss of credibility in diplomatic circles, or his disagreement with the policies of the administration. But these reasons provide no basis for the moral condemnation that punishment or even guilt implies. The fact that many people would regard his leaving office as an act more deserving of honor than blame casts further doubt on any effort to make resignation serve the function of punishment. It is not clear that even the European officials whom he allegedly deceived could legitimately criticize him since many agreed that they would have done the same for their governments. Even on the assumption that the deception is a wrong that calls for social recognition, the problem remains that citizens themselves—the only judges who have the final authority to condemn the deceiver—must be presumed to endorse the deception.

It might be suggested, nevertheless, that officials stand closer to the immoral action and are therefore more tainted by it than citizens are. There is something specially bad about the doing of the action, or at least about the kind of person who is capable of doing it.[22] This seems most plausible with respect to wrongs, such as justified killing, that are rare in private life. Citizens may regard differently someone who is capable of killing and someone who is capable of lying, even if citizens recognize the necessity of both actions in public life.

Still, why should officials who use violence be viewed differently from citizens who approve its use? The difference may rely on the greater revulsion that most people feel toward the idea that they might personally kill another person than toward the idea that they might bring about that person's death. If so, the difference would have some moral basis, at least for moral positions that respect a fundamental distinction between acts and omissions.[23]

Since most official violence is not simply brought about but is deliberately caused, however, the difference between officials and citizens cannot rest on that distinction. It would have to depend on a distinction among acts themselves. One such distinction turns on psychological distance. The more psychologically remote one is from the evil deed, the less morally culpable one is. The judge who imposes the death sentence suffers less opprobrium than the executioner who carries it out. The bomber pilots who loyally implemented the British government's policy of terror bombing in World War II were denied the honors granted other soldiers and the politicians who ordered the bombing.[24] Inside the U.S. military today, most regular officers eye with suspicion the men of Delta Force and the Green Berets, who are recruited and trained to carry out missions that may call for morally disagreeable actions in face-to-face encounters. As an Air Force colonel explains, special operations forces are regarded as "a bit wild, 'good killers, but bad officer candidates'."[25]

The examples that illustrate this psychological tendency, however, also reveal its moral inadequacy, especially for judgments about politics. In large-scale organizations, those who are most distant from the action are often the most responsible for it. If anyone should have dirty hands, it should be the top officials who make the dirty decisions.[26] If we regard a policy as morally unjustified, as did many the bombing of North Vietnam, we do not blame the soldiers who execute it more than the officials who plan it, if we blame the soldiers at all. A fortiori, if the policy is justified but requires immoral means, we should not blame those who employ the means more than those who decide to employ them. We are not obligated to choose as friends the doers of dirty work, but neither are we entitled to treat them as specially guilty persons for their part in the policies that their superiors make and that citizens approve.

Yet another sense of moral distance might be proposed to distinguish the guilt of high-level officials from that of citizens. Unlike citizens, those officials, day after day, confront the immediate effects of their decisions. If they do not see the effects firsthand, they hear about them in vivid detail. In this respect, their situation resembles that of the lower-level officials who carry out the policies. But unlike the lower-level officials, they may believe, often correctly, that they contribute more than anyone else to effects they observe, and could do something to try to prevent the effects. We may suspect that anyone who can continue in such a position regularly making decisions that cause suffering, however necessary, is morally callous. We may also fear that anyone who can continue to order death and destruction when it is necessary is more likely to order it when it is not necessary.[27] For these reasons, public morality may come to condemn the officials who make the dirty-handed decisions more than it condemns the officials who implement them or the citizens who approve them. If so, it would be a dubious public morality. It would give psychological proximity too prominent a place in judging public officials. We should not want the moral sensitivity of high-level officials to vary with the immediacy of their experience of immoralities. Some of the worst wrongs, especially in politics, are the most remote in time and place.

Nor would it be necessarily desirable to try to make officials more aware of the wrongs they commit by confronting them more directly with the harms they cause. It was often said of the decision makers who planned and ordered the bombing during the Vietnam War that their distance from the damage they caused kept them from considering more humane policies. But when McGeorge Bundy, President Johnson's national security assistant, went to Vietnam in February 1965 to review the military situation in person, many of his associates (including the president) believed that he became more hawkish.[28] While he was there, the Vietcong attacked the base at Pleiku, killing eight Americans and destroying several aircraft. Before his trip, speaking regularly by phone from Washington to officials in Vietnam, Bundy had seemed, so the officials had thought, sympathetic but somewhat cool, as if he did not entirely believe that the situation was as bad as they said it was. Now, on the ground in Vietnam after an attack, he immediately ordered a retaliatory strike and helped initiate a new policy of reprisal strikes that soon led to a major increase in bombing, the so-called second phase, known as Rolling Thunder.[29] At Pleiku, those "who worked for him and with him were surprised by the intensity of his feeling (as if he had blown his cool); since this sort of thing had been going on for some time, had not Washington realized that there would be killing?"[30]

Bundy's reaction is hardly unique among public officials in these circumstances.[31] Nor is it illegitimate in itself. To react emotionally to the killing of one's fellow citizens may be quite appropriate. The point is rather that proximity may encourage, as much as discourage, officials in the use of violent means. If an immediate experience gives rise to an intense desire to stop the killing, that desire can lead to a decision to order more bombing as easily as to a decision to stop the bombing. If proximity does not and should not necessarily produce reluctance to use violent means, then we cannot condemn officials just because they respond violently in close encounters with violence.

The Assumption of Accountability

So far we have found no basis for distinguishing officials from citizens in a way that the problem of dirty hands requires. The problem presupposes that officials stand in some distinctive relation to the wrongs that politics sometimes necessitates. But as long as officials are assumed to act with the democratic approval of citizens, officials cannot be burdened with any greater responsibility than citizens. Although the paradox would remain—politicians must sometimes do wrong to do right—the problem of dirty hands would no longer be a problem about how citizens should regard political leaders who commit wrongs. It would turn into a problem about what citizens and their leaders should do for the victims of their collective wrongs. The central questions would concern compensatory justice—for example, the nature and amount of reparations due the persons harmed by certain social policies. Focusing more attention on these questions would not be undesirable. Questions of compensation are important, and deserve more discussion than they often receive.[32] But if we were to permit such questions to exhaust the problem of dirty hands, we would miss an even more significant question that the problem, properly understood, poses for a democratic society.

What has so far prevented us from distinguishing officials from citizens with respect to dirty-handed decisions is the implicit assumption that in a democracy these decisions would not be justified in the absence of the approval of citizens. As used in the argument, the assumption seemed, and generally should be considered, uncontroversial. It could be satisfied by only minimal forms of democracy: for example, some kind of fair election in which citizens have a chance to accept or reject the officials who have the power over dirty-handed decisions. But there is a subset of dirty-handed decisions that by their nature cannot meet even this minimal criterion—those that cannot be made public. If citizens cannot know what officials have done, they cannot, in any substantial sense, approve or disapprove of their actions. In the case of these decisions, the hands of officials would be dirty in a way that the hands of citizens are not, even if officials act in the name and for the benefit of citizens.

These decisions should be understood as those that cannot be made public without defeating their own purposes, not simply those that are not made public through some abuse of office or failure of the democratic process. They are decisions that officials make in secret not because citizens are apathetic or ignorant, and not because officials seek to cover up their mistakes or misfortunes. Officials cannot decide openly because what they decide would fail if it were known, even if it were approved by citizens. President Carter could not have announced the decision to rescue the hostages in Iran without increasing the risk of its failure. These, then, are decisions that have, as a necessary condition of their efficacy, secrecy that anyone who accepted the decision would approve. Their legitimation would be self-defeating because publicity would preclude their success. In this class of decisions, the problem of dirty hands would persist. Officials must do wrong in order to do right, and they cannot claim that citizens endorse what they do because citizens cannot know what they do.

Furthermore, because government conducts so much of its business in the open, nondisclosure may not be enough to protect the secrets. This is why the vices of concealment are so commonly implicated in dirty-handed decisions. Officials may have to resort to deception and manipulation to keep the decisions secret. If officials do not dirty their hands in making the decision itself, they are likely to do so in trying to keep it secret. When both the decision and the effort to conceal it require morally questionable means, we have a case of doubly dirty hands. In the hostage crisis, one wrong—Vance's alleged deception—is added to another—the risk to innocent lives that the rescue posed. But with either kind of wrong, we have a problem of democratic dirty hands.

The most familiar instances of decisions that involve concealment do not seem inherently problematic. Officials cannot publicize certain decisions about military preparations, such as troop movements or the methods of operation of intelligence agents. They cannot describe plans for undercover surveillance of criminal conspiracies, or announce enforcement tactics such as unmarked police cars. They may have to conceal decisions about certain kinds of economic policies, such as plans for devaluation, or information about economic conditions, such as the extent of debt during a fiscal crisis.

The decisions in these examples could perhaps be treated as general types of policies that citizens could approve under assumed conditions of informed and disinterested judgment. The type of policy would thus be legitimated through some form of hypothetical consent. But the actual instances of the type cannot be so readily treated in the same way. For many of the policies, what is legitimately controversial is their application in particular circumstances. It is possible to imagine that reasonable citizens would consent to the necessity of covert operations in certain circumstances (for example, to prevent nuclear terrorism), but it is harder to see how such consent could be presumed in many of the more common cases in which such operations are likely to be contemplated (for example, to support friendly or subvert hostile governments). The justifiability of such policies depends on judgments about the value of the ends they promote (compared to other ends and compared to the disvalue of the means necessary to promote them). These judgments are usually too contestable to be resolved through assumptions about human nature or shared beliefs and interests under plausible hypothetical conditions.[33]

If the examples do not appear troublesome, it is because we assume that in each instance of the policy citizens have ways of *actually* holding officials accountable for the decisions. Citizens may not be able to know about the specific decision at the time, but they can review the decision at a later date, or they can approve in advance the general policy of which the decision is part, or they can authorize an intermediary representative to oversee the decision for them.

These three methods—retrospection, generalization, and mediation—are ways of reconciling secrecy with democracy. If they were fully adequate, they would eliminate the problem of dirty hands even in its revised form. If they are interpreted more rigorously than is usually done, they go some way toward solving that problem. But insofar as they fail, we are forced to choose between dirty-handed policies and democratic processes.

Reviewing the Decision

First, consider retrospective accountability. Its difficulty is that by the time citizens have a chance to review the decision, the damage may have been done. Many decisions, especially those that order military action or diplomatic intervention, have irreversible consequences. These consequences include not only direct harms such as the death of civilians or the fall of governments, but also indirect effects such as the creation of precedents and commitments. Because of these indirect effects, citizens may find themselves forced to continue a policy they dislike and would have rejected, had they known earlier about the decision that initiated it.

But even when the effects of the decision are more isolated and even where citizens might be expected to approve of the decision, the retrospective judgment may still come too late to have any political significance. A case of justified deception illustrates the difficulty. At a press conference in November 1962, shortly after the Cuban missile crisis had passed, President Kennedy denied that any matters other than Cuba had been discussed in negotiations with Soviet officials during the crisis.[34] But in fact Kennedy not only promised Khrushchev that the United States would not invade Cuba if the Soviets withdrew their missiles, but also assured him through "back-channel" communications that the United States would remove its missiles from Turkey. This assurance was not strictly a deal, since well before the crisis (as the Soviets were told) Kennedy had ordered these missiles removed.

If Kennedy could have spoken only to the American people, he might have been able to explain the negotiations honestly (though even telling Americans the truth could have caused many to believe falsely that the United States had made a deal under pressure). But Kennedy had to calculate the effects of his answer on the Turkish and especially the Soviet leaders. It was quite possible, for example, that Khrushchev had managed to persuade his hard-line colleagues to accept the settlement by telling them that Kennedy had in fact made a deal. A complete report on the negotiations, candid enough to persuade Americans, could have undermined Khrushchev's precarious position with his suspicious colleagues, re-igniting the crisis.

Kennedy's deception served an important end that most citizens would accept. No other less deceptive alternative (such as "no comment") was available. The intended victims of the deception were potential enemies, not U.S. citizens. It was an isolated instance rather than part of a permanent practice. Considerations such as these might very well have justified Kennedy's deception during the crisis and for some time afterward.

Yet neither the deception nor the agreement that it concealed was made public until years after the need for secrecy had passed. The president's advisers reported the episode publicly for the first time in a magazine article in 1982—long after they and their party had left office.[35] Not only could citizens no longer effectively sanction those who made the decisions or those who engaged in the deception, citizens could not call for timely measures to change how officials might conduct themselves in similar crises in the future. Thus, in those limited circumstances in which deception is justified, officials should reveal the deception as soon as the end that justified it has been accomplished and no further equally important ends would be defeated by the revelation. If officials have the discretion to deceive, they also have the duty to disclose the deception. The license to deceive expires.

Strengthening the standards for justifying deception (and other morally suspect means) in this way could overcome some of the difficulties of retrospective judgment. But for many decisions, especially those that cause major irreversible changes, judgment after the fact often leaves citizens with the opportunity to express regrets, not with a chance to influence events.

Generalizing the Decision

The possibility of some kind of prior judgment is therefore preferable as a method of accountability for dirty-handed decisions. Generalization is meant to serve this function. If a particular decision cannot be disclosed in advance, the general type of decision can be discussed publicly, its justifiability in various hypothetical circumstances considered, and guidelines for making it in those circumstances formulated. The paradigm is the policy of deploying unmarked police cars. It would obviously defeat the purpose to decide in open debate when and where the cars will patrol, but the policy itself, as well as constraints on it, can be publicly debated and promulgated.

The trouble is that the paradigm is of limited applicability. The policy has two characteristics which, though not unique, are shared by few other deceptive policies. First, the means are intended to apply more or less equally to all citizens within a given jurisdiction. The question of who should be the target of the enforcement is not critical. Second, the end can secure wide acceptance not only when stated in general terms, but also when applied in particular circumstances. That speeding should be an offense and what should count as speeding, once stated in advance, can in most circumstances be interpreted in a relatively objective way.

Not even all cases of covert law enforcement, the cases that one would expect to resemble the paradigm most closely, have these two characteristics. "Operation ABSCAM," the massive investigation of official corruption begun by the FBI in 1978, is in these respects more typical of the undercover methods that police in this country have increasingly employed in recent decades.[36] For nearly two years, some one hundred FBI agents took part in the investigation, which sought to expose corruption in Congress. Armed with tape recorders and hidden cameras, agents posed as Arab sheiks offering bribes in return for legislative favors. The investigation implicated seven members of the House of Representatives and one United States senator. Although ABSCAM may have been justifiable, it was properly controversial—and in ways that distinguish it from the paradigm of unmarked police cars.[37]

First, it can be argued that legislators should not be targets of this kind of investigation. Even if we should hold public officials to a higher standard of conduct, we might not wish to permit an executive agency on its own and in secret to choose which members of the legislature to investigate. Although in this case there is no evidence that the FBI targeted specific legislators for political reasons (the legislators evidently came forward on their own in a fortuitous display of nonpartisanship), the potential for political abuse in such circumstances is great. Other undercover investigations pose a similar problem. Since they typically involve specific groups (for example, Medicare doctors, executives in certain industries, racketeers in certain businesses) rather than a broad class of citizens, the choice of who should be investigated may reasonably affect whether we think the investigation should be conducted at all.

Second, in many undercover investigations, including ABSCAM, the fact that an offense has been committed is not so easily determined as it is in the case of drivers who exceed the speed limit. It has been argued, though a majority of the Supreme Court has never accepted the view, that if the government instigates the crime the defendant can legitimately claim that he was entrapped and escape conviction.[38] Even on the more established legal doctrine that only persons already disposed to commit a crime should count as criminals, ABSCAM and similar undercover operations come closer to creating than catching criminals.

Decisions outside of law enforcement depart even further from the paradigmatic cases that allow for prior judgment by means of generalization. A decision to intervene covertly in a foreign nation depends significantly on factors that cannot readily be stipulated in advance. Even those who would accept a policy that the United States should act to prevent a strategically important government from falling to the Communists would disagree about which countries and what moments should qualify as instances of the policy. Observers weigh risks differently according to how they value, for example, national independence compared to political freedom in the country in question.

Might we do better with a rule prohibiting certain *kinds* of intervention—perhaps covert intervention itself? As long as citizens believe that open intervention is both generally undesirable and occasionally necessary, they would be foolish to rule out all covert methods. Those methods could reduce the occasions on which open intervention would be necessary. Even so prudent and moral a rule as one proscribing political assassination is less straightforward then it seems. Its difficulties are in evidence in the ambivalence of the author of one of the most careful critical studies of assassinations allegedly planned or carried out by the CIA.[39] The author first comes out in favor of an absolute prohibition. Although he believes that there may be occasions on which assassination would be justified, he doubts that any government should be trusted to act only on those occasions, since most believe they will never be called to account. But then, still wanting to allow for the rare exception to the absolute rule, he concludes that if an assassination is truly necessary, "the agency asked to perform the deed can be counted on to break the rules, just as the CIA did when the rule was only implicit."[40]

Some rigid rules against U.S. officials' using methods such as assassination, if more rigidly enforced than they have been in the past, could serve the interests of both American democracy and American foreign policy.[41] The possibilities of this kind of accountability in advance have not been fully realized. But they leave much unjudged even among the specific activities to which they refer. The question of assassination rarely presents itself as a decision about whether U.S. agents should kill foreign leaders. More commonly, U.S. officials decide whether to support foreign nationals who intend to overthrow their own government.

Dissidents in the Dominican Republic several times in 1960 secretly asked U.S. officials there for weapons to help in their plan to kill Rafael Trujillo, the country's dictator who had by all accounts ruled repressively and brutally for many years.[42] They asked for a large assortment of weapons, some of which officials in the State Department and the CIA ordered sent, though only a few pistols and rifles were actually delivered.

After the Bay of Pigs, a new administration in Washington had second thoughts and refused to provide any more weapons. But the new U.S. consul, believing in the dissidents' cause but also perhaps believing that the United States had incurred an obligation to them, continued to urge support. The dissidents went ahead on their own, and assassinated Trujillo, probably using an American-supplied weapon.

In these changing circumstances, it is difficult to see how any kind of policy established publicly in advance could have served to guide U.S. officials. Even if one believes that the United States should never have supported the dissidents in the first place, one might appreciate the claim that by its earlier actions the United States had committed itself to some kind of continuing support. When the issue becomes whether and to what extent to encourage dissidents in such circumstances, general policies approved in advance usually do not address the critical contingencies, and therefore do not serve well as a method of accountability. Officials will dirty their hands on their own, and citizens will not be able to call them to account, except after the fact. There is no substitute for the consideration of particulars in these activities. If there is no way to discuss the particulars without defeating the decisions, there may be no alternative to refusing to make the decisions at all. If we wish to ensure that dirty hands stay democratic, we must either abandon covert actions of this kind, or we must find another form of accountability.

Mediating the Decision

Mediation is another such form, exemplified in the oversight activities of congressional committees. If the policy cannot be made public, legislators, substituting for citizens, oversee the actions of executives who make and carry out the decisions. The executives cannot themselves serve as surrogates for citizens. They are less likely than legislators to take an unbiased view of the decisions they and their colleagues make, and they are less likely to reflect the views of citizens.

This familiar political rationale has a less familiar moral counterpart. Oversight approximates the criterion of publicity that many philosophers since Kant have recognized as a test of moral judgment.[43] The criterion implies that moral deliberation take place among persons whose views represent as much as possible the differences of principle that prevail in the society. In the case of necessarily secret policies, officials may not be able fully to meet the criterion. But even an attenuated kind of publicity can, as Mill suggested more generally, "compel deliberation and force everyone to determine, before he acts, what he shall say if called to account for his actions."[44] To defend a judgment before an audience that more closely shares the interests and principles of citizens more nearly replicates the public debate that would have taken place if the policy could have been made fully public.

The difficulty with this kind of mediation, however, is that it is inherently unstable. There is no principled place to locate the limits of participation in the deliberations. Since the moral purpose of the oversight committee is to represent a wider range of perspectives, members of the committee, as well as members of Congress, legitimately press for greater publicity when they believe the issue before the committee calls for a still wider range of perspectives. (They most naturally tend to do so when they expect the publicity to serve their own political advantage, but their motives do not necessarily annul the good reasons there may be for their action.)

When the members of the oversight committee share the perspective of the officials they oversee, the process works only too smoothly—at the expense of accountability. For many years, executive agencies (such as the CIA) enjoyed cozy relations with their congressional overseers (such as the joint subcommittee of the Armed Services and Appropriations Committees). In the aftermath of Vietnam and Watergate, members of Congress who took a more critical view of these agencies began to play a greater role in their oversight. They not only asked tougher questions and demanded more information, but they (or members of their staffs) disclosed more information to the public, sometimes through leaks to the press. The agencies responded by trying to keep the committees from receiving information they legitimately required.

Few executives went as far as CIA Director Richard Helms, who refused to tell two congressional committees what they wanted to know about the agency's activities in Chile. After his conviction for failing to testify "fully and completely" before the committees, Helms implied that he did not trust the members of the committee to keep the secrets they asked him to reveal.[45] Later directors have managed to stay out of court, but not out of trouble with their congressional overseers, who suspect them of withholding important information about covert activities.

One response to this breakdown of trust is to criticize Congress for failing to respect the requirements of secrecy. This response in effect seeks a principled boundary to restrain the inherent tendency toward wider and wider publicity in deliberations about public values. The first step is to distinguish between Congress' right to know and the public's right to know. Congress' right, it is said, rests on the "special claim" to have more information necessary to perform its duties in the legislative and administrative processes, while the analogous right of citizens rests on the "broader claim that publicity . . . is necessary for popular control over government."[46] Although the latter claim is "broader," it turns out to grant citizens access to a narrower range of information. Citizens supposedly do not need to know as much to choose their representatives as their representatives need to know to make the laws and oversee their administration.

If the distinction implied only that Congress should receive some information (such as classified documents) that should not be released generally to citizens, it would be cogent enough. But it is usually taken to imply more than that. One political scientist invokes it to condemn Senator Mike Gravel and Congressman Ron Dellums for causing excerpts from a top-secret report to be read into the *Congressional Record* in 1972.[47] Prepared for President Nixon in 1969 by the staff of the National Security Council, the report discussed policy options during the Vietnam War. There is no evidence that the release of the report compromised national security, and there is some reason to believe that it contributed to public debate about foreign policy in the early 1970s.

The critics of disclosure typically concentrate their attack on its indirect consequences—in this case the risk that executive agencies will be less likely to give Congress such information in the future.[48] The use of the argument from indirect consequences in such cases is troublesome. It rests on a principle that public officials should not do what they otherwise believe is right if, as a result of their doing right, other officials will do wrong. Generalized under imperfect conditions where some officials inevitably do wrong, this principle would generate a great deal of mischief. It would give rise to many grave harms of omission, as well-intentioned officials tread lightly to avoid provoking their ill-intentioned colleagues.[49] The argument serves at best as a reason for temporarily maintaining secrecy until the miscreant agencies can be persuaded or forced to provide the information they ought to provide.

The End of Dirty Decisions

Like other forms of accountability, mediation goes some distance toward making dirty hands democratic. Each form, if more strongly interpreted than it usually is, gives citizens some knowledge about, if not some influence on, the making of dirty-handed decisions. Retrospection can be strengthened by limiting the duration of secrecy. Generalization can be enhanced through prohibitions on certain kinds of activities. Mediation can work better if in major disagreements of principle legislators expand the public that deliberates on the decisions.

But none of these forms of accountability covers the whole class of secret dirty-handed decisions, and for those left uncovered, the traditional problem of dirty hands persists. Officials act on their own when in making these decisions they break the rules of conventional morality. They do not have democratic dirty hands, shared with citizens. They have doubly dirty hands, all their own. The decision itself incorporates a wrong, and the making of the decision without democratic legitimacy represents a further wrong.

If we accept the paradox of dirty hands, the first wrong is inevitable, but what about the second? It could be eliminated if we prohibited the making of any dirty-handed decisions about which citizens could not know enough to hold the decision makers accountable. Such a prohibition could have far-reaching effects on government, preventing (as suggested above) many practices that officials now readily adopt, especially in the conduct of foreign affairs.

To decide whether the effects would be justified would require a closer examination of each practice. That examination would compare the relative value of preserving the democratic procedures compared to protecting national security or other important goals in various types of decisions. If citizens could take part in this examination and set standards in advance to determine the way officials make this trade-off in the future, then citizens could reassert democratic control. But this effort would suffer from the same limitations that plague all of the forms of accountability (especially generalization, on which this effort would have to rely).

The choice, then, is starker than it is usually presented. To continue making decisions that do not meet even minimal criteria for democratic accountability is not simply to choose security or some other value over democracy. It is to abdicate in many important instances the right to make that choice at all as a democratic society. If this conclusion is correct, it makes more urgent even such drastic steps as abandoning many widespread and useful practices of concealment in modern government.

But however desirable these steps may seem, they stand beyond our reach in some critical cases. We may simply have to accept, indefinitely, that officials will dirty their hands without democratic legitimacy. The necessity and implications of living with the problem of dirty hands in this form can best be shown in the policy of nuclear deterrence, the most extreme but most significant case of unavoidable, undemocratic dirty hands. The dirt not only attaches itself to isolated decisions, but pervades the succession of decisions that comprise the policy.

Democratic Deterrence

The problem of dirty hands in the policy of nuclear deterrence takes the form of a paradox, but not the form that has usually been assumed. The standard paradox is expressed in the proposition that an effective conditional intention to retaliate against a nuclear attack may be both wrong and right.[50] The intention seems wrong because it threatens the death of innocent persons, but it also seems right because it helps prevent that threat from being carried out. To escape the paradox, some have denied that the intention is wrong (implying that nuclear war may be morally acceptable). Others have denied that the intention is right (implying that deterrence, however effective, is morally unacceptable). The American Conference of Catholic Bishops' Pastoral Letter searches for a way to live with the paradox by temporarily accepting deterrence only on the condition that we make conscientious efforts to eliminate the need for it in the future.[51]

It is sometimes suggested that in the world of actual policy the paradox does not arise. One philosopher argues that in practice the paradox is "completely bogus."[52] We would not be justified in intending an all-out retaliatory salvo, he suggests, but we would be justified in intending a retaliatory response if it would serve some useful purpose, such as destroying the weapons and resources that could give the enemy control over the postwar world.[53] The latter intention is all we need to intend in order to make deterrence work. In the chaos of nuclear war, neither we nor our enemy can know what we will do in response to an attack, or even what we are doing in responding to an attack. This "existential uncertainty," it is said, is our best protection against a first strike.[54] It is also supposed to constitute the resolution of the moral paradox. To prevent war, we need intend only what is morally justifiable.

But even if this approach correctly represents what is necessary for deterrence, it does not dispose of the moral problem.[55] The threat that deterrence expresses may be wrong because simply making it creates a morally unacceptable risk.[56] At some point, the risk that the threat itself creates becomes as grave as the risk it is intended to reduce. To assess the risks, we should consider not only the likelihood that we might carry out the threat in response to an attack, but also the chances that in carrying out the threat we would do more than we threatened. We should also count the risk that we might launch our missiles for other reasons, or for no reason at all.

A proper moral assessment of these risks must recognize their institutional context. The analogy that seems to shape many discussions of deterrence—one individual threatening another—is misleading even if the individuals are understood to be nations. The fact that the threat is not an isolated decision of a single-minded agent, but a continuing policy supported by an organizational structure contributes in two ways to making deterrence a problem of dirty hands. The structure affects the wrong in the threat itself, and it thereby gives rise to a wrong in the process of judging the threat.

The structure in which the threat is made—the personnel, organizations, weapons systems, and strategic plans that support it—should significantly affect our estimate of the risks of making the threat. U.S. nuclear planning includes "massive attack options" that even the defenders of deterrence agree would be wrong to exercise. Those who try to justify the threat point out that intentions should not be inferred from plans.[57] They argue that having the plans may serve deterrent purposes, and indeed they may. But having them may also increase the chances of using them. Having the plans means having the institutions to carry them out.[58]

The very uncertainty on which the defenders of deterrence rely to maintain the credibility of the deterrent tends to undermine its control in an organizational setting. The uncertainty reduces our confidence that the options in the more limited strategies (such as flexible response and counterforce) can be kept from escalating to a full-scale nuclear exchange. The vulnerability of the institutions of command and control, for ex-

ample, may produce "powerful incentives within the U.S. milit̃
ning system to conduct full-scale strategic operations at the outset of any
serious crisis."[59]

These considerations do not prove that the threat embodied in the
strategy of deterrence is morally wrong. But they cast doubt on the claim
that it is right, and that doubt is enough to sustain the second wrong—
the democratic illegitimacy of deterrence. To decide whether the wrong
in the threat itself is justified, citizens would have to assess the risks of
the policy, and would therefore need to know about the institutional
structure that supports it. They would need, on a continuing basis, knowledge that is quite specific—including information about the people who
function within the institutions and the strategic plans that they devise.
To what extent do command structures and weapons configurations favor
massive attack options? How vulnerable do key decision makers really
believe our forces are? To what extent are command and control facilities
capable of surviving an attack? Answers to other equally detailed questions would be necessary to assess the various risks of the threat (the
chances of accident, mistake, and proliferation).

Yet if citizens acquired such knowledge, so would enemies, and the
deterrent effect could be lessened. It might remain sufficient to prevent
a nuclear first strike, but it probably would not be adequate to discourage
more limited action that could lead, step by step, to nuclear war. Thus,
to exploit the general uncertainty that makes the nuclear threat strategically credible and morally acceptable, we must maintain a differentiated
uncertainty: citizens cannot know what political and military leaders
know. Not only must officials decline to disclose critical information
about nuclear policy, they may need to deceive citizens about the nuclear
policy in order to maintain the uncertainty on which the deterrent depends. Conventional military policy can also conflict with the democratic
process, but the conflict is not so intractable. The effects of conventional
policies, in time of peace as well as war, are more visible, and the influence
of citizens has more time to take effect. The dilemma of nuclear policy
is exacerbated because citizens see only its (apparent) success.

Nor can we escape the dilemma by choosing as leaders the kind of
persons whom we trust to make decisions about which we can never
know. First of all, we cannot be sure that the elected officials are in
complete control of the institutions that plan and execute nuclear policy.
Second, for deterrence to work, potential enemies must see our leaders

as the kind of persons who would order nuclear retaliation, or must at least be uncertain about whether they are the kind of persons who would order it. If enemies must remain ignorant of the character of our leaders in this essential respect, so must we. As citizens we cannot know what we need to know in order to judge the morality of the policy of nuclear deterrence or even the morality of those to whom we might delegate the making of that policy.

The paradox of dirty hands thus returns in the revised form that implicates the democratic process. To the extent that citizens are permitted to judge whether the threat is morally acceptable, it becomes less acceptable because less uncertain. Yet to the extent that citizens are not permitted to judge the threat, it becomes less acceptable because less legitimate.

The paradox does not imply that citizens should have less influence than they do now on the making of nuclear policy. On the contrary, its force partly depends on recognizing the value of democratic control of that policy. Many aspects of nuclear policy—including choices among strategies—can be the subject of public debate without weakening the system of deterrence.[60] In recent years citizens have begun to take a greater interest in nuclear issues, and they could play a still larger role in the making of nuclear policy. Greater participation would call for some significant changes in the attitudes of the elites who now dominate nuclear policy making and the institutions in which it takes place. Such changes would be desirable and perhaps even more feasible now than before.[61]

Insofar as citizens gain more influence over nuclear policy, they could have more voice in the dirty-handed decisions that comprise that policy. To this extent, the dirty hands would be less undemocratic. But since the efficacy of deterrence itself places an inherent limit on public participation, the dirty hands can never be completely, or even sufficiently, democratic. It is therefore tempting to invoke the principle stated earlier: if the dirty-handed policy cannot be legitimated, it should not be adopted. We would then conclude that nuclear deterrence, like some of the other kinds of policies that preclude democratic legitimation, should be abandoned.

However desirable its abolition might be as a goal, no nation alone, and no likely combination of nations, could soon bring about its end without creating even graver risks than those imposed by its continued existence. Must the conclusion be simply that we should learn to live with deterrence and the terrible moral tension it expresses? We can, of course, qualify our acceptance of deterrence, making it "conditional" on the conscientious pursuit of the end of deterrence.[62] But recognizing the nature of the democratic dirty hands inherent in the practice of nuclear deterrence suggests a stronger conclusion. That recognition may shift the balance of moral and political burdens in the relations among nations that maintain the system of deterrence.

Insofar as effective deterrence denies citizens the knowledge they need to assess defense strategy, deterrence imposes a moral cost on democracies that it does not impose on nondemocracies. The problem of dirty hands in this form arises only in a democracy. This asymmetry has implications for nuclear policy that have not been sufficiently appreciated. If democracies have more to lose from deterrence, they have more to gain from reducing the reliance on it. (They would also have more to gain from eliminating the need for it, if that were possible.) This implies that a democracy should be more willing to take the first step or the first several steps toward what has been called the "denuclearization of international politics."[63] A democracy has greater reason to structure its nuclear arsenal to serve the limited purpose of deterring others from using nuclear weapons than to serve the broader purpose of fighting wars. Another implication is that a democracy should be more cautious in employing "extended" deterrence to preserve its political influence elsewhere in the world.

The democratic reason for reducing reliance on nuclear deterrence may not seem so important compared to the reasons of survival that all nations share. Decreasing the risk of nuclear war surely is reason enough for any nation. But the democratic reason has an important and distinctive role. First, it reveals a cost that democracies incur, no matter how limited, or how successful, their strategy of deterrence. The damage to the democratic process is not simply a risk; it is continuous and actual. Second, the democratic reason stands in an important sense prior to any of the other reasons for adopting a nuclear policy. It is not simply another cost to be counted in the calculus of policy making; it subverts the possibility of a society's conducting that calculus. When deterrence diminishes democracy, citizens cannot adequately weigh the deadly risks of the various forms of deterrence under which they might live, or the various steps that their government might take to reduce the reliance on deterrence.

That a democracy has a further reason to deemphasize deterrence suggests that it should be braver in its pursuit of denuclearization. But it does not, of course, imply that a democracy should surrender to an enemy or abandon its democratic allies. One of the implicit premises of the argument from asymmetry is that democracy itself is an important moral value worth preserving. Nevertheless, in concrete circumstances the implications of the argument may shift the balance of risks in ways that could encourage a democracy to take greater chances in negotiations on arms control and perhaps even to take some unilateral steps in the reduction of arms.

Whether acting on these implications would make much practical difference in actual negotiations depends on social and political developments that are hard to anticipate. To achieve a mutually beneficial agreement, democratic negotiators may have to conceal from their adversaries the fact that they believe that democracies have more to gain in the negotiations. But the implications of this shift in the balance of risks suggest a perspective on deterrence that concentration on the moral paradox alone does not provide. Because of its effect on the democratic process, deterrence—even while it works—should look particularly pernicious to democrats. Deterrence is not democratic.

The policy of nuclear deterrence exemplifies in the most acute form the general dilemma that the problem of dirty hands poses for the democratic process. We face not simply a problem of dirty hands, but a problem of democratic dirty hands. When officials do wrong in order to do right, they act, with respect to a small but significant class of decisions, without the consent of citizens. Officials may even deceive citizens in order to ensure that the decision accomplishes its end. If citizens cannot discuss a decision in a public forum, they cannot collectively determine whether officials are correct in deciding that morally wrong means are necessary to accomplish morally right ends. Citizens cannot know whether officials have made a dirty-handed decision or just a dirty decision.

In politics, the vices of concealment—deception, secrecy, and manipulation—are the most insidious of all. They prevent us from reaching a collective judgment about the other wrongs of government (including the vices of violence). They obstruct judgments about officials who would use immoral means to accomplish moral ends. They even sometimes prevent us from knowing that we cannot make these judgments. The possibility of judging dirty-handed decisions—at least judging with any claim to democratic authority—depends on keeping the decisions clean in one respect. The wrongs they effect cannot include concealment that would preclude accountability.

Understanding the democratic dimension of the problem of dirty hands need not make the problem more intractable. It does not necessarily reinforce the view, affirmed by many believers in the paradox of dirty hands, that political morality is inherently incoherent. The Machiavellian portrait of the politician caught between two incompatible moralities may well depict some of the dilemmas that modern officials face, but it does not fully represent the repertoire of responses that democrats can deploy. Democratic citizens must teach democratic princes how to be responsible.

Democratic citizens should first try to stop the making of decisions that cannot be justified in public, even those decisions that officials regard as justified. For those decisions that cannot be eliminated, citizens should seek to strengthen the devices of accountability, even if they know that such efforts can never completely resolve the problem of dirty hands. Partly democratic dirty hands are less bad than just plain dirty hands.

2

The Moral Responsibility of Many Hands

The portrait that dominates discussions of the moral dilemmas of public officials presents a solitary figure, agonizing alone when making moral choices, and acting alone when executing them.[1] It is a picture that lacks a significant political dimension, and thereby obscures an important problem of political ethics—the problem of many hands. Because many different officials contribute in many different ways to decisions and policies of government, it is difficult even in principle to identify who is morally responsible for political outcomes. Even if we can decide that a policy is morally wrong, we may not be able to locate anyone who made it.

The first chapter suggested that dirty hands create a problem for democracy because citizens cannot know the content of certain kinds of policies that governments pursue. The nature of the policies precludes accountability. Many hands also give rise to a democratic problem: the nature of policy making itself obstructs accountability. When citizens look for officials to call to account for a policy, they rarely find anyone who single-handedly made the policy. They often cannot even discover anyone whose own contribution to the collective outcome seems significant enough to warrant credit or blame for it.

This chapter argues that the conventional ways of ascribing responsibility in politics—represented by the hierarchical and the collective models—are not satisfactory responses to the problem of many hands; and that personal responsibility, properly interpreted, can be imputed to officials more often than these models imply. The criteria for personal responsibility adopted here are common to a wide range of moral theories. The criteria hold persons responsible for an outcome insofar as they cause it and do not act in ignorance or under compulsion. On these criteria, we can say that one official is more or less responsible than another without implying, as in the law, that degrees of fault correspond to proportionate shares of compensation, or that they fit exactly the standard categories of criminal liability. Legal responsibility, though suggestive, is not a reliable guide to moral responsibility.[2]

Corresponding to each of the criteria of personal responsibility are types of excuses officials use to eliminate or mitigate their responsibility for political outcomes.[3] By examining the conditions under which the excuses seem to be acceptable or unacceptable, we can see how the criteria serve to establish personal responsibility in the context of collective action. We should not expect to derive anything so systematic as a general theory of political responsibility or even of political excuses, but we should be able to formulate a set of considerations that can help identify the presence of personal responsibility in a variety of specific political circumstances. The examples on which the considerations build are drawn mostly from the executive branch, where officials encounter the problem of many hands most regularly.[4]

In most political contexts, these considerations or criteria and their corresponding cases would have to be supplemented with substantive principles of political theory grounded in concepts such as justice and the common good. But an analysis of excuses, even by itself, can serve to inform our judgments about those who govern us, and thus enrich our understanding of political responsibility.[5] Its use might even influence the conduct of public officials. Those who took the idea of personal responsibility seriously would perhaps make decisions with greater care, and if they did not, other officials and citizens who did could enforce its requirements. They could employ sanctions, including public criticism, dismissal from office, permanent exclusion from office, or (as chapter 3 suggests) criminal punishment.

Hierarchical Responsibility

According to the hierarchical model, responsibility for a political outcome falls on the person who stands highest in the formal or informal chain of authority. Weber provides the classic statement of the model. He holds, first, that modern government recognizes "fixed jurisdictional areas" and "office hierarchy" in which "there is a supervision of the lower offices by the higher ones."[6] Second, he sharply distinguishes administration and politics: administrators merely execute the policies set by politicians.[7] Finally, the administrator and the politician are therefore subject to "exactly the opposite principle of responsibility": "The honor of the civil servant is vested in his ability to execute conscientiously the order of the superior authority, exactly as if the order agreed with his own conviction . . . The honor of the political leader . . . however, lies precisely in an exclusive personal responsibility for what he does, a responsibility he cannot and must not reject or transfer."[8]

Weber's model vastly simplifies the task of ascribing responsibility to public officials since it places most public officials most of the time beyond the province of moral responsibility. As long as they follow the orders of their superiors and the procedures of the organization, they are not responsible for any harmful results of their actions. We are of course still left with the chore of sorting out the responsibility of the various politicians who have a hand in making the policies that the administrators carry out. But because the hands are fewer and the jurisdictions well defined, the problem is much more tractable.

Weber's model, however, does not correspond to the vision of politics that emerges from modern studies of the making of public policy. Instead of functioning within well-defined jurisdictions and settled lines of authority, officials act within overlapping "issue networks" whose membership is shifting and partially drawn from outside government.[9] They engage in a "bargaining game" where victory depends more on "skill and will in using [other] bargaining advantages" and "other players' perceptions" than on positions in a hierarchy.[10] Instead of respecting a clear distinction between politics and administration, bureaucrats exercise discretionary authority either delegated to them, or simply assumed by them, to shape and often to make policy. Meanwhile, elected politicians concern themselves with the details of implementation.[11]

The empirical deficiencies of the hierarchical model do not necessarily defeat it as a normative standard. Weber himself anticipated some of the institutional developments that impugn the model.[12] Later writers continue to commend the model in spite of—or because of—the growth of administrative discretion and the dispersion of authority in the modern state.[13] But even if a more hierarchical structure of government is desirable, the hierarchical model is not a satisfactory basis on which to ascribe responsibility in the structure of government that now prevails. Where discretion and dispersion abound, the model obscures the identity of the officials who actually exercise power.

Insofar as officials holding the top positions in a hierarchy cannot be expected to have control over political outcomes, hierarchical responsibility does not coincide with moral responsibility. In these circumstances, to impute moral responsibility according to hierarchical position would violate a fundamental presupposition of morality—that persons should be blamed only if they could have done otherwise. The difficulty is not that it would be unfair to hold top officials responsible for failures beyond their control. Officials know in advance that they may lose their jobs because of events over which they could have had little or no influence, and they thus tacitly consent to the risk of this kind of political "punishment." Such risk, furthermore, may be a useful feature in the design of political institutions, encouraging officials to take every possible precaution to avoid mistakes.

These considerations show only that strict liability in politics may sometimes be morally justifiable; they do not establish that such liability is equivalent to moral responsibility. When we hold officials strictly accountable in this way, we usually do not condemn them morally. Nor is such accountability sufficient to capture many of the decisions and policies that citizens may wish to criticize. The higher the level of the office, the less significant is any particular decision in an overall appraisal of the performance of an official. Hierarchical responsibility leaves citizens without anyone to hold accountable if, for example, they generally approve of a president but believe that his decisions on welfare policy are immoral.

That hierarchical responsibility imparts scarcely any moral force explains why political leaders are often quite ready to declare themselves fully responsible for some pernicious results of some decision or policy. Taking responsibility becomes a kind of political ritual that has no negative effect on a leader. Indeed, leaders can often turn this ritual to their advantage.[14] With regular incantations of "I accept full responsibility," an official strengthens his or her own political standing—by reassuring the public that someone is in charge, and by projecting an image of a courageous leader who does not pass the buck. Also, as a leader becomes known as one who takes the blame for subordinates, the leader gains the gratitude and secures the loyalty of those subordinates.

Most significantly, the ritual often quells public debate about a controversial decision or policy, effectively blocking further inquiry into the moral responsibility of all the officials involved, especially that of the leader. After the failure of the Bay of Pigs invasion, President Kennedy privately blamed the CIA, the Joint Chiefs, and just about everyone who knew about the invasion in advance. But publicly he accepted the "sole responsibility" and objected to anyone's "attempting to shift responsibility" away from him.[15] Reinforcing the ritual taking of responsibility, the hierarchical model in this case not only cut short public inquiry into other officials' responsibility for the failure of the invasion, but also forestalled public debate about each official's failure to consider whether subversion of this kind is morally justified at all.

Accepting responsibility in American government does not usually include resigning from office, as is common in European political practice. It more often represents an attempt to silence demands for resignation. The more personally blameworthy an official, the more strenuously the official is likely to insist on accepting hierarchical responsibility. In the spring of 1973, as Watergate intruded more and more into the office of the president itself, Nixon invoked the ritualistic formula of responsibility in its almost pure form: "Who is to blame for what happened in this case? . . . The easiest course would be for me to blame those to whom I delegated the responsibility to run the campaign. But that would be a cowardly thing to do . . . In any organization, the man at the top must bear the responsibility. That responsibility, therefore, belongs here in this office. I accept it."[16]

Collective Responsibility

The argument underlying the collective model begins by posing a form of the problem of many hands. Many political outcomes are the product of the actions of many different people, whose individual contributions may not be identifiable at all and certainly cannot be distinguished significantly from other people's contributions. The second step is the claim that no one individual can be morally blamed for these outcomes. At the final step, proponents of the argument seem to diverge, offering two different conclusions. One states that every individual associated with the collectivity should be charged with moral responsibility, and the other holds that only the collectivity can be so charged. But the conclusions (and the two versions of collective responsibility they support) share a fundamental assumption. Neither ascribes responsibility to persons on the basis of their specific and distinctive connections to an outcome.

The first version of the collective model can be illustrated by Herbert Kaufman's effort to pin the blame on all citizens for the consequences of bureaucratic "red tape": "It would not surprise me . . . if [public officers and employees] are merely scapegoats . . . We may accuse them because, intuitively, we want to divert the guilt from the real cause: ourselves. No one element of the population is responsible for all red tape or even for most of it . . . we all have a hand in it."[17]

One philosopher defends this kind of dispersion of responsibility partly on the grounds that it avoids the ascription of individual responsibility. He rejects all noncollective ideas of moral responsibility because they incorrectly assume that the individual is "self-contained and self-subsistent."[18] We are morally responsible for the actions of people with whom we have any "special relationship."[19] That includes all our fellow citizens, even earlier generations, but fortunately does not encompass all humanity. We are not culpable, this philosopher concedes, for the actions of Genghis Khan. While radically expanding the responsibility of citizens in this way, this approach drastically diminishes the responsibility of officials. Because officials act as representatives, limited by the demands of citizens and bound by long-standing commitments their predecessors have made, their decisions are not fully voluntary, and they are therefore not fully responsible for the decisions.

This version of the collective model cannot account for many distinctions that we intuitively wish to draw in apportioning credit and blame. We normally distinguish degrees of responsibility that citizens and officials bear for actions of the government or the groups with which they are associated. Those who do not protest against an unjust policy, for example, are normally thought to be more responsible for it than those who do. Among those who do not protest, those who have greater resources with which to influence the policy are more responsible than those with fewer resources. These and many other similar distinctions presuppose a principle that the collective model must reject (at least with respect to citizens): responsibility for an outcome depends in part on the contribution an individual actually made, or could have made.

The second version of the collective model—blaming the collectivity rather than any specific member of it—is sometimes represented by the hypothetical example of an old-time train robbery.[20] An armed bandit holds up a carful of passengers and escapes with their money. All of the passengers, or even a few of them, could have prevented the robbery, had they coordinated their actions. In this way the passengers were collectively responsible for their own losses, but since no passenger was obligated to resist the bandit, none was individually responsible. The fault lay not in individual acts or omissions, but in the structure of the group.[21]

Similarly, a political system may suffer from structural faults that block the efforts of any individual to accomplish morally respectable ends. An example appears in "The Blast in Centralia No. 5," the introductory case in a widely used casebook in public administration. "Responsibility [for the mine disaster that killed 111 men] here transcends individuals. The miners at Centralia, seeking somebody who would heed their conviction that their lives were in danger, found themselves confronted with officialdom, a huge organism scarcely mortal . . . As one strives to fix responsibility for the disaster, again and again one is confronted, as were the miners, not with any individual but with a host of individuals fused into a vast, unapproachable, insensate organism. Perhaps this immovable juggernaut is the true villain in the piece."[22]

The responsibility of the private and public officials in this case and most actual cases, however, differs from that of the passengers in the train robbery example. Officials act in the context of a continuing institution, not an isolated incident, and they or other officials therefore may be culpable for creating the structural faults of the institution, or for neglecting to notice them, or for making inadequate efforts to correct them. The responsibility of officials is no more temporally bounded than is the existence of the institutions in which they act.

Because both versions of the collective model distort the idea of responsibility, neither can serve as the foundation for judgments we wish to make about public officials. The first version blurs moral distinctions not only among various officials but also between officials and citizens. The second version recognizes no connection between structural fault and individual responsibility for supporting structural criticism and reform. The hierarchical model has the advantage of locating responsibility in determinate positions, but it neglects the problem of many hands. Proponents of the collective model take that problem all too seriously, reproducing it in the model itself and thereby weakening democratic accountability. When everyone in the collectivity or only the collectivity itself is responsible, citizens have no one to call to account.

We do not need to deny that hierarchical position is relevant in imputing responsibility, or that collective responsibility sometimes makes sense. But for the purposes of democratic government, we should seek an approach that preserves a traditional notion of personal responsibility. Its advantages for democratic accountability are plain if it can accommodate many of the complexities of a political process in which many different officials contribute to policies and decisions.

Personal Responsibility

Ascribing responsibility to officials as persons, rather than simply as occupants of certain offices or as members of a collectivity, relies on two criteria of moral responsibility. An official is morally responsible for an outcome only if (1) the official's actions or omissions are a cause of the outcome; and (2) these actions or omissions are not done in ignorance or under compulsion.[23] The first refers to causal responsibility; the second to volitional responsibility.

The criterion of causal responsibility, as interpreted here, is deliberately weak. A person qualifies as a cause if the outcome would not have happened but for the person's act or omission.[24] To say that a person is a cause merely connects his or her action with the outcome, along with the action of many other hands and the influence of many other forces. It does not establish that the person is the most important cause or even an agent to whom we should ascribe responsibility at all. If we wish to select one individual from among all the other causal factors in this chain of causation, we have to invoke other moral and political considerations, including the volitional criterion.

Some philosophers have objected that we should not use the causal criterion at all to assign moral responsibility in organizations.[25] The causal contribution that any single official makes to an organizational outcome is rarely significant. Therefore, to require, as a necessary condition of responsibility, that an official be a cause of the outcome is to "give aid and comfort to officials who want to avoid responsibility."[26] These philosophers are right to resist assimilating moral responsibility to causal responsibility. We should not want to say that an official is less responsible to the degree that he or she is less causally effective. But the weak causal criterion does not have this implication since it is not a sufficient condition of moral responsibility and does not determine degrees of moral responsibility.[27]

The causal criterion might still seem to eliminate moral responsibility in some circumstances where it ought to be maintained. When an outcome would have happened no matter what any individual did or failed to do, who can be identified as a cause? The criterion can be legitimately extended to cover some of these cases, notably those where the outcome is overdetermined. It should be understood to allow a person's action to qualify as a cause if the action would have been necessary to produce the outcome, had no other action sufficient to produce the outcome been present.[26] Other cases turn on how the outcome itself is described. If we characterize the outcome in very general terms—say, U.S. policy in Vietnam—we may not be able to identify any individual as a cause. But if we describe the outcome more specifically—the bombing of North Vietnam—we may have more success in locating responsible individuals. Ascribing moral responsibility calls for specificity in characterizing outcomes as much as in identifying agents. This specificity, furthermore, does not preclude responsibility for patterns of decisions and decision making. The outcomes for which we hold officials responsible include the continuing practices and structures of government.

The second criterion—volitional responsibility—stipulates in its most general form that a person is responsible for an action insofar as he or she could have done otherwise.[29] Unlike the causal criterion, which only sets a threshold for responsibility, the volitional criterion can also determine degrees of responsibility. Inability to act otherwise takes many different forms, ranging from general incapacity (such as insanity) to specific defects in particular actions (such as inadvertence). Most relevant for assessing the actions of public officials are these more specific faults, which may be considered under the traditional Aristotelian categories of ignorance and compulsion.[30]

Ignorance of what one does (not knowing that a certain description applies to one's action) counts as an excuse only if the ignorance is not negligent. In the case of public officials, the standards of negligence depend on moral and political considerations, such as the importance of the outcomes in question, and the efficacy of deterrence in the circumstances.[31] So does the question of whether compulsion should count as an excuse. The compulsion that public officials cite to excuse their conduct is rarely the extreme physical and psychological kind that philosophers and lawyers usually discuss. When officials claim that they had no choice, we do not take them literally. They can usually be understood as implying that they did not choose the *range* of alternatives within which they made some decision. Like Aristotle's sea captain, they confront two undesirable options (jettisoning the cargo or sinking the ship).[32] The duties of office conspire with the forces of nature to pose a choice between disagreeable alternatives. Limitations on the range of alternatives do not eliminate an official's responsibility, but they do warrant our specifying, in any ascription of praise or blame, what alternatives were realistically accessible.

The meaning of these criteria can best be explained through an analysis of the validity of the excuses that officials use to deny responsibility. Insofar as the criteria and their corresponding excuses help identify officials who should be held accountable for the decisions of governments, they serve to demonstrate the possibility of personal responsibility in politics.

Alternative Causes

In "Centralia No. 5," one of the persons blamed for the deaths of the miners was Inspector Scanlan, who had the authority to close the mine he knew to be unsafe but failed to do so. Scanlan's defense (in part) was that, "had he closed the Centralia mine, [the director of the Department of Mines and Minerals] simply would have fired him and appointed a more tractable inspector."[33] This is an example of the excuse from alternative cause: "If I hadn't done it, someone else would have," or "If I don't do it, someone else will." The excuse is more common in official than in personal life because in organizations the empirical assumption on which it depends is more likely to be true. In organizations, persons often are fungible.

In a general and unqualified form, the excuse is incoherent. To relieve one person of responsibility, the excuse asserts that other people (the alternative causal agents) would be responsible for the action. But if the excuse is valid, each of the other people would be exonerated, seriatim, in the same way as the first person. If the excuse is valid, no one is responsible; but the excuse cannot be valid unless someone is responsible. In any case, the excuse evidently has not been accepted in civil or criminal law,[34] and moral judgment seems to agree with the law in this regard.

The excuse may sometimes be acceptable in a modified form. One such form is as a criterion of causal relevance. Here an official claims, not that someone else would have made the same mistake, but that someone else would have made a different mistake sufficient to cause the harmful outcome. The excuse is thus used to show that the respect in which the official's action is faulty is not a cause of the outcome.[35]

In the political process, however, judgments about causal connections or their absence are often uncertain. Consider the case of an FDA official who permits a drug, which subsequently turns out to be unsafe, to be placed on the agency's list of substances generally recognized as safe. Assume that the official did not order the standard laboratory tests on the drug. We might perhaps not blame this official for any harm suffered by users of the drug if we believe that the technicians charged with performing the tests would eventually have approved the drug. But to the extent that the causal relevance remains uncertain (say, we doubt that the technicians would have approved the drug), then other factors will influence our judgment about the validity of the excuse.

Specifically, we will be more likely to accept the excuse if the fault is relatively minor (such as failing to order the tests because of some technicality rather than because of accepting a bribe), or if the consequences to which the fault allegedly contributed are relatively harmless. It is perhaps odd that these factors should affect our judgment at all, since they are not strictly relevant to deciding whether a fault was a cause of the outcome. But given the inevitable uncertainty of causal connections in organizations, we may be justified, as a practical matter, in considering these other factors when assessing even causal excuses.

The excuse from alternative cause is also acceptable if it is combined with certain kinds of justifications. To the plea that other officials would have committed the wrong anyhow is added the claim that they would have committed a worse wrong (or in some other way would have made the consequences worse). This excuse comes naturally to officials who do not resign from a government that is pursuing an admittedly wrong policy. During the Vietnam War, many officials, including Hubert Humphrey and Robert McNamara, privately told friends that they were staying on to keep the escalation from getting worse. Others, like Charles Frankel (assistant secretary of state for educational and cultural affairs) pointed to benefits they could accomplish that in their judgment out-weighed any effect their resignations might have on the war.[36]

We are right to be suspicious of such pleas. The heady mixture of exercising power while believing oneself to be doing good can easily forestall a sober assessment of the consequences of alternative courses of action. Still, the plea is sometimes acceptable. Even when the government an official serves is utterly evil, resignation may not be the most appropriate course. It has been argued that the S.S. officer Kurt Gerstein, by continuing in his post during World War II, "prevented worse things from happening."[37] If an official really cannot make any difference at all by remaining in office (or, for that matter, by resigning from office), the official would escape any judgment of responsibility for the regime. We could still criticize the official for continuing to hold office in a government that promoted immoral policies. Such criticism should be regarded, however, not as an ascription of responsibility, asserting that by some act or omission, the official actually furthered specific immoral policies of a regime. Rather, it should be considered an accusation of complicity, claiming that the official's association with this regime is itself immoral or dishonorable.[38]

In less extreme circumstances, the range of alternatives is usually greater, but an argument from the worse alternative may still seem plausible. After Attorney General Elliot Richardson and then his deputy resigned rather than carry out Nixon's order to fire Watergate Special Prosecutor Archibald Cox, Solicitor General Robert Bork decided to stay on the job and dismiss Cox. Bork argued (in part) that he would be more likely to protect the integrity of the Justice Department and the independence of any future special prosecutor than anyone Nixon would appoint as his replacement.[39] In this way, the justifiability of Bork's use of the argument from the worse alternative comes to depend on his subsequent conduct.

It might be argued that the validity of this excuse-cum-justification should not turn on simply a comparison of the consequences of an official's actions and the consequences of the actions of alternative causal agents. Bernard Williams maintains that this way of imputing responsibility (which he associates with utilitarianism) ignores the value of personal integrity.[40] He argues that a young scientist who opposes research on chemical and biological warfare should not take a job in a government laboratory engaged in such research, even if as a result another scientist will take the job and pursue the research more zealously. Agents should be primarily responsible for their own "projects" (actions based on commitments that form part of their personal character) and should not abandon them simply for the sake of social utility.[41] While Williams may be correct in criticizing utilitarianism for permitting an impersonal perspective to dominate a personal one, his own account of personal integrity remains insufficiently developed to support the radically circumscribed responsibility he evidently favors. Acting to protect one's personal integrity, at the expense of avoidable and serious harm to other people, seems too close to moral self-indulgence. It could represent an effort to keep one's hands clean no matter what happens to the rest of society.[42]

Causing and Advising

A second category of causal excuse comprises those pleas that would remove an official completely from the chain of events leading to a harmful outcome. These may be called excuses from null cause. In a common form of this excuse, an official cites a *novus actus interveniens*.[43] This refers to a subsequent act by another official who can control whether the first official's action has any effect and therefore supposedly bears the entire responsibility for any harmful consequences. The role of advisers in government best illustrates some of the many faces of this excuse in action.

In other times and other places, advisers often bore the responsibility for the consequences of their rulers' decisions—and with a vengeance. When for whatever reason the decisions of the Chinese emperors went awry, their counselors could expect to have their hearts cut open, their feet cut off, or to be pickled in brine.[44] Today, advisers to government officials have less cause to worry. Rather than strict liability for the advice they give, advisers are commonly assumed to have no responsibility at all for the consequences of decisions made on the basis of their (properly given) advice.[45] Since the advisee remains free to accept or reject the advice, the adviser escapes blame for anything the advisee does.

This interpretation of the causal criterion fails to capture the complexities of the process of advising.[46] The key assumption of the interpretation is that causing advisees to act is incompatible with their acting voluntarily. The assumption seems plausible only if one concentrates on instances in which an adviser makes an advisee do something, and ignores the great variety of other ways an adviser may influence an advisee. Advisers often contribute significantly to the final decision their advisees make. The way the advisers frame the alternatives, the weight they give to various arguments, the language and the illustrations they use (chosen perhaps to appeal especially to the advisee)—all these forms of influence may make the final decision different from what it would otherwise have been.

The influence of advisers, moreover, need not always take the form of giving explicit reasons or arguments. Officials may adopt a proposal because they trust their advisers personally—as President Roosevelt is known to have followed Louis Howe's advice on political patronage, or as President Kennedy is said to have decided on the Cuban blockade because those with whom he was "personally most compatible" recommended it.[47] In such cases, we would impute some responsibility to the advisers and do so without necessarily canceling or even reducing the responsibility of the official who made the decision. An advisee's responsibility is not nullified by the causal influence of the adviser, and the adviser's responsibility is not eliminated by the voluntary decision of the advisee.

There is, however, another way that advisers may limit their responsibility, and it illustrates a second form of the excuse from null cause. In this form, advisers accept a place in the chain of actions leading to an outcome but insist that it is not a very important place. It is so unimportant a place, they imply, that it does not deserve to be cited as a cause at all.[48] Underlying the excuse in this form is an appeal to normal expectations. Causal explanations of particular human actions typically focus on the factors that depart from the ordinary course of events.[49] As long as advisers merely advise in accord with the norms of their office, they act as we expect them to act, and we do not cite their acts or omissions as causes of decisions that go wrong.

The classic source of a definition of the responsibility of advisers based on the requirements of their office is (or should be) chapter 25 of *Leviathan*.[50] There Hobbes clearly recognizes that special conditions must obtain if a role is to shield an adviser from responsibility for the consequences of the advice. Hobbes distinguishes counsel that is consistent with, and counsel that is contrary to, the duty of a counselor. The latter consists of counsel that is "vehemently pressed," in which the adviser appeals to "common passions and opinions" instead of "true reasoning."[51] A counselor who in this way acts contrary to the norms of his office may be accused and punished, and presumably may also be blamed for consequences that follow from this advice.

This sharp distinction between two kinds of counsel is intelligible within the bounds of *Leviathan,* where shared standards of objective reasoning prevail in politics and where advisers speak to a single sovereign who authoritatively determines the public good. In modern democracies where these conditions do not exist, such a distinction, as a basis for insulating advisers, is difficult to maintain, even with respect to scientific advisers, whose role most closely approximates that of Hobbes's dutiful counselors. The view nevertheless persists that some advisers can completely escape responsibility if they confine themselves to giving merely technical analysis (advice about means), and conversely that they risk blame if they overstep this role by recommending one general policy over another (advice about ends).

In a report on the role of scientific advisers in the controversy over the Anti-Ballistic Missile System in the late 1960s, the Operations Research Society distinguished between analysts and advocates in a manner that recalls Hobbes's contrast between two kinds of counselors. The analyst restricts himself to the "quantifiable and logically structured aspects of the problem only," while the advocate need not admit the weaknesses of his positions and may put forward "unsupported allegations."[52] The report sharply criticized those scientific advisers who became advocates in the ABM debate.

Even on the highly technical questions in this debate, however, the kind of questions that advisers on both sides chose to address betrayed their partisanship and became a form of advocacy. Pro-ABM scientists concentrated on an analysis of the need for an ABM system, while the anti-ABM scientists stressed the evidence showing the inadequacy of an ABM system to meet this alleged need.[53] If on scientific questions such as this advisers are not able to purge their analyses of partisanship, we can hardly expect advisers on issues with even more economic and political content to sustain the role of Hobbesian analyst.[54]

It is of course possible (and often desirable) for an adviser only to analyze, not advocate. But even an adviser who presents a completely neutral analysis does not thereby escape moral responsibility for the consequences of the analysis. Under non-Hobbesian conditions, what the role of an adviser should be will often be contestable—morally so. A procedural controversy over the proper role of an adviser often simply reflects the substantive controversy in which the various advisers are engaged. The reaction to the ORS Report, and its criticism of the scientists who advocated instead of analyzed, seemed to follow the divisions of the ABM controversy itself. The pro-ABM scientists favored the report, and the anti-ABM scientists disapproved of it.[55] When the nature of the role remains in such serious dispute, advisers are responsible for the consequences of their choice to play one role rather than another in the controversy.

The responsibility is, if anything, greater when scientists themselves have contributed to the development of the technologies that the government would apply. It may be difficult to determine how far that responsibility extends, especially when the consequences of the discoveries are not only remote but ambivalent, promising great benefits as well as holding great risks. But the case for ascribing responsibility to scientists for their discoveries is clear if, like J. Robert Oppenheimer, they continue to have opportunities to influence how politicians use the discoveries. Defending himself in 1954, Oppenheimer disclaimed any such responsibility: "I did my job . . . I was not in a policy-making position . . . I gave the views for and the views against. Our statutory function was to give technical advice."[56] But eight years earlier he evidently accepted a much more extreme form of responsibility. According to President Truman, Oppenheimer "came into my office . . . and spent most of his time wringing his hands and telling me they had blood on them because of the discovery of atomic energy."[57] Moving from one extreme to the other, Oppenheimer passed by the requirements of a more moderate and plausible kind of personal responsibility—the continuing obligation to use opportunities to influence the uses to which one's discoveries are put.

Beyond the realm of technical and scientific analysis, advisers less commonly rely on the distinction between analysis and advocacy to limit their responsibility. Instead, advocacy itself becomes a duty of advisers, and the more advocates, the better. We leave the territory of *Leviathan* and enter the world of *On Liberty*. The system of governmental advising is seen as a kind of microcosm of Mill's vision of a liberal society, where the free expression of many different perspectives is supposed to offer the best chance for arriving at policies that promote the public interest. An advisory system based on this model would populate government with advisers of diverse views, and encourage each to advocate a partial perspective.[58]

Within such a system, advisers may well claim that they should not be held responsible for the decisions an official makes after listening to their advice, even if the official happens to follow the advice. The advisers themselves may not subscribe to the positions they are advocating, but may be merely putting forward the partial point of view required by the role they play in the advisory system. If such a system exists and is understood to exist by advisers and the officials they counsel, any particular adviser's responsibility might be plausibly limited in this way.

But no system of this kind is likely to be so well tuned that it will always produce an optimal balance of advice (let alone decisions in the public interest).[59] To cope with failures of the system, we need a second-order rule of responsibility that specifies when advisers should abandon their normal role of advocacy. We might say that when advisers have good reason to believe that the advisory system in which they are participating is not yielding a reasonable balance of opinions or is otherwise distorting decision making, and their advocacy of partial points of view is contributing to that distortion, they should abandon their normal role and seek to remedy the distortion in the process. If they fail to do so, they cannot, simply by appealing to the norms of their role, disclaim responsibility for their part in the harmful decisions that the system produces.[60]

These limitations of the excuse from null cause apply not only to advisers but also more generally to all officials who, to remove themselves from the causal chain, plead "it's not my job." The excuse relies on a definition of role that may be appropriate for government as usual (when normal expectations prevail), but is not suitable for government in crisis (when normal expectations fail). If many officials are not doing their jobs, others may be obliged to do more than their jobs. Even if all are doing their jobs, some officials may be obliged to do more if the circumstances are exceptional. The excuse from null cause ignores such obligations by assigning officials their place in the causal chain strictly according to the normal expectations of their offices.

The plea "it's not my job" cuts short any argument about whether an official could have made any difference, or could make any difference in the future. If the duties of the official's role do not concern the policy in question, failure to take any action—to oppose the policy or to resign from office—is treated as if it has no causal connection to the policy. As George Ball said in an interview in 1973, "Why *should* I have resigned in protest over Vietnam policy just because I disagreed with it? My main responsibility . . . was Western Europe. Perhaps five percent of my time was spent on Vietnam. It simply wasn't my responsibility . . . it wasn't as if I were the Honduras desk officer being put in the position of having to approve a U.S. military action in Honduras."[61]

Ball is right to suppose that the nature of an office circumscribes an official's responsibility to some extent. One cannot be culpable for all the policies on which one could have had any influence. That Ball's "main responsibility" did not concern Vietnam at least counts as a reason for blaming him less than those officials whose main duties did involve Vietnam. By the same token, as a high-ranking State Department official, Ball shares more blame than (say) an official in the Department of Health, Education and Welfare. But these differences in responsibility are more a function of the knowledge and power of the officials than of the norms of their offices. Rather than being an excuse in its own right, the appeal to role ultimately relies on other excuses (ignorance or compulsion). It is these excuses that operate when officials are obliged to depart from the normal expectations of their offices. In any case, even if the norms of office can affect degrees of responsibility, they cannot eliminate responsibility. They do not remove an official from the causal chain.[62]

Good Intentions

The volitional excuses come into play after the causal criterion establishes that an official is a cause of an outcome. To escape blame for an outcome, an official who is a cause of it would typically plead ignorance or compulsion. But the official may invoke a more general defense: "I didn't intend that." Since this defense can obviate the excuses of ignorance and compulsion, we need to see if it has any validity in politics before considering those excuses.

Some theories of responsibility support the defense by making officials responsible only for what they intend, not at all (or at least never as much) for what anyone else does as a result of their decisions. Kant expresses this view in its most absolute form. Kant insists, for example, that you must tell the truth even to a murderer who asks where your friend, his intended victim, is hiding.[63] You are responsible for your own intentional act (truth-telling or lying), and if you tell the truth you cannot be blamed for what other people do as a result of your honesty.

The implausibility of this view in ordinary moral life is magnified in public life. Perhaps we should deny that public officials should let consequentialist calculations determine whether they lie or commit other acts that are absolutely wrong on a Kantian view. But we should surely still hold the officials morally responsible for failing to take precautions to avoid the harmful consequences of the actions of other people when those actions are predictable responses to the officials' own actions. Even a traditional morality, which otherwise downplays consequences, holds that we consider what bad consequences flow from following its principles and what dispositions we can develop to avoid those consequences.[64]

Some philosophers defend a qualified version of the Kantian doctrine, conceding that we are morally responsible for some of the unintended consequences of our actions but insisting that we are "primarily" or "personally" responsible only for what we intend.[65] This responsibility evidently implies that we may never do intentional harm in order to avoid greater unintended harm.[66] But shrinking responsibility in this way would insulate officials from criticism for many harms for which we should want to blame them. On this view, public officials who negligently or even corruptly divert money that should be spent for police protection are not morally responsible for any criminal assaults that occur as a result of the reduced protection. The officials would not be responsible even if they could have anticipated that the assaults would occur.[67]

Even if such theories could coherently make room for moral criticism of unintended consequences, the priority the theories give to intention distorts the nature of responsibility in the institutions of government, where unintended consequences are so rife they might well be regarded as an occupational hazard.[68] Officials in the Johnson administration who consistently opposed expansion of the Vietnam War and urged the withdrawal of American forces certainly did not intend their dissent to have the effect of strengthening Johnson's resolve to continue the war. Yet the dissenters became "domesticated," and their participation in the process helped to legitimize the decisions they opposed.[69] They were welcomed as devil's advocates, their presence reassuring the president and his collaborators that objections to their policy were receiving serious consideration. Contrary to their own intentions, these dissenters became part of the set of causes that sustained the policy.

It is of course difficult to know at what point one's objections serve mainly to further purposes one opposes, but at the point where we could expect any reasonable politician to recognize that dissent has become counterproductive in this way, we should consider a dissenting official at least a moral accessory.[70] Good intentions may make us less critical of officials who oppose than of officials who support the questionable policy, but the intentions do not absolve the dissenters of responsibility for any consequences to which they contribute. Insofar as we are inclined to cancel or mitigate responsibility, we would do so, not by citing an absence of intention, but by accepting either a plea that the officials could not be expected to realize that they are promoting the result they oppose, or a plea that they could do nothing to prevent that result.

To say that intention is not a necessary condition for charging an official with responsibility is not inevitably to embrace the doctrine that we are all "equally morally responsible for all consequences."[71] It is simply to recognize that, at least for public officials, the contours of responsibility are likely to be more irregular than the criterion of intention would draw. In tracing the bounds of responsibility, we have to pay attention to other criteria, specifically those of ignorance and compulsion.

The Ignorance of Officials

If ignorance in general were a valid excuse, the innocence of some public officials would be irreproachable. But the kind of ignorance relevant to the problem of many hands concerns an official's lack of specific knowledge about the actions of other officials. An official who admittedly contributes to an objectionable outcome may seek to excuse the contribution by claiming that he or she did not know, and should not have been expected to know, that other officials had acted wrongly or would act wrongly. When as U.N. Ambassador in 1961 Adlai Stevenson stated that the United States did not have anything to do with the invasion of Cuba, he could not have been expected to realize that his statement was false. He escapes responsibility for any wrong that was committed.[72]

Whether Stevenson should have been told is another matter, but ambassadors, press secretaries, and others in similar roles have to trust that they are being told the truth, or at least that they are being told everything they need to know about the governmental activities within their purview.

At the other end of the causal chain, an official may sometimes be excused for consequences of a decision when he or she could not be expected to foresee the wrongs that other officials would commit in implementing the decision. After the surrender of Germany, President Truman signed an order terminating the shipment of food, clothing, and other goods that our allies had been receiving under Lend-Lease. The abrupt disruption of these supplies threatened significant hardship for many citizens in these countries until Truman rescinded the order. Truman defended his original order by claiming that his aides had executed it too literally.[73]

Such an excuse does not work when officials are the instruments of their own ignorance. They may, for example, encourage subordinates not to tell them about certain possibly objectionable plans so that they can deny knowledge of the plans if they go awry. Or officials may elicit misleading information from subordinates by indicating, sometimes unwittingly, what kind of conclusions they wish to hear. Considering an American intervention in the Dominican Republic in 1965, Rusk and McNamara asked the acting U.S. ambassador to the Dominican Republic if "he agreed with their view that a rebel victory would probably lead to a pro-Communist government."[74] Not surprisingly, the acting ambassador agreed.

To reject a plea of ignorance, we do not have to show that an official should have foreseen the specific act of some particular official (for example, that an aide would misinterpret an order in exactly one way rather than another). It is sufficient that the official should have realized that mistakes of the type that occurred were likely. In bureaucracies, certain patterns of fault are common enough that we should expect any competent official to anticipate them and to take reasonable precautions to avoid them or at least to minimize their harmful consequences.

During the early months of the Peace Corps, Sargent Shriver, disappointed in the small number of requests foreign governments had submitted for corps programs, urged his "programmers" to seek out more requests. According to one account, those who failed to come back with programs "in their pockets" were fired or fell into disfavor. As a result, some programmers created fictitious programs. It has been argued that Shriver should bear some responsibility for these consequences since he should have foreseen that his own injunction could induce such behavior by some of his staff.[75] When a superior puts great pressure on subordinates to produce results and gives the impression that questionable practices to achieve these results will be condoned—as allegedly occurred in the army recruiting scandals reported in the fall of 1979—then the blame falls at least equally on the superior. Ignorance ceases even to mitigate responsibility.

But that an official apply pressure, even of the mild sort Shriver evidently exerted, is not a necessary condition for making an official responsible for the subsequent actions of others. Officials who set in motion bureaucratic routines cannot escape culpability for the consequences even if they are no longer involved in the process when the consequences occur. The system of double bookkeeping that Henry Kissinger approved in 1969, supposedly to conceal a single bombing attack on Cambodia, persisted "by rote and without a special new decision" and led other officials in 1973 to give Congress false information.[76] Even if the initial bombing and secrecy could somehow be justified, Kissinger would not escape blame for the subsequent deception. Whether the bureaucratic routines are pathological or conventional (or both), they can be anticipated. That they have a life of their own, often roaming beyond their original purpose, is a fact of organizational behavior that officials should be expected to appreciate. The more the consequences of a decision fit such bureaucratic patterns, the less an official can plausibly invoke the excuse from ignorance.

The Compulsion of Offices

Yet an official may still have an escape. Some of the most normal and expected patterns of behavior in bureaucracies are also the most difficult to change, and some of these patterns may force an official to continue to act in harmful ways despite the fact that the harm is foreseeable. Just as the excuse from ignorance begins to falter, the excuse from compulsion comes to the rescue. Of the many kinds of constraints that officials cite to reduce their responsibility for decisions, those that derive from the actions of other officials, rather than from forces of nature or reactions of the public, bear most directly on the problem of many hands.

The question of responsibility certainly arises when an official issues an explicit order to carry out a morally objectionable policy, but this kind of compulsion is relatively rare in the workaday life of administrators in modern bureaucracies.[77] More common are cases where no explicit order has been given, but subordinates believe that a superior expects them to pursue a morally dubious course of action. This is the gray area between command and discretion. When a superior relies on subordinates to know what to do without being told, the superior should no more escape responsibility for the actions of subordinates than should the subordinates. No one ordered FBI Director L. Patrick Gray to destroy the incriminating files from E. Howard Hunt's safe. But, as Gray later testified, "The clear implication . . . was that these two files were to be destroyed."[78]

A kind of constraint even more common than the orders or expectations of a superior is that created by various practices established by officials who may no longer be identifiable. Such practices can circumscribe an official's range of choices, and thus may mitigate his or her responsibility. Consider Mayor Beame's dilemma during the New York City fiscal crisis just before the market for city securities collapsed in the spring of 1975.[79] Among other charges, critics accused Beame of misleading the public by failing to disclose the true state of the city's finances. Beame insisted that it was not his fault if the budget misrepresented the city's financial condition. He had inherited the questionable accounting practices ("gimmicks," the critics called them) that gave rise to any misrepresentation. Those practices that he knew about, he could neither change nor even publicize without (he believed) risking the bankruptcy of the city, and jeopardizing the livelihood and welfare of millions of the city's residents. For example, the budget overstated the amount of federal and state aid the city expected to receive because city officials recorded as "receivable" funds that federal and state officials did not intend to allocate. Beame argued that if he had removed the disputed receivables from the books, or even had conceded that they were in dispute, he would have significantly reduced the chances of collecting these funds from the federal and state governments. There were other such "gimmicks"— nearly all difficult to change, and none of them of the mayor's making.

We may be prepared to excuse Beame as mayor for the existence of these practices, and blame him less for any decisions they constrained. We would normally impute more responsibility to the mayor's predecessors. But in this case there is a twist: among his predecessors were Abe Beame, Controller, 1969–73, 1962–65; Abe Beame, Budget Director, 1952–61; and Abe Beame, Assistant Budget Director, 1946–52. Personal responsibility, unlike role responsibility, pursues officials through time.

Some bureaucratic practices, unobjectionable in intent, turn out to limit the performances of officials in harmful ways. Such constraints particularly affect those officials who have been called "street-level bureaucrats"—social workers, police officers and others who deal frequently with citizens, and exercise considerable discretion in an uncertain environment.[80] Because these officials face demanding standards of job performance and rarely have sufficient resources to meet them, they develop "bureaucratic mechanisms" to evade responsibility for their failures. Because the performance of officials in the Job Corps program was measured by the number of trainees who received a job after completing the program, officials tended to recruit those youths who already seemed disposed to succeed in a job. These turned out to be youths with more of a middle-class than a lower-class orientation.[81] A seemingly neutral procedure of evaluation thus gave rise to discriminatory bureaucratic conduct.

In these circumstances, we would want to impute major responsibility to the higher-level officials who set up the procedures—if we could locate those officials. But the street-level bureaucrats themselves cannot be considered blameless. Even within the constraints of fixed routines, some officials perform worse than others, and these variations open some space for ascribing responsibility. A measure of actual variation—for example, an average performance—would not serve as a satisfactory base line from which to assess responsibility since all officials may be doing less well than they could, even given the constraints. We would need a criterion based on a hypothetical average performance—what the average official could reasonably be expected to do under the circumstances (a "reasonable bureaucrat" test?). Furthermore, when these lower-level officials come to recognize how certain bureaucratic routines cause them to perform in morally questionable ways, they acquire, as do other officials who work within defective structures, a specific responsibility to call attention to the defects, even if they cannot correct them.

Insofar as we locate the officials who are personally responsible for public policy, we refine and fortify the praise and blame that, as democratic citizens, we direct toward governments. To discover the individuals who are most closely connected to decisions and policies, citizens must go beyond the simpler standards of hierarchical and collective responsibility, and must avoid formulas (such as alternative cause or pure intention) that would overly simplify personal responsibility itself. Personal responsibility may require citizens to know more about what more officials do, and to make more nuanced judgments about what they do. Yet it offers a stronger foundation for democratic accountability.[82]

Personal responsibility can support accountability for decisions and policies that are less attributable to any current officials than to the bureaucratic structures in which the officials act. Because personal responsibility attaches to persons, not to offices or collectivities, it follows officials wherever they go. We can trace it through time—to the past when the mayor was the controller, or to the future when the solicitor general makes good on his claim that he was the least bad alternative. Furthermore, when we assess officials' responsibility for harmful decisions made within a defective structure, we consider the efforts they make to criticize and change the structure. Even if officials do the best they can in circumstances not of their making, they do not escape blame if they simply and indefinitely accept those circumstances.

The grounds for extending moral responsibility in these ways derive from the volitional criterion. Officials who operate the faulty machinery of government may be presumed to know more than others about its faults. The excuse of ignorance is therefore usually less accessible to them. They are also often in the best position to fulfill or to frustrate the claim that no one can do anything about the faults. Hence, the excuse from compulsion becomes less plausible to the extent that an official fails to promote criticism and reform. To extend responsibility, we thus have to modify in these general ways some of our conventional assumptions about personal responsibility. The specific kinds of modifications that this extended responsibility requires, and the corresponding changes it calls for in the practice of government, emerge most clearly in the use of the criminal law to enforce the responsibility of public officials, the subject of the next chapter.

We can hardly expect to identify officials to hold responsible for all, or perhaps even the worst, evils that governments visit upon their citizens. Nor for that matter can we always identify officials to praise for the good that governments occasionally accomplish. But the pursuit of personal responsibility provides the best foundation for understanding the role that human agency plays in good and bad government, and the strongest basis for enhancing the accountability that democracy should demand of officials of government.

3

Official Crime
and Punishment

When public officials act contrary to their trust, the liberal tradition offers citizens the ultimate remedy of an "appeal to Heaven."[1] It provides less surely for an appeal to earthly judges. In no case is this more evident than in the punishment of official crime. The criminal law has served better to punish the crimes of citizens than the crimes of government against citizens. One reason no doubt is that governments manage the means of punishment. A more fundamental reason is the focus of this chapter: governmental crime does not appear to satisfy the moral conditions that justify the application of the criminal sanction.

In origin and rationale, the criminal law is directed against offenses committed by individuals acting as ordinary citizens. Governmental crime often lacks either an individual criminal or a citizen criminal or both. There may be no individual criminal when the crime is the product of organizational structures rather than of deliberate decisions by individuals. There may be no citizen criminal when the crime can be imputed only to individuals or organizations acting within the scope of their official authority. These two differences between governmental crime and ordinary crime give rise to the theoretical problems examined here.

The first difference creates a problem of moral responsibility: how can we justify punishing individuals or organizations for structural crime which appears to lack the "guilty mind" the criminal law morally requires? This problem plagues the use of the criminal law to control any kind of complex organization, corporations as well as governments. The second difference points to a problem of political responsibility: how can we justify punishing individuals or organizations for crimes committed in their official capacity as agents of a democratic government? This problem affects the use of the criminal law in government more than other organizations. Governments and their officials are granted discretion to act on behalf of all citizens, and they sometimes are permitted to adopt methods (such as violence) that would be punishable if used by private parties. They seek immunity for their dirty hands.

This chapter argues that neither of these problems stands in the way of using the criminal sanction against public officials. Both reveal, however, a need for broader notions of personal responsibility and public office, and both undermine the idea of organizational responsibility for crimes of government, at least on most conceptions of punishment.[2] One implication of the argument strengthens the central contention of chapter 2. If the severe sanction of criminal punishment can be justified to enforce personal responsibility in government, then a fortiori the application of milder sanctions should be acceptable in many instances. But on its own terms, the criminal sanction deserves a more secure place in the arsenal of accountability. Between revolution and submission, no other way of calling public officials to account fulfills the same purpose as the criminal law. Without it, citizens are limited to measures that are either less discriminate or less stringent. Criminal punishment is both specific and severe in condemning, on behalf of a democratic community, the violation of shared standards of public office.

The Problem of Moral Responsibility

Since the problem of moral responsibility in government arises from characteristics that governments share with other complex organizations, we should consider the problem in the context of organizations in general. In the law it is the corporation that has provoked the most sustained discussion of the problem. Several writers in recent years have pointed out the existence of structural crime in corporations, and noted that the criminal law in its standard form does not cope well with this kind of crime.[3] These observations themselves are consistent with many different theories of responsibility, including the view to be defended here. Certainly any search to discover the causes and any reforms to prevent the recurrence of such crime cannot focus exclusively on individuals. But the existence of structural crime is often alleged to have more far-reaching implications. It is taken to dictate a particular answer to the general question of responsibility in complex organizations—what may be called the structuralist thesis.[4]

Proponents of the structuralist thesis make two distinct claims. First, they deny that individuals can be held criminally responsible for many crimes of organizations. Second, they affirm that organizations can be held criminally responsible. These two claims must be distinguished because, though the first often leads to the second, the second may be maintained alone. We may assert, for example, that both individuals and corporations are liable for different types of crimes or even for the same crime.[5] (Less plausibly, we might hold only the first claim, in effect implying that no agent can be held responsible for most organizational crime.)

Structuralists share some of the assumptions of the model of collective responsibility discussed in chapter 2. Their claims are more limited, however. They refer to the responsibility of members of organizations for crimes of those organizations, not to the responsibility of members of whole societies for all kinds of moral wrongs. Structuralists are not committed to the conclusion that no one, or everyone, is morally responsible for many of the harmful consequences of organizational decisions and policies. Nevertheless, the notion of personal responsibility deployed against the collective model also serves to undermine the first part of the structuralist thesis.

Personal Responsibility

Consider, then, the claim that we cannot legitimately ascribe personal responsibility for crimes in organizations. Like moral responsibility, criminal liability requires that an individual charged with an offense have the ability and knowledge to act otherwise than he or she did. The requirement of a guilty mind for many crimes consists of either the "intention to do the immediate act or bring about the consequences of (in some crimes) recklessness as to such act or consequence."[6]

The structuralists who reject personal responsibility for organizational crime presumably do not mean that we can never legitimately bring criminal charges against individuals in organizations. Structuralists need not deny that we can punish illegal conduct that is plainly outside the scope of office. An official who takes a bribe or extorts money from a client, in the absence of any authorization or encouragement by the organization, is surely guilty of a crime as an individual. The difference between personal and official crime is not always clear, but it is best captured by the distinction in French administrative law between a *faute personnelle,* for which an individual alone is blamed, and a *faute de service,* for which the organization is also culpable. The former reveals "a man with his [personal] weakness, his passions, his imprudence," whereas the latter manifests an "impersonal" official who, like anyone in the position, is "more or less subject to error."[7] The distinction is not primarily one of motives (acting for one's own ends or for the organization's goals) since most illegal conduct in organizations probably embodies many different motives at the same time.[8] Official crime is better conceived as conduct authorized or supported by the organization, either formally through instructions and procedures or informally through the norms and practices of the organization.

But not all official crime in this sense creates a problem of responsibility. That an official was merely following orders will not usually protect him from criminal liability, even when he had reason to believe that the order came from the highest officials in the organization.[9] In defense against a conspiracy charge involving the break-in at the office of Daniel Ellsberg's psychiatrist, John Ehrlichman pleaded that he reasonably believed that the president had authorized the entry. The Federal District Court held that even if the president had done so Ehrlichman would still be liable for failing to recognize that the break-in violated the law.[10]

Nor does the problem of responsibility arise simply because many individuals take part in a crime. The ways the criminal law distinguishes among degrees of participation, including individual roles in conspiracies and other inchoate crimes, more or less conform to the principles of moral responsibility.[11] Even in cases of collective omissions—as when all the officers in an organization fail in a duty to prevent a harm that any one of them alone could have prevented—the common law generally agrees with morality in holding each of them responsible.[12] If the structuralist thesis is to have any plausibility, its objection to personal responsibility must be stated more specifically.

The problem that seems to worry the structuralists springs from two characteristics of organizations—specialization and routinization. Because of the first, individuals who have knowledge of a crime (usually lower-level officials) may not have the ability to do anything about it, and the individuals who have the ability (higher-level officials) do not have knowledge of it. The division of organizational labor thus becomes a division of moral agency: any particular role allows an individual to satisfy only one of the conditions necessary for moral and legal responsibility. Police officers, for example, may observe their colleagues taking bribes but fail to report them out of fear of retaliation, or in the belief that their supervisors will do nothing about the corruption.[13] Subordinates believe, often correctly, that their superiors do not want to know about illegal behavior in the organization.[14] In such cases, prosecuting only those officials who most obviously satisfy the conditions of responsibility will serve neither to prevent the corruption not to provide just punishment. As long as we insist on personal responsibility, we can, it seems, bring no more than weak charges against those who fail to report a crime, and no charges at all against the superiors who know nothing about it.

Routinization also poses an obstacle to ascribing personal responsibility for organizational crime. Contrary to anyone's intentions, practices and norms of an organization may contribute to criminal activity. A practice may have been originally intended to serve respectable purposes, but eventually come to promote criminal projects. The city of "Rainfall West" adopted stringent health and safety standards for restaurants and cabarets, presumably better to protect the health and safety of citizens. But the standards were so stringent that almost no business could satisfy them. City inspectors, police, and prosecutors enjoyed enormous discretion in deciding which businesses to charge with violations. These conditions invited the selective prosecution, extortion, and bribery that occurred.[15] In other instances, no one consciously establishes the practices. Routines simply develop piecemeal over the years, as part of the informal culture of an organization.[16] Organizational routines appear to take on a life of their own and to play a greater role in creating crime than do decisions of any individuals. It would not make sense, according to the structuralist view, to impute responsibility to any individual in these circumstances, certainly not criminal responsibility.

Even in the case of structural crime, however, the structuralist claim does not seem warranted. The mistake the structuralists make is to take an overly static view of organizational behavior, looking at only one crime at a time. If we adopt a more historical perspective, routinization and specialization can actually aid the ascription of personal responsibility. Because organizations develop routines, their mistakes recur in predictable ways. Their designs may not be dark but their crimes are reiterated.

The patterns of pathology known to theorists of organizations can be, and often are, just as well known to those who work in organizations. Higher officials may not be aware of specific crimes in their organization, but they know, or should know, that certain structural conditions (such as discretion in enforcing strict standards) give rise to organizational corruption. Individuals who could be expected to know about these conditions and take steps to correct them could be morally blameworthy and in some cases properly subject to criminal sanctions. At the least, officials could be required to inform legislators that the conditions may be contributing to corruption.

Where the causes or conditions cannot be diagnosed in advance and where higher-level officials must rely on lower-level officials to report and check corruption, we still need not despair of assigning responsibility to individuals. Here specialization can be an ally of personal responsibility. The law can require that organizations establish offices specifically charged with discovering and preventing crime in the organization and protecting officials who seek to report criminal activity there. Inspectors-General, Merit Systems Protection Boards, Ombudsmen, Parliamentary Commissioners, and Vulnerability-Assessment Task Forces already go some way toward establishing institutions that could hold specific individuals responsible for failure to prevent organizational crime, and virtually all individuals in the organization responsible for at least reporting such crime.[17] Failure to maintain and protect institutions that help expose crime would itself be a crime. In these various ways, the very characteristics of organizations that make it difficult to hold individuals criminally responsible for isolated crime make it possible to hold them responsible for the reiterated crime that organizations commonly occasion.

But a problem remains. The personal responsibility that we can accommodate in this way falls short of the standard of *mens rea* that the criminal law normally requires. By making officials liable for crime they should have known about, regardless of whether they actually knew about it, we establish negligence as a principal basis for criminal culpability. Although many legal systems punish negligence, most confine the practice to offenses involving serious and direct physical harm, and even in this limited form it has been subjected to persistent criticism.[18] When we punish negligence, it is said, we violate a fundamental moral principle of the criminal law—that persons should not be punished unless they have "made a conscious choice to do something [they] knew to be wrong."[19] In the view of the critics, the boundary of criminal liability might extend to recklessness (a conscious disregard of risk), but it would stop short of negligence (an unreasonable failure to be aware of a risk).[20]

Stated in this form (as it usually is), the objection against punishing negligence is too broad. The moral principle that underlies criminal liability does not imply that a person must have had in mind at the time of acting the desire for, or awareness of, the harm prohibited by the law. Rather, it requires that the act must have been voluntary in the sense that the person could have done otherwise.[21] "What is crucial," as H. L. A. Hart has shown, "is that those whom we punish should have had, when they acted, the normal capacities, physical and mental, for doing what the law requires and abstaining from what it forbids, and a fair opportunity to exercise these capacities."[22] The law may legitimately punish negligence if a reasonable person would have taken the precautions that the accused failed to take, and the accused had the capacities to take those precautions. Following this approach, we would draw the boundary of criminal responsibility between negligence and strict liability. While the latter disregards moral responsibility (punishing a prohibited act regardless of efforts the accused made or could have made), the former still respects it.

That negligence may be justifiable grounds for punishing some crimes does not show that it is an acceptable basis for punishing organizational crime. Most commentators who endorse the idea of criminal negligence limit its application to "gross" rather than ordinary deviations from a reasonable standard of care, and many organizational crimes result from negligence that seems quite ordinary.[23] The section chief in the Bureau of Mines who fails to assign inspectors to a company with an uneven record in compliance, or the FDA official who ignores an internal memorandum that warns of danger in a drug about to be approved hardly seems guilty of "a failure to exercise even that care which a careless person would use."[24] Furthermore, even proposals such as the revised versions of the U.S. Criminal Code that would criminalize some supervisory failures adopt a standard of recklessness ("willful default") rather than negligence.[25]

There are, nevertheless, several reasons for adopting the stricter standard of negligence in judging organizational crime. First, a view that justifies punishing negligence directs our attention beyond the current state of mind of the criminal and the immediate occasion of the crime to the prior circumstances in which the negligence originated. In this way, the view expresses a concept of responsibility that better represents human relationships in a moral community. On this view, we do not conceive of officials confronting citizens as isolated individuals at discrete moments, sharing only an awareness that they should not intentionally harm one another. Instead, we regard them as persons having characters shaped over time in association with each other, sharing an understanding that officials owe citizens a more stringent and constant concern. In such a community, citizens would judge officials according to standards of care that the community has evolved, and in light of the past efforts that each has made to satisfy those standards. Organizations provide the order and continuity necessary to sustain such standards. For practical reasons, the criminal law may confine its attention to the immediate context of a crime, but its underlying conception of moral responsibility, at least as applied to organizational life, should be understood to have greater temporal extension.

A second reason that negligence in organizations may deserve the criminal sanction derives from the nature of the harm that the negligence can cause. The degree of care demanded by a standard of conduct has traditionally been set in proportion to the apparent risk. That risk may be higher in organizational crime.[26] The magnitude and persistence of the harm from even a single act of negligence in a large organization is usually greater than from the acts of individuals on their own. The greater risk comes from not only the effects of size but also from those of function. In the common law of official nonfeasance, for example, public officials whose duties include the "public peace, health, or safety" may be criminally liable for negligence for which other officials would not be indictable at all.[27] Because of the tendency of organizational negligence to produce greater harm, we may be justified in attaching more serious penalties to less serious departures from standards. Although the departure may be ordinary, the potential harm is gross.

A related reason for imposing stricter standards in organizations is that officials are more likely to underestimate the harm that their negligence may cause. The division of labor and remoteness of outcomes combine to create a psychological distance that may make efforts to take precautions seem less important than they are.[28] To compensate for this discounting effect, the law may have to attach more severe sanctions to some kinds of negligence than would be warranted either solely by the harm produced in any particular instance or by the harm produced by this type of negligence in general. It is sometimes claimed that negligent harms do not call for such severe sanctions as do intentional harms because any specific negligent act is less likely anyhow to be repeated than the equivalent intentional act.[29] Whatever the merits of this distinction in ordinary life, it does not hold in organized activities, where persistent harm is at least as likely to be caused negligently as intentionally. The careless bureaucrat is probably more common than the malicious one.

Finally, the idea of consent justifies imposing the stricter standards of negligence on officials who violate them in any particular instance. In organizations we have a stronger basis for claiming that negligent conduct is voluntary. The standards that an official is supposed to observe can be made more explicit and better known in organized than in unorganized activity. Also, the decision that an individual makes to hold office in an organization can be more plausibly taken to signify acceptance of those standards. How far these considerations warrant our regarding an act of negligence as voluntary depends on how strongly the organization and the law support the standards. It also depends on how readily officials can take steps in advance to prevent organizational crime or to avoid participating in it.

When we cannot reasonably expect an official to take such steps, we may wish the law to condemn only continuing participation in crime. But even here, the law may demand some further action from participants. They may be required to report the activity to appropriate officials or to persons outside the organization, and perhaps even to resign from office and publicly denounce the activity. While we would hardly want to insist that officials resign whenever they should foresee any risk of involvement in crime, we can surely expect that they resign when they see a pattern of crime in which they are likely to play a part and which they cannot otherwise avoid. Even Talleyrand, one of the most brazen apologists for holding on to power, recognized as much. While rationalizing his own decision to remain in office when ordered to commit a crime, he conceded that an official would have to resign if the crime were not isolated.[30] The moral responsibility of office, moreover, does not wholly terminate upon resignation. We may wish to insist that former officials make some effort at least to bring the negligence of their former colleagues to public attention. There is a moral life—and perhaps there should be legal liability—after resignation.

Despite the complications to which any standard of negligence would have to attend, we have stronger reasons for attaching criminal penalties to negligence in organizational than in ordinary life. If these reasons were better appreciated, citizens and officials might come to view negligence in office more harshly than they do now. Stronger legislation against official negligence would become possible, and its successful prosecution more practicable. In any case, these reasons provide theoretical grounds for extending the criminal liability of officials in organizations, and to this extent undermine the structuralist claim that individuals cannot be held personally responsible for organizational crime.

Organizational Responsibility

The second structuralist claim makes organizations themselves the object of the criminal sanction.[31] While organizations cannot be imprisoned, they can be punitively fined and sentenced to probation, and they can suffer the stigma of a criminal conviction. Some versions of the claim would hold an organization responsible even when we can identify no individual fault, but most would charge the organization, on the doctrine of *respondeat superior,* only when an individual acting on its behalf commits an offense.[32] The latter view thus still has to rely on some notion of individual responsibility in order to establish organizational guilt.

Organizational responsibility, it is claimed, provides a more efficient deterrent than individual responsibility. An organization stands in the best position to discover and discipline the misconduct of its own officials, and will do so efficiently if the law threatens the organization with sufficiently stiff penalties. Critics have pointed out that a fine large enough to deter corporations would usually exceed their ability to pay. It would therefore serve as no deterrent at all when, as often is the case, the risk of discovery is low and the expected gain is high.[33] Also, the higher the penalty, the greater are the internal pressures to conceal the illegal conduct from officials who might be able to do something about it.

These criticisms cast doubt on the efficacy of organizational responsibility, but they are not decisive. We lack the empirical evidence that would show the effects of different schedules of penalties on the frequency and variety of organizational crime. The question of the moral status of organizational responsibility therefore takes on critical importance. Three objections to holding organizations morally responsible deserve to be considered.[34]

First, it is argued that an organization by its nature cannot be a moral agent in the sense required by the criminal law because organizations lack minds. The notion of a "mental state has no meaning when applied to a corporate defendant since an organization possesses no mental state."[35] Partly for this reason, in virtually all civil law countries the general rule is that corporations are not criminally liable.[36] Organizations do not have minds in the same sense that persons do, and the efforts to show that corporations have characteristics that resemble aspects of the mental states of individuals do not dispose of this difficulty.[37] The existence of a decision-making structure or a capacity for long-range planning yields at best only partial analogies. The "intention" of an organizational "mind" exists only by virtue of conventions stipulating that the statements and actions of individuals in certain positions in the organization count as expressing the purposes of the organization.

Although organizations do not have minds of their own, they might still be morally blameworthy. The law requires *mens rea* for persons because they have minds, but from this requirement it does not follow that *mens rea* is necessary for punishing entities that do not have minds. Since the "minds" of organizations differ so fundamentally from the minds of persons, we should expect the criteria for ascribing organizational responsibility also to differ. The criteria are likely to refer partly to the states of mind of individuals (for example, the principal officers of a corporation). But there is no reason to suppose that the criteria can be reduced to statements referring only to individuals, and therefore no reason to deny that an organization can be held liable as a collectivity, independently of any responsibility that we may also wish to impute to its members.[38] When we blame Hooker Chemical for dumping hazardous chemical waste at Love Canal or the Niagara Falls Board of Education for permitting a school to be built on the site, we are partly condemning (past and present) officials of the corporation and the board.[39] But we are doing more than that. We are also criticizing the practices of the organizations—the internal and external patterns of relationships—that persist even as the identities of the individuals who participate in them change.

That we may morally criticize organizations, however, does not imply that we should criminally punish them. A second objection to organizational responsibility maintains that the effects of punishing organizations are unfair.[40] The unfairness results not from the direct punishment of an organization that may not be a moral agent, but from the indirect punishment of individuals associated with the organization who may not be morally responsible. When the law fines a corporation, many persons suffer who could have done nothing to prevent the crime—among them, shareholders, employees, and consumers. The heaviest burdens, moreover, do not necessarily fall on those who benefited the most from the corporate misconduct. It is important in any event to preserve in the law the moral difference between benefiting from a wrong and contributing to it by an act or omission. It is one thing to make the beneficiaries of misconduct pay the costs of damages when the costs must fall somewhere. It is quite another to impose punitive damages and the stigma of punishment on persons who had neither the knowledge of the crime nor the capacity to do anything about it.

The validity of this objection plainly depends on the kind of punishment the law prescribes. The objection is most cogent when the law imposes a fine or penalty that impairs the performance of an organization and spreads the costs of the impairment indiscriminately among all connected with the organization. The objection is less persuasive when the law directs the sanction more specifically toward the source of the criminal activity, as in the proposals for corporate probation or the equity fine.[41] But no matter how precisely targeted the sanction, the stigma of conviction falls in some measure on everyone associated with the organization. If the sanction does not in some sense convey the idea that the organization was a bad one of which to be a member, the sanction seems no more than a civil penalty. But if the sanction carries the moral force of punishment, it should respect the moral constraints of justifiable punishment. Punishing the organization spreads the blame beyond the responsibility and is to that extent without moral justification.

A third objection to organizational responsibility concerns its implications for organizational autonomy. We can begin to see the danger of these implications in the work of some of the philosophers who justify punishing corporations. They are ready to grant some valuable prerogatives to the corporations they regard as fit to assume full moral responsibility for violating the law. If corporations are "like persons" with respect to criminal liability, then, one philosopher suggests, "they should also have the rights that people have" and therefore, he implies, they do not have to be so closely "watched and regulated."[42] Accepting organizational responsibility does not entail conferring on corporations full personhood with all its attendant rights. But the practice of holding organizations responsible does have some troubling implications—for organizations that could be punished as well as for those that actually are. The practice implies that all organizations (at least those with the status of moral agents) deserve to have their autonomy respected on terms similar to those enjoyed by citizens. Seeking a warrant to punish criminal corporations, the advocates of corporate responsibility may find that they have granted all corporations a moral license to resist many desirable forms of legal and political control.

Just because we punish corporations, we do not of course have to grant them all the rights we accord persons. The problem is that as subjects of punishment, rather than of only civil penalty, corporations have a stronger moral basis than they should have on which to press claims for autonomy. It is not the extension of rights that is objectionable but the basis on which the extension takes place. The legal rights of a corporation (as distinct from the rights of its members) should rest mainly on social utility, and they should be able to be overridden when they conflict with the legitimate claims of a majority of citizens.[43] The rights of persons have an independent moral basis and cannot be so directly set aside.[44]

This and other important differences between corporations and individuals are obscured by the assumption that both similarly deserve to be held morally and criminally responsible. Such an assumption leads courts and commentators to extend to corporations a wide range of personal rights—often without insisting that these rights be justified on a basis fundamentally different from the rights of individuals. This tendency is especially noticeable in criminal procedure,[45] but it also reaches into other areas, including even First Amendment rights.[46]

Because organizational responsibility distributes punishment beyond moral responsibility and because it encourages unjustified organizational autonomy, we should be wary of it. We should rely instead on personal responsibility to provide the foundation for the punishment of crimes in organizations.

The Problem of Political Responsibility

Governments are a special kind of organization: they and their agents claim various forms of immunity from the law. Their special status, it is argued here, should not shield governmental officials from the personal liability that individuals in other kinds of organizations incur. On the contrary, the officials of government may have to meet even stricter standards of responsibility. Similarly, the objections to imposing criminal sanctions on organizations apply even more strongly to imposing the sanctions on governmental organizations. The objections apply more strongly, not because governments enjoy any special immunities, but because they must accept special duties.

Insofar as officials and organizations outside government share the characteristics of those in government, these conclusions cover them as well. Where we draw the boundary between government and nongovernment (or between public and private institutions) does not critically affect the argument. What matters here is that we do not permit claims of immunity to stand in the way of ascribing criminal responsibility to governmental officials, or to provide a basis for withholding it from governmental organizations.

The rationale for the immunity of governmental organizations differs somewhat from that for the immunity of officials, but both appeal to the same characteristic of government—its sovereignty in the making and enforcing of the laws. Justice Holmes put forth the classic judicial statement of the rationale: "There can be no legal right as against the authority that makes the law on which the right depends."[47] As his chief authority for this principle, Holmes cited chapter 26 of *Leviathan*, where Hobbes maintains that "the sovereign . . . is not subject to the civil laws."[48] Since in Hobbes's preferred commonwealth the sovereign is a monarch against whom citizens have no (effective) rights, democrats could hardly embrace the doctrine of sovereign immunity on these terms.

But there is a more nearly democratic version of the doctrine, in which the sovereign consists of a majority of citizens.[49] Such a majority (and any public ministers acting in its name) enjoy the privileges of sovereign office, which includes immunity from certain laws. The sovereign may prescribe standards for the proper exercise of governmental authority, and establish penalties for its abuse. But because the standards cannot be specified in detail in advance, officials must have considerable discretion to act on behalf of the sovereign. To permit any other officials of government to prosecute what they regard as abuses of this discretion would be to allow them to substitute their own judgment for that of officials directly acting for the democratic sovereign. The sovereign itself could authorize the punishment, but a sensible sovereign will not do so because of the danger of "overdeterrence."[50] The mere general threat of the punishment and the conflicts it can produce among the sovereign's representatives may discourage even conscientious officials from vigorously carrying out the duties of their office, and may dissuade worthy persons from accepting appointment to public office. Therefore, the democratic version of the immunity doctrine would subject governmental agencies and their officials to criminal sanctions only in the most flagrant cases of personal crime, where wrongdoing takes place completely beyond the scope of office. For all other misconduct, the sanctions of the political process—elections, administrative discipline, legislative oversight, impeachment—would be applied.

The notion of sovereign immunity has left its mark, sometimes in subtle ways, on many different practices in modern democracy. It appears more often in the civil than in the criminal law, but even in civil cases, judges often state the doctrine of sovereign immunity so broadly that it would, if taken seriously, protect officials from criminal liability as well. In *Nixon v. Fitzgerald,* the opinion of the Court, according to the dissenters, places the president above the law; it revives the doctrine that the king can do no wrong: "Taken at face value, the Court's position that . . . the president is absolutely immune should mean that he is immune not only from damages actions but also from suits for injunctive relief, criminal prosecutions and from any kind of judicial process."[51] Members of Congress enjoy immunity under the Speech and Debate Clause, which on recent interpretations shields them from prosecution even for some crimes (such as bribery) that are clearly beyond the scope of their office.[52] While executive and administrative officials cannot so easily escape prosecution for such gross personal crimes, they rarely face charges for official crimes.[53]

Even treating officials exactly as citizens can have the effect of conferring immunity in those activities in which only officials engage. The most pervasive manifestation of this kind of immunity is the absence of any provisions in the law to prohibit many of the harms that officials and agencies cause—those that result, for example, from supervisory negligence in the control of corruption, the inspection of mines, or the certification of dangerous drugs. The criminal law hardly takes notice of the special duties of public office. The sections of the U.S. Criminal Code dealing with public officials refer almost exclusively to bribery, conflict of interest, and fraud.[54] The common law of official misconduct is infrequently invoked.

Although we may wish to preserve some of the practices of immunity on other grounds, we should not rely on the rationale of sovereign immunity even in its most nearly democratic form. That rationale is seriously flawed in several respects. It may be true, as Hobbes and Holmes imply, that the idea of the criminal responsibility of a government as a whole is unintelligible except in an international system. We would have to imagine the government holding itself responsible, simultaneously punishing and being punished. But the absurdity disappears if instead of viewing the government as an indivisible entity, we think of it as composed of various parts (executive and judicial branches, or local and state jurisdictions). From this perspective the criminal responsibility of government simply means that one part of the government pronounces judgment and imposes sanctions on another part (agencies as well as officials). If a democratic constitution assigns these duties to prosecutors and courts, they act in the name of the democratic sovereign no less than the officials whose conduct they judge. As long as the criminal laws and the constitutional arrangements remain open to review through the democratic process, we cannot plausibly argue that the idea of democratic government itself calls for any kind of criminal immunity for anyone.

The argument that the possibility of prosecution for misconduct will "overdeter" officials and agencies depends largely on empirical assumptions that have not been supported with any substantial evidence. Officials and their judicial defenders repeatedly invoke that argument in favor of civil immunity, but they never show the actual effects that civil liability has on the legitimate activities of officials (for example, by comparing jurisdictions that grant greater and lesser degrees of immunity).[55] Some indirect evidence suggests that such effects may occur, and this may provide a reason for granting officials some form of civil immunity.[56] But it does not establish the claim that the criminal sanction overdeters officials. The inhibiting effects of civil actions are likely to be more extensive than those of criminal charges because so many more people can bring civil suits.

Tough penalties for misconduct may discourage some people from accepting public office, but they may also encourage more worthy people to accept office by making public service a more honorable calling. Evidence does not support, for example, the common belief that the stringent disclosure and conflict-of-interest provisions of the Ethics in Government Act have impeded the recruitment of political executives. The act may in fact serve to protect honest officials from false charges, and help persuade them to stay in public office.[57]

Finally, political sanctions are not adequate to the task that advocates of immunity assign them. The basic problem is that a political judgment may fasten on almost any feature of the whole performance or character of an official or an organization. Clever officials can usually point to other achievements which, even if not outweighing their crimes, will at least divert their judges. When the assembly of the Roman people asked Scipio to "render his accounts," he talked instead of his great military victory and led the people to the Capitol to thank the gods. Bentham remarked that "had I lived at that time, most probably I should have gone up with the rest to the Capitol, but I should always have attained a little curiosity with respect to the accounts."[58]

Present-day politicians do not need to distract voters with military .victories. Even without immunity and even after conviction, officials can evade political punishment. Convicted of accepting a bribe while mayor of Union City, New Jersey, William V. Musto pleaded that his crime was "victimless," that his wrongdoing was trivial compared to the corruption that goes on in other cities, and that he had already suffered enough from the publicity. The judge was not persuaded, but enough voters evidently were; they reelected him decisively.[59] However permissively we may interpret the right of citizens to elect anyone they choose, we should not suppose that the criminal sanction and the political sanction serve precisely the same purposes.

Neither are quasi-judicial procedures such as impeachment an adequate substitute for criminal prosecution. Even when successful, they only remove the official from office and (sometimes) bar him from holding office in the future; they do not impose any further punishment. Impeachable offenses, furthermore, are not identical to crimes.[60] Also, disciplinary proceedings against permanent officials are notoriously ineffective in punishing misconduct partly because accused officials have so many procedural protections. Indeed, the possibility of a criminal charge may often be required to set in motion an adverse action against an official.[61]

Personal Responsibility in Government

Instead of looking to Hobbes for the foundation of official responsibility, we should attend to Locke. Neither Hobbes nor Locke conceives of the relation between citizens and the government strictly as a contract, which would imply a reciprocal recognition of rights. Hobbes does not, because he wants to deny that citizens have any effective rights against the sovereign. Locke does not, because he wishes to deny that rulers have rights against citizens.

For Locke, the relationship between citizens and the executive, and between citizens and the legislature, resembles a fiduciary trust.[62] Locke in effect transfers the concept from private law to public law, merging the trustor and the beneficiary into one party (the citizenry). The government as trustee incurs a unilateral obligation to citizens to act for their good. The concept implies that citizens can at any time change the terms of the trust or revoke the power that confers the trust.[63] If we adopt the concept of trust as the basis for the responsibility of public officials, we are not likely to be tempted by the claims of governmental immunity. Although for practical reasons we may decide (democratically) to grant some protection to certain offices or certain functions, we would not accept a theoretical principle that confers on public office any independent rights or privileges.

The idea of trust also has a more far-reaching implication: it justifies a more exacting conception of public office. As Justice Cardozo wrote: "Many forms of conduct permissible in a workaday world for those acting at arm's length are forbidden to those bound by fiduciary ties. A trustee is held to something stricter than the moral of the market place. Not honesty alone, but the punctilio of an honor the most sensitive, is then the standard of behavior."[64] Public office, conceived as a trust, thus imposes higher standards of conduct than does citizenship. Actions that may be permissible or civilly wrong when performed by private citizens could be criminally wrong when done by public officials.

This conception would rejuvenate the common-law offense of official misconduct. In the seminal English case, an official accountant, charged with neglecting and refusing to disclose an item that should have been in governmental accounts, pleaded that his conduct rendered him liable only for a "civil injury, not for a public offense."[65] Lord Mansfield concluded to the contrary: "if a man accepts an office of trust and confidence, concerning the public . . . he is answerable to the King for his execution of that office; and he can only answer to the King in criminal prosecution, for the King cannot otherwise punish his misbehavior, in acting contrary to the duty of office."[66]

The notion of office as a trust has reappeared in American law in recent years under the curious aegis of the federal mail fraud statute.[67] Three state governors, charged with schemes to defraud the public, have been convicted on principles relating to a breach of fiduciary trust.[68] These cases suggest that such a breach can occur even if the scheme defrauds no one of any money or property and even if it enriches no one and was not intended to do so. It is sufficient if in specifiable ways the scheme defrauds citizens of their "right to . . . disinterested and honest government."[69] In the case of Governor Mandel of Maryland, "concealment of material information" about political favors he did for his friends seemed to be enough for conviction.[70]

Commentators have objected to this use of the concept of trust.[71] They argue that, by turning aspirational standards into criminal prohibitions, this application of the concept threatens to discourage "robust" political activity. It could do so, first, because incumbents can exploit its vague standards to harass challengers and other political opponents. Second, the standard may have a chilling effect on political participation and "interfere with the delicate process of coalition formation," which requires the "striking of deals."[72]

These concerns about overcriminalizing the political process cannot be lightly dismissed. But whether the expansion of the legal liability of officials would inhibit legitimate political activity surely depends on what standards of trust we establish for various public offices, and how precisely we formulate them. It may well be that we should carry out any expansion only through explicit legislation rather than judicial interpretation, currently the most common method. We certainly should not seek to support all, or even most, of our moral judgments about politics with the force of the criminal sanction. But from punishing the conduct exemplified in the cases of the corrupt governors—which involved secretly giving favors of office to friends—it is a long way to prohibiting all political deals and all political patronage. Even if the implication of this line of decisions is to turn the mail fraud statute into a "truth-in-government" act, as one critic fears,[73] that result could help citizens know better what kind of "robust" politics is going on so that they can decide what kind of deals and favors they want to tolerate.

To move toward stricter standards of responsibility for public officials, we should consider at least two general kinds of misconduct. First, in accord with the previous analysis of negligence, we could penalize the failure to take reasonable steps to discover and prevent conduct that is already designated criminal. Officials would be liable for supervisory negligence if they held offices that explicitly required oversight of the specific activity in which the crime occurs. Such oversight need not be the exclusive concern of one office, but could also be part of the duties of general supervision.

This approach would extend to government officials a modified form of a doctrine some courts have already applied to corporate officials. Officials who stand in a "responsible relationship" to a crime are liable even if they did not participate in it.[74] What this relationship actually requires remains unclear, and presumably would differ in corporations and governments. But determination of responsible relationships in governmental organizations is precisely the kind of task that democratic theory assigns to legislatures. They are well situated, if any institution is, to fix these relationships in ways that allow for the proper measure of administrative discretion and subsequent judicial review. Legislatures are also in the best position to ensure that greater supervisory liability would not encourage overly cautious, rule-bound administration. They could fashion a package of sanctions that would balance penalties for negligence and rewards for excellence in administration.

A second kind of misconduct is the official obstruction of the democratic process. The concern would be not mainly the protection of procedures in the legal or electoral processes, which are already covered by numerous criminal laws, but the promotion of broader features of the political process such as openness and access. A prime instance of such obstruction would be an official's failure to disclose important information to the public or to designated authorities. Concealing the true state of a city's financial condition, for example, might very well be made a crime even in the absence of any act of perjury. It is perhaps not surprising in our society that failing to disclose certain information to investors in the financial marketplace has long been illegal, but refusing to reveal information to citizens in the political arena has rarely been penalized.[75] There is, of course, a need to protect classified information that officials keep secret for legitimate reasons, but there is equally a need to publicize information that officials conceal mainly for personal or partisan motives. The law pays more attention to the former than to the latter. The U.S. Criminal Code contains many sections that meticulously proscribe unauthorized disclosure of information but virtually none that require disclosure.[76]

A related kind of obstruction of democracy occurs when officials prevent citizens from reporting information or expressing their views to government agencies. Such intimidation may take more subtle forms than the law now normally prohibits. After Cora Walker reported that New York City housing inspectors solicited a bribe as a condition of granting her a certificate of occupancy for her new rooming house, the superintendent of housing immediately filed criminal charges against her for renting rooms without the proper permit. Although she eventually won on appeal, nothing happened to the superintendent or other officials who initiated the criminal proceedings against her.[77]

Officials sometimes improperly discourage not only citizens but other officials from coming forward with important information. Because the Fitzgerald cases posed the issue of the civil liability of officials, the court and the litigants focused on the harm that Fitzgerald suffered in losing his job and having his constitutional rights violated.[78] They gave less attention to the most disturbing consequence of the episode—the inhibiting effect on future officials who, like Fitzgerald, should expose the mistakes and misconduct of their colleagues. To deter and punish such intimidation, the criminal sanction is in principle (though not always in practice) better suited than the civil suit.

Another form that obstruction of the democratic process can take is the encouragement of violations of properly enacted governmental regulations. When the administrator of the Environmental Protection Agency privately promised a small oil refinery in 1982 it would not be penalized if it violated Federal lead standards, she evidently violated no law herself.[79] While the democratic process should grant administrators considerable discretion, it surely does not authorize them selectively to encourage citizens to ignore legitimate regulations, even if administrators plan to change the regulations in the future. These and other instances of official misconduct constitute candidates for offenses under an expansive approach to the criminal responsibility of public officials. That approach, as we have seen, is better guided by a concept of trust than by a concept of immunity.

Organizational Responsibility in Government

That officials should be held criminally liable for some governmental crime does not necessarily imply that governmental organizations should be. To reject the general arguments for immunity that shield both the officials and the organizations of government is not yet to dispose of some claims that would specifically protect governmental organizations.

Both the Model Penal Code and the National Commission's Study Draft of a new Federal Criminal Code explicitly exempt governmental entities from criminal liability, but their rationale for the exemption is obscure. The code's commentator says merely that "corporate liability is generally pointless in such cases."[80] The only reason the commission's staff offers is that public agencies receive closer scrutiny than do private corporations. This is a doubtful distinction, which in any case may be overwhelmed, as the staff seems to recognize, by the similarities between the conditions of criminal activity in public and private organizations.[81]

There have been few domestic cases in which a governmental organization has been a criminal defendant, and apparently only one in which a court has seriously examined the theoretical issues that such status raises. In that case, the Australian High Court overturned the conviction of the manager of a government-owned factory, who was charged with being an accessory in a crime imputed to the government.[82] Although other considerations played a part, three of the five justices suggested that they would not convict the government of a criminal offense (at least in the absence of explicit statutory permission to do so). Apart from some technical points of Australian law, the chief arguments appealed to the "absurdity of supposing that the Executive Government . . . is to be brought before magistrates to receive punishment, a punishment which the Executive may enforce or remit."[83] This claim in part relies on the Hobbesian point rejected above, but it also invokes the practical paradox of punishing the authority that controls the means of punishment and the power of pardon. This "absurdity" may seem more difficult to avoid in the absence of a system of separation of powers, but even in its absence in this case, only one justice considered the paradox to be insurmountable in principle. As one of the dissenters pointed out, the legislature could authorize the funds to pay the fine, and the courts could direct that at least a portion of the fine be paid to the aggrieved parties.[84]

The most substantial objections to organizational responsibility in government are variations on two of the objections already raised against organizational responsibility in general. First, the problem of the dispersion of punishment is even more serious in government than in other organizations. Not only does the punishment fall on citizens who, like shareholders or employees of corporations, had nothing to do with the crime and may not be able to do anything about similar crimes in the future, but it also often falls most heavily on those citizens who have the least opportunity to do anything about such crimes. To assess a fine or punitive damages against the budget of a negligent governmental agency, as some reformers have proposed,[85] would be almost to guarantee that the agency's clients with the least political clout would find their governmental benefits reduced the most. We would perhaps not regret this consequence in the case of some agencies (say, the Department of Commerce), but we should disapprove of it in the case of others (Health and Human Services).

The sanction of probation that some legal reformers would impose on corporations seems inappropriate for governmental organizations.[86] Here we might reasonably object that the judiciary would be usurping functions that the legislature or citizens more generally should exercise. Judicial oversight, even the increasingly common use of "special masters," may be warranted in some instances. But if the structures and procedures of a whole agency are the source of persistent crime, the agency is likely to require massive reorganization and continual review. Such extensive intervention should fall within the province of a legislature, which can consider what changes are appropriate in light of the needs of other governmental agencies and the exigencies of other public policies. Furthermore, if the legislature takes temporary control of an agency in this way, the stigma of a criminal conviction would probably lose most of its significance since the agency would have become a different organization in critical respects.[87] To the extent that the stigma has any force, it could unfairly discredit officials in the agency who are working to improve it, and discourage others who are considering whether to join it. The social harm could be greater from these effects in government than in corporations since a discredited governmental agency may be the only provider of certain essential services for citizens.

If the practice of punishment implies a respect for the rights of all agents potentially subject to its sanctions, then we should be even more hesitant about accepting the practice for governmental than for other kinds of organizations. There are dangers in granting any organization the kind of autonomy we recognize in persons. But nongovernmental organizations can sometimes claim independent rights against government insofar as the organizations express the rights of particular individuals or groups in society. Democratic theory, at least in its liberal versions, assumes that individuals and groups do not have to justify their autonomy by showing that every activity they pursue positively contributes to the good of the whole society. Any autonomy that governmental organizations enjoy, however, must be justified on precisely these grounds. An agency may legitimately claim rights against the rest of the government only when citizens, through the democratic process, determine that these rights would ultimately serve collective purposes.

As long as we wish to treat the organizations of government as solely means to our common ends, we should deny them the status of moral agency, and therefore exclude them from the practice of punishment. This exclusion does not imply that we should not impose sanctions on such organizations. Indeed, in grave cases of reiterated crime, we may have recourse to the analogue of capital punishment—the elimination of the agency. But this and similar sanctions are not, or should not be understood as, punishment. They are political policies, and they need neither respect the same moral constraints nor express the same moral force as the practice of punishment. To suppose otherwise would be to misapprehend the moral and political foundations of criminal responsibility.

Limits of Criminal Responsibility

The practice of punishing public officials (though not public organizations) can help sustain moral responsibility and democratic accountability. But the practice has some significant limitations. The most obvious ones arise from the practical problems of enforcement and deterrence.[88]

Governmental crimes may leave few traces since the victims (sometimes all citizens) do not realize they have been harmed. Prosecution may be under the control of officials who do not wish the crimes to come to light. High-level officials can track the progress of investigation and secretly subvert it. Juries are often hesitant to convict, and judges reluctant to impose stiff sentences on, respectable-looking defendants who plead that they were only doing their duty. To some extent, these problems can be overcome by institutional reforms (such as authorizing special prosecutors) and by changes in public attitudes (such as recognizing the seriousness of negligence in public office). All of the problems concern the capacity of the criminal process to achieve its aims on its own terms. More fundamental are its limitations in serving other purposes of morality and democracy.

First of all, many of the wrongs that governments inflict upon the world are by their nature beyond the reach of the criminal sanction. Some of these wrongs are not appropriately deemed criminal either because none of the decisions that produce them is in itself wrong, or because they are not produced by any decision at all. Extending the argument of chapter 2, the analysis here has suggested that on a proper understanding of responsibility in public office fewer wrongs escape the criminal sanction for these reasons than is usually assumed. But no doubt some still do. The most obvious are those that lie beyond the capacity of any government to correct. Governments sustain the social and economic structures that contribute to disease and famine, but though governments and their officials can sometimes ameliorate this suffering and sometimes exacerbate it, they rarely can change the underlying structures. At least they cannot do so in any period of time that could even in principle fall within the scope of a criminal judgment, however broadly conceived.

Other wrongs are the product of identifiable decisions but cannot be crimes because society disagrees deeply about how serious they are, or about whether they are wrongs at all. Perhaps an act does not have to be "universally disapproved of" by all members of society, as Durkheim maintained,[89] but it cannot be widely approved of by a substantial portion of the society. Many practices that we may wish to regard as criminal must remain the objects of only moral and political condemnation. The injustice of the distribution of wealth in modern societies may be partly attributable to policies of governments and decisions of officials, but its perpetrators are not yet all criminals. Finally, some wrongs that are almost universally considered crimes may not be punishable. In the absence of an international system of criminal justice, high officials who commit war crimes are likely to be able to escape criminal sanctions.

A second set of limitations concerns compensatory justice. The criminal conviction of officials does not help the immediate victims of governmental crime; a civil suit for damages is supposed to serve this aim.[90] Citizens may initiate civil actions themselves, and may do so without having to show that the harms are intentional and without having to go through the cumbersome procedures of a criminal trial. The aggrieved citizen will still encounter a (more explicit) doctrine of sovereign and official immunity.[91] But the doctrine does not, or at least should not, have the same implications in the civil as in the criminal process. In an optimal system, the immunities conferred in one process would be just the reverse of those granted in the other. Officials would be civilly immune but criminally liable, and government would be criminally immune but civilly liable.

The interrelationships among these forms of immunity and their effects on deterrence and justice are complex, but the basic reasons that the civil and criminal process should treat governments and officials differently can be mentioned. Civil sanctions fall more effectively and justly on government (all taxpayers) than do criminal sanctions, but are more likely to "overdeter" individual officials than are properly designed criminal sanctions. An adequate scheme of civil liability for government almost certainly will have to rely on an expanded system of criminal sanctions, but for the purpose of deterring officials rather than satisfying victims.

Perhaps we should not expect the criminal process to ensure that justice is done for innocent citizens, but we should expect it to see that justice is done to guilty officials. An important reason for bringing public officials to trial has traditionally been to demonstrate that all citizens are equal before the law. This is so even if the crime is political, and the punishment capital. In the debates preceding the execution of Louis XVI, the Girondin leaders argued forcefully against proscription and for prosecution under the law: "because every man is a citizen, every man can also be a criminal; because no man is without peers, no man is exempt from judgment."[92]

Despite great inequalities in resources, officials today still are less likely in the courtroom than in other arenas to receive more favorable treatment than ordinary citizens. Indeed, the worry may be that officials stand in greater danger of unfair treatment. They are more visible and therefore perhaps more vulnerable to politically motivated charges. The "political trial" has a long (not wholly unworthy) history in modern government.[93] But most democracies have given judicial institutions sufficient independence to protect against the most blatantly political prosecutions of officials, if not of citizens. Whatever we may think of the FBI's techniques in the ABSCAM investigation of members of Congress, we should not forget that the convicted legislators received at least as much impartial judicial review of their claims of unfair treatment as citizens would have enjoyed in similar circumstances.[94]

Former officials seldom suffer as much as ordinary citizens from the subsequent effects of a criminal conviction. Most of the Watergate criminals, especially those who served in the higher offices, have found respectable positions in the private sector.[95] Some have realized substantial profits from lectures and books about their experiences, and some have gained nomination to public office again.[96] Frank Wills, the alert night watchman who started the chain of events that led to the Watergate convictions, could not for many years find a regular job.[97]

It is often said that the disgrace of conviction is greater for a public official. But if this is so, it should be thought of as merely compensating for the undeserved prestige the official enjoyed while his criminal activity remained undiscovered. Many officials, moreover, elude the disgrace— at least in the circles that matter to them. Charged with failing to testify "fully, completely and accurately" before a senate committee, CIA Director Richard Helms pleaded *nolo contendere* (itself a device corporate and government officials commonly use to avoid the stigma of conviction).[98] Helms implied that he would wear this conviction as a "badge of honor." "I don't feel disgraced at all," he said, "I think if I had done anything else, I would have been disgraced."[99] Helms believed that he had acted out of loyalty to the CIA and the agents he led. It is hard enough to cause the full force of punishment to fall on officials who commit personal crimes in government. It is still more difficult to make it felt by officials who commit crimes of state with the approval of professional colleagues. The criminal sanction can accomplish its purposes in government only where officials can count on the support of colleagues and citizens who share their concern for the integrity of public office, and where officials can rely on institutions that promote collegial cooperation toward this end.

The practice of punishing officials contributes, though in a limited way, to the democratic process. The trial of a public official can dramatically focus public attention on crimes of government. It can, upon occasion, stimulate broader reforms that may help citizens hold officials more accountable in the future. Watergate and other investigations of the early 1970s spurred efforts to strengthen control over the FBI and CIA and to toughen the standards governing the financial dealings of federal executives and legislators in office as well as in campaigns.[100]

But criminal investigations and prosecutions only rarely give rise to such vigorous movements of reform. The exposure to which political authority in the United States was subjected in this period, according to one account, was "unique in modern history, aside from investigations by revolutionary regimes of their predecessors."[101] In any case, the criminal trial itself fixes its attention on particular individuals even when they are charged with structural crimes. Although prosecutors and witnesses may incidentally expose patterns of misconduct, they confine themselves primarily to the offenses of individuals, and to facts that can survive the stringent standards of criminal procedure.

In their efforts to hold officials accountable, citizens should care as much about honoring faithful officials as condemning felonious ones. Although legal reformers at least since Beccaria have criticized the widespread obsession with punishment and the corresponding neglect of reward, our formal institutions remain better suited to denunciation than commendation. Yet the sanction of reward offers several benefits that punishment does not. Bentham noticed that reward serves better to produce "acts of the positive stamp," and is more likely to be self-enforcing because candidates have an incentive to bring forward the necessary evidence.[102] A system of reward could also help check the dangers of overdeterrence by counterbalancing the excessive caution that officials are said to show when working under the threat of the criminal sanction.

Rousseau identified an even more important benefit of a system of reward. In such a system, citizens give "more consideration to persons than to isolated deeds [and can therefore honor] sustained and regular conduct . . . the faithful discharge of the duties of one's station . . . in sum deeds that flow from a man's character and principle."[103] Perhaps robust institutions of reward, such as the Rosière de Salency that Rousseau and Bentham had in mind, are possible only in small, homogenous communities.[104] But something like the broader assessment of character and career that such institutions provide is essential in the democratic process. The institutions of punishment not only fail to serve this function, but because of their preeminent position in the processes of public judgment, they may also prevent other institutions from serving it.

The criminal process is not so inhospitable to democratic participation as is sometimes supposed. It is, after all, the home of the quintessential democratic institution—the jury. There also may be ways of encouraging citizens to take part in the earlier stages of a criminal proceeding. Some political scientists have suggested that recipients of governmental benefits (such as medical care and welfare) could organize so that they could discover and report corruption in the administration of these programs.[105] Criminal proceedings, nevertheless, remain a process in which the government usually must initiate the formal charges, few citizens can actively participate, and no one may officially discuss many of the significant implications of the crime being tried.

None of these limitations of the use of the criminal sanction in government shows that it is in itself unjustified, only that it is insufficient as a method of realizing moral responsibility and democratic accountability of public officials. How significant a place we should assign it in the pursuit of these goals depends in large measure on how we evaluate its merits compared to those of civil, administrative, and political sanctions. One of its most valuable roles may turn out to be as a sanction of last resort for standards that are established and enforced through other institutions and by citizens more generally. The Office of Government Ethics, for example, reviews and clears the financial disclosure reports that high-level officials in the executive branch file to comply with conflict-of-interest rules set by Congress. According to a former director of the office, this process "amounts to prospective enforcement of criminal laws by requiring nominees [for public office] to take precautionary steps to stay out of harm's way."[106] Here, as in many other circumstances, the practice of punishing public officials functions best if no official needs to be punished.

Despite its limitations, criminal responsibility remains an important resource for judging and controlling democratic governments. Through the practice of punishing public officials, a democratic community seeks not only to deter official misconduct, but also to define its collective sense of the standards of public office. The denunciation that punishment expresses is the most solemn statement of what a betrayal of those standards means to the community. We may not always be able to discover the officials who deserve such denunciation, but we should not suppose that the principles of moral responsibility or political democracy stand in the way of bringing them to justice. Neither the organizational complexity nor the sovereign status of democratic governments precludes our holding officials personally responsible for crimes of government.

4

Legislative Ethics

Is legislative ethics possible? The doubts that this question raises go deeper than the cynicism we customarily express about politicians. The greed and ambition of some legislators, no less than that of others who exercise political power, no doubt impede the pursuit of the ethics in public life. But the question is meant to point to a more general problem—one that would arise even if all legislators tried to act ethically. The problem is that the ethical demands of the role of the legislator conflict with the generic requirements of ethics. Ethics demands a general perspective, but legislators are also obligated to look after their own particular constituents. Ethics requires autonomous judgment, but legislators are also expected to defer to electoral decisions. Ethics calls for action on public principles, but legislators who always act publicly may act less generally and autonomously.

Other public officials, too, confront conflicts between obligations to the good of particular persons and obligations to a public good. Their roles sometimes permit, or even require, actions that would be wrong if performed outside of the role. But the predicament of legislators is especially perplexing, not only because of their electoral connection to constituents, but also because of their relationship to colleagues.[1] Compared to administrators and most executives, legislators enjoy more independence from their colleagues. Legislators themselves normally do not control who will become or who will remain a legislator. Their relations are more collegial than hierarchical. But compared to most judges and some executives (who could be seen as similarly independent), legislators count more on their colleagues to accomplish their primary function. Legislators cannot legislate at all without the cooperation of their colleagues. Thus, legislators have less control over each other at the same time that they have more need for each other.

This further tension in the collegial relationship makes the problem of legislative ethics more complex. It suggests that the problem cannot be understood, let alone resolved, by considering legislators in isolation from their colleagues—whether as individuals alone, as individuals in relation to constituents, or as individuals in relation to principles. Each of the conventional approaches to the problem adopts one of these perspectives, and each therefore fails to take seriously the collegial dimension of legislative life.

Minimalist Ethics

The most familiar form of legislative ethics consists of rules that prohibit conflicts of financial interest. This is the form that dominates the practice of ethics in the Senate, the House and most state legislatures.[2] The appeal of a minimalist ethics is clear enough. It proscribes only a small area of conduct, and it prescribes relatively objective rules, which can be accepted by legislators who disagree on fundamental moral and political values. It does not dictate any particular role or any substantive political theory on which representatives must act. By circumscribing the scope of ethics in this way, it gives greater play to the give-and-take of pluralist politics.[3] The conflict between the generic requirements of ethics and its representational requirements is thus reduced.

But a minimalist ethics also has a minimal rationale. The price of keeping its demands modest is making its justification incomplete, if not incoherent. By itself, the idea of conflict of interest in democratic representation is paradoxical. To avoid a conflict of interest, legislators are not supposed to do anything that would appear to further their own interests. Yet, as Madison emphasized, a legislator must share a "communion of interest" with his constituents.[4] A legislator cannot adequately represent the interests of constituents without also representing some of his or her own.

The most common way of resolving this paradox has been to say that a conflict of interest exists only when the representative would personally benefit from some piece of legislation in a way or to a degree that other people would not.[5] In practice, however, virtually the only conduct such a rule would exclude is a member's voting on a controversy about his or her own seat in the legislature. This way of resolving the paradox therefore would not help much even in grounding the provisions of conflict of interest and financial disclosure. More recently, codes of ethics have defined a slightly different standard: members should not support legislation, with the principal purpose of furthering their own "pecuniary interest" or that of their family or friends.[6] Such a standard is no doubt worth establishing and enforcing, since we would hardly want to say that personal profit should be the main goal of the legislative life. But none of these standards captures much of the conduct legislative ethics should aim to prevent, and in fact none concentrates on the relevant aspects of that conduct.

The exclusive focus on the conflict of *financial* interest, though perfectly understandable historically, distorts the rationale of legislative ethics. The rationale (even for conflict-of-interest provisions) must be both narrower and broader than this focus suggests. We should not object simply because a legislator personally gains from holding office. After all, many office-holders in private as well as public life exploit the prestige of their positions and institutions to further their careers or fortunes. As long as legislators do not take bribes, why should they not enjoy financial benefit from their public service? The objection must be not to personal gain as such, but to its effects on legislative judgment. Only some kinds of financial gain therefore should be prohibited. To determine which kinds, we need to look at patterns of financial influence, not simply the finances of individual legislators.

If a central purpose of prohibiting conflicts of interest is to protect legislative judgment, the prohibitions should reach beyond the realm of financial gain. Legislators who always use their office zealously to pursue the legislative goals of single-issue groups with which they are associated may be distorting legislative judgment no less than those who accept contributions from special-interest groups. Whether single-issue representation should be condemned depends in part on how many legislators are engaging in it, and with what effect on the conduct of legislative business. Many kinds of influence can erode legislative judgment, and to determine which kinds should be discouraged, legislative ethics needs to attend to the legislative process as a whole.

As long as we concentrate on the personal financial motives of individual legislators, we cannot make sense even of the conflict-of-interest provisions that a minimalist legislative ethics favors. As soon as we begin to formulate a rationale for such provisions, we are forced to examine the patterns of conduct among legislators and the people whom they represent. The individual legislator alone with his bank account cannot be the main subject of legislative ethics.

Functionalist Ethics

Does the *role* of a legislator—the individual in relation to constituents—provide a more suitable subject? The natural place to look for instruction about the role of the legislator is in the tradition of political theory, specifically in trustee and delegate theories of representation.[7] That tradition offers the best source for what might be called a functionalist basis for legislative ethics. Such an ethics defines the duties of legislators in terms of their function as representatives.

Some legislators invoke the ideas of delegate and trustee to legitimate their legislative activities to themselves as well as to their constituents.[8] But many representatives refuse to see themselves as either delegates or trustees, and deny that they experience any conflict between these roles. They believe that they think as their constituents do, and see no point in distinguishing between exercising their own judgment and following the desires of their constituents.[9] One political scientist who asked members of Congress whether they should act as delegates or trustees received responses like these: "Who dreamed up these stupid questions?" and "I refuse to answer these high-school questions."[10]

It should not be surprising that many representatives resist the categories of delegate and trustee. These roles simplify the activity of representation as it is actually practiced and as it should be portrayed in any adequate legislative ethics. Theories of representation, at least sophisticated ones such as those of Burke and Mill, hold much more complex views of the representative's role. They recognize that any representative must choose among several aspects of a role, or (we could say) several different roles. As Burke emphasized, a representative owes allegiance to many different principles and many different groups of people. In our time, the number and variety of these principles and groups have expanded significantly. We should take notice of at least three dimensions of the representative's role.

First, there is a distinction that corresponds to the traditional contrast between trustee and delegate. We may distinguish trustees from delegates according to the reasons for their decisions—whether they decide according to expressed preferences of the persons they represent, or according to representatives' judgment about the interests of the persons they represent. Since preferences and interests may coincide, delegates and trustees may in fact act in the same way some of the time. But when preferences and interests do not coincide, the problem resembles that of paternalism in professional ethics.[11] Under what conditions and for what reasons may an agent act beyond or even contrary to the wishes of a principal? As in professional ethics, we should maintain a strong presumption against overriding the preferences of principals, but we would not want to deny that the presumption could be rebutted under some circumstances.

Another dimension of the role considers not *how* citizens should be represented, but *which* citizens should be represented. Along with the traditional categories of nation and district, others complicate the life of the legislator. Sometimes legislators owe allegiance to a political party, either because they owe their election to the party label more than anything else, or because they need the party's support for their own legislative programs. Some legislators properly see themselves partly as representatives for groups such as blacks and women, who are underrepresented in the legislature. The obligation to the district is also more complex than is usually supposed. Because a representative's electoral constituency is a majority of the electorate in the last election, the representative faces the question of how much he owes to other groups, including those who voted against him, and even those who would compose the current electoral majority. Furthermore, many legislators find themselves bound to local elites whose interests may diverge from those of other groups in the district. Representing such an elite could sometimes be justifiable—for example, when the elite promotes economic development that would benefit the poor in a district.

So far, then, we have not just two roles of the representative, as is often suggested, but at least eight, taking into account nation, party, district, and district majority in combination with the categories of delegate and trustee. Even this simplifies the representative's role. A more accurate account would add a third dimension—indicating the types of issues with which a representative must deal. We may wish to say that a particular legislator, for example, should act as a delegate on welfare issues that would allocate funds to the poor in the district, but that the legislator should act as a trustee on foreign policy—especially if the constituents are both impoverished and bellicose. If the legislator then decides to follow the district majority on civil rights, we begin to see the complexity that a choice of role presents.

In face of the many roles that any one legislator might legitimately choose and the many factors that affect that choice, we should not expect legislative ethics to specify which role representatives should adopt. No general principle prescribing one role, or even a combination of roles, is likely to prove adequate.[12] The reason that such a principle has proved elusive is not only because there are so many roles from which to choose, but also because the choice depends on what else is happening in the legislative system. In an ideal system, we could assume that each legislator does what he or she ought to do, and that the system as a whole functions as it should. But under actual conditions, neither of these assumptions holds. In choosing how to fulfill the duties of the role, a legislator therefore must take into account the actual conduct of other legislators, as well as that of other agents and the general features of the political system as a whole.

Some traditional theorists of representation recognize that representation is not simply a one-to-one relation between constituents and legislators but is a collective process involving systematic interaction among many people holding different roles. It is this pattern of conduct in the representative system as a whole that should ultimately determine our judgments about legislative ethics. When Mill served in Parliament, he refused to be the spokesman merely for his constituents or even for his party. He took instead a more visionary stance, advocating causes such as female suffrage well before they stood any chance of enactment. Yet he did not think that every representative should be as independent as he was. According to his own theory of representation, legislators should follow the wishes of their constituents on matters involving "fundamental convictions."[13] Some legislators, he thought, should play the role he himself did, but most should not. What we should seek, Mill suggests, is a representative assembly that is well balanced among various kinds of representatives. The duties of any single representative depend on what other representatives do or fail to do, and thus the proper role of a representative cannot be determined without reference to the state of the legislative system.

Because legislators must choose among many different roles, and because the rightness of that choice depends on the state of the system in which they make it, legislative ethics cannot specify in advance a particular set of duties for a representative. Legislative ethics cannot tell the representative whether to act as a trustee or delegate even on a given issue. It follows that legislative ethics will grant considerable discretion to legislators in their choices of role and their decisions on policy. To this extent, theorists who with Burke would give scope to the independent judgment of legislators are correct. But it does not follow that legislative ethics is reduced to the study of the character of legislators. We do not simply say, as Burke's theory suggests, that citizens should seek the best men (and women) and tell them to exercise their best judgment. The very fact that so much discretion is necessary implies that the conditions under which the discretion is exercised are critical. The primary focus of legislative ethics thus again should be the legislative process itself.

Rationalist Ethics

A third approach—which seeks what may be called rationalist foundations for legislative ethics—fails in a different way to take the legislative process seriously. Rationalists would base legislative ethics on substantive principles of political theory, such as justice, liberty, or the common good. Such principles are attractive since they seem to provide a more comprehensive and secure foundation than the other approaches offer. The principles are more coherent than the prohibitions of minimalist ethics. They are less vulnerable to the variability that functionalist prescriptions manifest because their validity does not depend so much on what other legislators are doing, or what else is happening in the legislative system.

The trouble with the principles of rationalist ethics, however, is that they turn out to be either indeterminate for a wide range of significant legislative conduct, or restrictive of a wide range of legitimate legislative choice. In either case the legislative process is slighted. Either the principles say too little about what should happen in the process, or they say too much. A less-known part of a well-known theory of justice illustrates this difficulty.

John Rawls holds that the "rational legislator is to vote his opinion as to which laws and policies best conform to principles of justice."[14] Like trustee theory, this view grants legislators the discretion to choose among various laws and policies, independently of what constituents prefer. But notice that this discretion itself may be limited by the principles of justice. The legislator has a right to "his opinion" about which laws satisfy the principles of justice, not about about which principles are the principles of justice.

Many decisions that legislators face cannot be said to be clear choices between a policy that is just and one that is unjust, or even between a policy that is more or less just than another. Tax reform, tariff rates, social security rules, occupational safety regulations, and similar welfare policies may raise questions of fairness, but they seldom admit of clear answers on any theory of justice as refined as Rawls's. Rawls himself concedes that such policies are "commonly subject to reasonable differences of opinion," and that "often the best we can say of a law or policy is that it is at least not clearly unjust."[15] In Rawls's constitutional system, furthermore, legislators spend most of their time considering social and economic policies of this kind. Their chief task is the promotion of welfare, not the protection of rights.[16]

When questions of justice *are* relevant and determinable, Rawls's theory presents the opposite difficulty: it limits the role of the representative too much. Legislators are bound to act on Rawls's whole theory of justice, and exclusively on that theory when it comes into conflict with other theories that citizens may hold. Although more than almost any other philosopher Rawls takes seriously the problem of accommodating many different conceptions of the good, his theory would still remove some important views from the political agenda. Excluded by Rawls's theory are a number of other theories of justice, some of which are widely held and which have respectable philosophical pedigrees. The alternative theory that he is most concerned to reject is utilitarianism, which in various forms underlies many of the justifications of modern public policy. It is doubtful that we can justify limiting the role of the representative to acting on a single (controversial) theory of justice.

To prove that Rawls's theory is philosophically superior to alternative theories is not to establish that representatives should act exclusively on its principles. Those principles must be actually accepted at some time by citizens. In the absence of some act of acceptance, there is reason to doubt that they are principles of our society.[17] It might be wrong for representatives to enact a policy that can be justified only on utilitarian principles, but that it is wrong must be argued in, among other forums, the legislature. Principles contrary to Rawls's cannot be excluded either from the deliberation in the legislature or from the menu of principles on which an ethical legislator acts. To determine a theory of justice for society in the definition of the duties of the representative would be to make collective choices by philosophical fiat.[18]

Nor should we suppose that more modest constraints on the substantive principles that representatives may choose escape this difficulty. Consider a view that holds that representatives may follow their constituents' preferences so long as the "negative" rights of other citizens are not violated.[19] Negative rights (which are claims not to be treated in certain ways) still derive from a substantive theory of justice, but they demand less than do "positive" rights (which are claims to have certain goods). As with a more general theory of justice, the problem is that the very definition of what is to count as a right in our society is itself a question that, to some extent, should be determined in the legislative process. A principle that tells legislators not to violate negative rights is not much help when they are considering whether to support legislation that would establish new rights. The growth of the welfare state has often been explained and defended as a progressive recognition that government should provide certain benefits (positive rights) in order to prevent certain harms to citizens (negative rights). Yet its opponents claim that the welfare state violates the negative rights of other citizens (property owners, for example). We expect legislators, among others, to resolve such disputes, and in doing so they do not merely follow, but sometimes change, the prevailing boundaries between positive and negative rights.

These objections are quite general in their implications. They apply to any legislative ethics that would limit the role of a representative to carrying out the dictates of any single substantive theory of fundamental values. The choices among these values are among the most important decisions that legislatures make, and the choices should not be predetermined by the definition of the role of the representative. A rationalist ethics sends each legislator into the legislative process, already committed to the principles on which all legislators should act. In effect, each legislator becomes the entire legislature.

The problem with all three approaches, then, is that they ignore the interrelationships among legislators themselves. The minimalists worry only about keeping each legislator honest. The functionalists search for a rule that relates each representative only to constituents. The rationalists recommend principles that each legislator is to pursue no matter what happens in the legislative process. None of the approaches takes seriously the interdependence of colleagues that is the key to the problem of legislative ethics. A more adequate foundation for legislative ethics must locate legislators in the legislative process, understood broadly to include not only lawmaking but also other political activities in which legislators typically engage.[20]

If we view legislators as interacting with each other as well as with their constituents, we can better understand the conflict between what their roles demand and what ethics requires. The requirements of ethics should be understood as constraints on the principles on which legislators act in the legislative process. The most promising source for such constraints is the criteria that any principle must meet to qualify as a moral principle at all. Criteria to serve this purpose may be drawn from what some philosophers call the conditions of the "moral point of view."[21] They require that a principle be general, autonomous, and public.[22] In philosophy these requirements seem quite weak since they exclude few moral theories that are seriously discussed, but in politics they can have more force since they rule out views (such as egoism) that are widely maintained (at least implicitly).

The problem of legislative ethics thus becomes a problem of reconciling these requirements with the roles of representatives in a legislative process. The requirements must be strong enough to ground prohibitions on a wide range of unethical conduct, but they must not be so strong as to preclude the legitimate demands of the role of the representative. They must leave legislators free to act on behalf of their constituents and free to choose among a wide range of moral principles.

The Particulars of Generality

A general principle is one that can be universalized: if it applies to one case, it applies to all cases that are similar in relevant respects.[23] The philosophical foundation of this idea owes most to Kant, whose various versions of the categorical imperative are meant to determine what is to count as an acceptable moral principle. If a principle cannot "stand the test of the form of a general law of nature," Kant writes, "then it is morally inadmissible."[24] Kant thought that this test would rule out the basic principles of many other moral theories, including utilitarianism, but most modern philosophers reinterpret it as a necessary condition that any moral principle, including the principle of utility, can satisfy.[25] In this form, it provides an approximate criterion for generality in legislative ethics.

Although the requirement of generality by itself does not exclude very much from legislative deliberation, it does exclude enough to create a problem for representation. By its nature, representation presupposes that representatives have some special responsibility to a particular set of citizens, namely their constituents.[26] This responsibility need not be so specific as delegate theory implies, but it must be specific enough to distinguish those whom a legislator represents from those whom he does not. Burke himself recognized that he owed more to the electors of Bristol than to the electors of Warwick or Stafford.[27] Even in a legislature that pursues general principles through moral deliberation, the common good does not spring full-blown from the collective brow of the legislature. It emerges only after each legislator expresses the views of particular groups within society, and it must be defended to particular groups by the legislators who represent them.

If representatives may legitimately act for particular citizens, how can we insist that representatives act only on principles that are general? The natural answer is that conduct favoring constituents *is* general in the sense that we can universalize the principle that each representative should give special weight to the welfare of his or her constituents. No representative claims any special privilege not granted to other representatives. But the appeal of this answer lies not so much in the formal test it satisfies as in the substantive assumption it makes. The key assumption is that a process in which representatives act primarily for parts of the whole functions best for the benefit of the whole. The particular is thus justified by its consequences for the general.

What can justify this assumption? The standard justification is not plausible, though legislators seem to act (and theorists seem to write) as if it were. It is based on the conception of the common good as the sum of particular interests. Even if this were an adequate conception of the common good, it would not provide the link we need to move from the particular to the general. The most single-minded advocate of this conception recognizes this problem. According to Bentham, the only way to find out what is in the public interest (his notion of the common good) is for each representative to express the views of his constituents. But since these views may be mistaken, representatives must be able to act on their own view of public interest. Bentham resolves these contradictory demands on the representative by means of one of his characteristically mechanical devices: the representative is to *speak* for his view of the public interest but to *vote* with the view of his constituents.[28]

Despite its obvious inadequacy, Bentham's proposal contains an important insight—and one that does not depend on his assumption that the public interest is simply the sum of particular interests. Speaking for the public interest is not just a way of fulfilling the duty to the public, but it can also "have the effect of working a change in . . . [the] opinion" of constituents, and "on a later occasion causing them to concur with" their representative.[29] The public interest does not emerge merely from the aggregation of subjective preferences; it must be created in the legislative process.

We can think of this creation as occurring in a reiterated, four-step process: representatives express particular views, modify the views in light of what other representatives say, act on the modified views, and then seek to justify them to constituents. The process begins again with the new views of the constituents if they have been persuaded, or their original views if they have not. In this kind of legislative process, a particular claim by a representative could count as a general principle, *provided* that the claim could be justified as contributing to a legislative process that seeks a common good. This is a strong proviso, one that the principles of legislators rarely satisfy. There are, of course, many notions of the common good, and many ways the process itself can fail to pursue them. But the implications of the generality requirement can be illustrated by three kinds of particular claims that it proscribes.

First, legislators could not justify representing particular claims of established groups without taking into account the state of the representation of less-established groups in the legislature. A persistent defect of liberal representative systems is the neglect of the interests of citizens who either cannot press their claims at all or cannot do so as effectively as citizens who possess greater resources. To be sure, it is hardly reasonable to blame a legislator for the fact that some groups never express their views in the political process. Even a legislator who with the best intentions looks for these silent groups may have trouble finding them. From the perspective of the legislator traveling in his district, "the people" are hard to find, though "certain people" are not. As one congressman observed, "You go where people meet. That means you spend more time talking to groups like the Chamber of Commerce than you do to people who live along the road here. The great mass of people you can't reach. They are not organized. The leadership, the elite, runs along the top of all institutions, and you can reach them, but not the people generally."[30]

But the very difficulty of locating "the people" makes it all the more important that legislative ethics call attention to the balance of voices represented in the legislature as a whole. Legislators should have to show that the pressing of particular claims of well-represented groups is consistent with satisfying the needs of ill-represented groups. To show this, some legislators may have to take steps to correct structural defects in the legislative process, and may have to give special attention to the unorganized, seeking them out, and helping them formulate their fair claims on government.

Second, the generality requirement has implications for the enforcement of legislative ethics. It would not permit legislators to ignore the misconduct of their colleagues on the ground that legislators should mind the business of their own constituents. Legislators would not be so reluctant as they have been to criticize and penalize their colleagues for transgressions of institutional standards. Although in recent years the Senate and the House have been somewhat more inclined to act against their colleagues who are guilty of gross violations of legislative ethics and the criminal law, neither body has shown much enthusiasm for establishing and enforcing stringent standards of conduct for its members. Many observers believe that it took the threat of no pay raise in 1977 to win the passage of the tougher rules in the present code, and since then some of these have been relaxed. Most legislators assiduously strive to avoid service on the Senate Ethics Committee and the House Committee on Standards of Official Conduct. Legislators rarely report improprieties of their colleagues or even of the members of their colleagues' staffs, and they even more rarely criticize colleagues in public for neglecting their legislative duties.

Some reformers have argued that a code requiring only disclosure of financial and other interests should replace the current elaborate set of prohibitions concerning conflicts of interest, gifts, and outside income.[31] On this approach, neither the Congress nor its committees would have to judge whether a member is guilty of a conflict of interest or other ethical impropriety. The legislature would simply ensure that all the information for making such judgments is available to the public. Each member's constituents would enforce, through the electoral sanction, their own interpretation of ethical standards. One of the chief attractions of this approach—in addition to its potential for vastly simplifying the task of writing and enforcing any code of ethics—is that it seems more democratic. It appears to appeal to a delegate theory of representation that would hold members strictly accountable to their constituents.

The appearance is deceptive, however. A delegate theory of representation does not entail that only constituents in one district or one state should control the conduct of the representative from that district or state. On a delegate theory, constituents in *any* state or district may quite properly instruct their representative to seek, through the procedures of the legislature, standards to govern the conduct of *all* representatives. Thus, even a delegate theory, properly interpreted, recognizes the interdependency of legislators. The approach that holds that disclosure is sufficient does not, however. A code requiring only disclosure puts other members of Congress—and all citizens who care about the moral health and political efficacy of the institution as a whole—at the mercy of the moral and political judgment of a few members and their constituents. This may be an appropriate form for representation in a convention (a "congress of ambassadors from different and hostile interests"[32]), but it hardly seems appropriate for an institution that, like the U.S. Congress, should function as a collegial process.

Another issue in the enforcement of legislative ethics is the role of an outside commission.[33] The usual arguments for—as well as those against—these proposals have been mostly political. Voters are more likely to believe that legislators are observing the provisions of a code of ethics if some quasi-independent body takes part in their enforcement than if the legislators try to do the job all by themselves. But there is a deeper reason that tells in favor of some outside participation in the enforcement of legislative ethics. Credibility is important not simply for making ethical standards effective; it is also necessary for making them valid. We should distinguish between two kinds of moral duties: those that are valid whether or not anyone is observing or acting on them (for example, the duty not to injure others; or the duty to help others in distress); and those that are not valid unless one has good reason to believe that others are also observing them (for example, the duty to pay taxes; or the duty to follow the rules in a game).[34] The validity of the second kind does not depend on everybody's actually fulfilling the duties, but it does presuppose the existence of some authoritative system to interpret and enforce them. Otherwise, individuals may reasonably claim that doing their duty would put them at an unfair disadvantage with respect to people who are not doing their duty. Many of the prohibitions of any legislative ethics are likely to refer to duties of this kind. That they are obligatory depends in part on each legislator's having reasonable expectations that other members will try to fulfill them.

In the absence of a credible form of enforcement for the legislature as a whole, any legislator has good reason to doubt the moral force of, say, restraints on the use of the franking privilege, limits on outside income, or the prohibition of activities that create conflicts of interest. These considerations do not add up to an irresistible case for an outside commission. There are possible constitutional objections to such a body, and the legislature itself may yet prove to be a credible enforcer. But the considerations suggest the kind of argument that would be necessary to satisfy the requirement that the particular conduct of each legislator must relate to the general conduct of the legislature.

The third illustration of the generality requirement is the failure of individual legislators to take responsibility for the collective product of the legislature. The requirement entails criticism of legislators who run *"for* Congress by running *against* Congress."[35] As Richard Fenno describes this practice: "It is easy for each Congressman to explain to his own supporters why he cannot be blamed for the performance of the collectivity . . . The beauty of the strategy is that everybody can use it and nobody will be called to account by those under attack . . . In the short run everybody plays and nearly everybody wins. Yet the institution bleeds from 435 separate cuts. In the long run, therefore, somebody may lose."[36]

Representatives not only blame the collectivity for legislative failures to which they might have contributed or could have helped prevent, but they also seek praise for legislative activities to which they contributed little or from which little resulted. They engage in position taking more than lawmaking.[37] When they do make laws, they favor legislation for which they can take some personal credit. Each congressman tries to "peel off pieces of governmental accomplishment for which he can believably generate a sense of responsibility."[38] One result is legislation that gives "particularized benefits"—new dams in the region, tariffs for local industries, or military bases in the district.[39]

The condemnation of this kind of conduct is the closest that contemporary political science comes to affirming a normative canon on political representation.[40] But before we let legislative ethics join in this chorus of condemnation, we should listen carefully to the tunes that are being sung. Many of the critics of legislative individualism are also advocates of an activist government and of majoritarian policies. The villain seems to be government that does not act at all, and policies that cater to single-issue groups.[41]

These may be among the consequences of the rise of legislative individualism, but they do not necessarily constitute the most compelling reason to suppress it. Citizens who do not object to these consequences— citizens who would make government more limited as well as those who would make it more responsive to minorities—can still deplore the individualistic behavior of legislators. Nor should we accept without qualification the stronger political parties that many see as the cure for legislative individualism.[42] Such parties may be necessary, but if they prevent legislators from exercising independent judgment, they may promote legislative generality at the price of legislative autonomy. The institutional design must be delicately balanced if it is to satisfy both of these requirements.[43]

The Autonomous Legislator

When representatives legislate, they should consider legislation on its merits. This principle seems simple enough, and (at least in public) most legislators claim to follow it. The reasons they give to justify their actions generally refer to the welfare or the rights of citizens, not to the pressures of lobbyists or the influence of campaign contributors. The principle plainly excludes bribery and extortion, in which legislators unequivocally act on reasons more related to the money they receive than to the legislation they support. But beyond such clear cases, the principle bristles with puzzles.

Like most people, legislators rationalize their conduct: the reasons they give may not be their real reasons. Their rationalizations are rarely the crude kind popularly ascribed to politicians. Congressmen do not typically keep their true reasons to themselves and give another set of reasons to the public. Nor are they inclined to fool themselves by accepting reasons that are not their real reasons for taking a position. Interpreting his extensive interviews with congressmen, John Kingdon concludes that most "like to believe that they are going through some sort of rational consideration which is connected to the issue of public policy they are deciding. They do not enjoy seeing themselves as being manipulated or pushed and pulled by forces beyond their control . . . [The congressman] must seize on some sort of argument that will justify his vote to himself and to others. For some congressmen, this is reinforcement; for others, persuasion."[44]

No doubt this search for reasons not only takes place, but also affects votes. But even when it does, it can hardly allay our suspicions about the reasons that representatives give, or the principles on which they act. One of Kingdon's own examples shows why. Tobacco-area congressmen, he suggests, could not have brought themselves to vote against the cigarette advertising bill if they believed that smoking caused cancer. They devoted a great deal of time to hearings to try to refute the evidence presented in the Surgeon General's Report. They finally gathered enough respectable testimony to convince themselves that a causal link between smoking and cancer had not been established, and thus to allow themselves in good conscience to vote against the bill.[45]

These congressmen may or may not have been sincere, but it is not the sincerity of representatives or even their motives that should be at issue. Both are difficult enough to appraise in personal interactions. In the distant and mediated relations of political life, they can hardly be the basis for reliable judgments of legislative ethics. If we are trying to establish whether reasons refer to the merits of legislation or arise instead from irrelevant causes, we should focus on the general conditions under which representatives give reasons, rather than on the connection between the reasons that representatives give and their motives in particular cases. We should judge differently the legislative conduct of congressmen who depend on tobacco interests for most of their campaign contributions, and congressmen who do not so depend. The less-dependent congressmen may still decide to vote for tobacco subsidies—perhaps to protect the jobs of workers in their district. But their decision could be understood as expressing a choice between the values of health and employment. It could be understood in this way because the congressmen would be acting in circumstances less contaminated by pressures unrelated to these values.

More generally, legislative ethics must attend to the conditions under which representatives give reasons because the conditions constitute the most reliable basis on which citizens can assess the actions of their representatives. Representatives must enjoy discretion, not only in their choice of policies but also in their choice of roles and principles, and citizens may not be able to judge the results of these choices for many years. What citizens are in a better position to assess are the circumstances in which the representatives make the choices. The requirement of autonomy is intended to rule out circumstances that give rise to irrelevant influences on the judgment of legislators.

Representation does not readily accommodate autonomy, however. The tension between the two would be impossible to accept if we were to adopt any of the leading philosophical standards of autonomy. If autonomy were thought to exclude, as Kant argued it should, any kind of desire as a basis for action, it would have little relevance to political life.[46] Even Rawls's concept ("acting from principles that we would consent to as free and equal rational beings") seems an inappropriate standard for representatives. It would "force [representatives] to consider the choice of principles unencumbered by the singularities of the circumstances in which [they] find themselves."[47] Some special obligation to a constituency is one singularity of circumstance that representation cannot do without; legislators, after all, must stand for election. Another, nearly as inescapable in modern politics, is the obligation to a political party.[48]

The criterion of autonomy therefore cannot demand, even as an ideal, a wholly unencumbered legislator, one who acts utterly unswayed by political pressures and partisan loyalties. It can, however, place some constraints on the kinds of reasons that would justify the actions of representatives. Such a criterion would require that a representative's reasons for acting be relevant to *either* the merits of legislation *or* the means necessary for adopting the legislation, where the means are consistent with a legislative process that generally considers legislation on the merits. On this criterion, legislators could still trade votes on legislation they think less important in order to win passage of legislation they think more important—but only if such logrolling did not prevent consideration of the more important measures on their merits. Similarly, reelection or party loyalty could also count as principled reasons, when they are consistent with this kind of legislative deliberation.

The Pecuniary Connection

Money is not the root of all legislative evil. Ideology, ambition, and sheer incompetence cause their share of distortions in the judgment of legislators. But in our culture the influence of money is the most notorious—and for the purposes of legislative ethics the most instructive—obstacle to legislative autonomy. The other kinds of distortions tend to parallel those caused by money. We have already noted the inadequacy of the conventional ways that legislative ethics has sought to control pecuniary influence. The concern should be not so much the personal financial gain of legislators but the effects of financial influences on their actions in the legislature. We should focus more generally on the connection between potential influence and legislative judgment.[49]

What kind of connection should we look for? Political scientists do not find very strong correlations between campaign contributions and roll-call votes in most policy areas. Where correlations appear, the policy areas tend to be narrow (e.g., milk price supports, maritime cargo preferences), and the effects tend to be weaker than other factors such as constituency and ideology.[50] It has been argued that even stronger correlations are not necessarily incriminating. The causal direction may be the reverse of what critics suspect: contributors simply give to those legislators whose policy positions they favor.[51] Campaign contributions do not buy votes, it is commonly said; the most they buy is access.[52]

These conclusions are not so reassuring as they are usually taken to be. Influencing the final vote, at least on the scale that is likely to be attempted, is not the worst offense against the legislative process. By the time the vote comes, the damage has usually been done. If big contributors dominate the legislative lives of congressmen, they influence the information legislators take seriously, the priorities they assign to issues, and the agendas that they adopt in committee as well as on the floor. Access can in these ways powerfully shape legislation. (Even more potent is its value in the activities that legislators undertake individually or informally—for instance, influencing decisions of an administrative agency.) The kind of influence that big contributors wield is not objectionable simply because it gives some citizens disproportionate influence. It is not simply that the choir of political contributors "sings with a strong upper class accent."[53] Our aim is not necessarily the pluralist ideal of equal influence for all interests. The objection is that legislation is substantially affected by a factor that bears little if any relation to the merits of the legislation. In the imperfect markets of modern America, no one has yet demonstrated that wealth corresponds to intensity of desire, let alone deliberateness of thought.

To eliminate the whole range of influences that are irrelevant to the merits of legislation, we would need to make comprehensive changes in the political process. As a beginning, we could seek a system of campaign finance that lessens the dependence of legislators on money—more precisely, on money that comes attached to defined interests. This could be said to be part of the aim of the decade of reform of which the Federal Election Campaign Act of 1971 and its later amendments stand as the most notable legacy.[54]

The results of the reforms have not unambiguously favored legislative autonomy, however. Among the unintended consequences are the growth of Political Action Committees, which arguably perpetuate in yet another form the dependence of legislators on special interests.[55] The reforms have another less direct but perhaps more insidious effect on autonomy. As they now stand, the restrictions on contributions and spending strongly tend to favor incumbents over challengers (at least in House races).[56] Any limit on the amount of money available to candidates gives an advantage to incumbents, even if incumbents could otherwise raise much more money than challengers could. There seems to be a kind of funding threshold, a point at which challengers' spending wins them enough recognition to threaten incumbents, and above which incumbents' spending usually does not improve their own standing with voters.

Consequently, ceilings on contributions and spending are likely to slow the turnover in the membership of Congress. Turnover is not valuable in itself, but a reasonable prospect of turnover is necessary for legislative autonomy. Autonomy requires exposure to vigorous opposition, not insulation from political pressure. Without some incentive to take seriously other points of view, legislators are likely to continue to act in the roles and on the principles they chose upon entering the legislature, regardless of whether the reasons for their original choices are still relevant. Since in broad terms the views and votes of individual legislators do not change much over time, the only way to create, or at least to consider, change in the roles and principles on which legislators act is to change the identity of the legislators.[57]

Accordingly, the regulation of campaign finance should at least not discourage turnover in the legislature. Instead of putting ceilings on campaign contributions, we should first build some floors. The reforms of the last decade stopped short of the public funding that would be required to support such floors in congressional campaigns. The major obstacles to public funding do not seem to be theoretically grounded, at least not directly. Public funding would benefit challengers. That is one reason congressmen are not rushing to enact it. But it is not a reason that citizens should accept, if they care about legislative autonomy.[58] Any system of public funding would, of course, have to achieve a balance between allocating funds to candidates and parties with established electoral reputations, and newcomers with some proven popular support.[59] But that is a constraint on the design of the system, not a reason against its establishment.

Public funding would also cost a great deal of money. Some critics as well as some reformers seem to be repelled by the very idea of spending large sums of money on elections—what they see as the "squalor" of "big spending."[60] They appear to believe that "it is shameful for a civilized nation to allow large amounts of money to be spent in electing its representatives."[61] We should, of course, want to make sure that the money is well spent, and that no other measures could accomplish our purposes at less expense. But in deciding whether public funding is worth the cost, we should not forget to count as a significant benefit the collective good of an ethical legislative process. In the absence of such a process, legislators may not even be able to decide against public funding without raising the reasonable suspicion that they are not making that decision itself autonomously.

The Necessity of Publicity

It was Kant who first emphasized the deep connection between morality and publicity. He presented the criterion of publicity as a fundamental test of morality, equivalent to one version of the categorical imperative. "All actions which relate to the right of other men are contrary to right and law, [if their] maxim . . . does not permit publicity."[62] That a principle can be made public is not sufficient to make the principle moral, but it is necessary. If a principle must be kept secret, it is because the principle cannot be generally and freely accepted on its merits. In this sense, publicity is a test of the other requirements of legislative ethics—generality and autonomy. A legislator could not legitimately act on the principle that he will tell the truth except when it could jeopardize his reelection. Making that principle public would defeat its purpose. That it must be kept secret shows that it is not general enough (it favors the legislator), and that it is not acceptable for relevant reasons (it presumes the ignorance of voters).

Because Kant considered the criterion to be "an experiment of pure reason," abstracted from all actual conditions, he did not insist that justifications *actually* be made public.[63] This formality prevents his criterion in its original form from serving as a requirement of legislative ethics. Especially in politics, the actual process of publicizing reasons differs significantly from the hypothetical process. Facing an actual audience, politicians are more likely to take into account arguments that they have not previously considered and are more likely to change their minds when they cannot answer those arguments. The reasons on which they act stand a better chance of being relevant to the merits of the legislation that they enact.[64]

Unlike the other two requirements, publicity does not directly conflict with representation itself. The practice of representation does not license secrecy in the way that it legitimizes particularity or dependency. On the contrary, the practice seems to entail that citizens know as much as possible about the conduct of their representatives. This is all the more true if we keep in mind the earlier argument that representatives must have considerable discretion in deciding how to interpret their roles. The more discretion they have, the more citizens must know about their decisions.

The problem that publicity creates comes instead from conflicts with generality and autonomy. The more public the activities of legislators, the more pressure they may face to pursue particular interests, and the more dependence they may develop on outside groups. We do not have to assume that legislators are ethical cowards who capitulate to political pressure when they must make difficult decisions in the open. The problem of publicity persists even if legislators act conscientiously. Indeed, it results partly from trying to follow the other standards of legislative ethics. When legislators act always in the glare of publicity, they are forced to justify their conduct continually. Consequently, the kinds of justifications they give are directed more toward immediate issues and momentary audiences. Both of these tendencies run counter to the requirement of generality, which would consider the legislative process as a whole functioning over time, and both also act against autonomy, which would prescribe deliberation on the merits of issues.

That publicity may conflict with these requirements does not justify banishing it from legislative ethics, however. On the contrary, the possibility of conflict itself provides a reason not only for preserving publicity but also for granting it status equal to the other requirements. The conflicts among the requirements reflect disagreements about the relative importance of various values. Is it more important to let citizens know what is happening in a conference committee, or to leave the members free to deliberate without citizens looking over their shoulders? To answer such questions is to make choices among fundamental values inherent in both processes and policies.

Even if legislators rightly choose secrecy over publicity in certain circumstances, they should make that choice openly. A decision for secrecy should not itself be secret. The decision must be justified to citizens, and that can only be done in public. To be sure, it can only be done with reasons that are also general and autonomous. But to judge whether the reasons are general and autonomous, citizens must know about the reasons. Publicity is a necessary condition for deciding how much weight we should assign to each requirement, including publicity itself, and a necessary condition for deciding whether in certain circumstances we should disregard any requirement, also including publicity itself.

What kinds of secrets may legislators keep? Legislators often invoke a right of privacy to justify withholding information about such matters as their medical condition, club memberships, and the finances of their family. But public officials should not enjoy the same right of privacy as ordinary citizens.[65] Publicity about a wide range of activities that would otherwise be private is justified because legislators enjoy considerable discretion in their exercise of power over us. Judging whether that discretion has been legitimately exercised requires examining carefully the conditions under which it has been actually exercised. Those conditions include any information relevant to the performance of the duties of public office—information that legislators often wish to keep secret.

Important as are the secrets that legislators would keep about themselves, still more significant are the secrets that they would keep about the legislature. It may hardly seem necessary to urge the importance of publicity in the U.S. Congress, generally regarded as the most open legislature in the world. Indeed, the problem of publicity, in the judgment of some observers, is that there is too much of it. In the early 1970s, as part of a general effort at self-reform, the House opened all committee meetings to the public (including television audiences), and provided that names could be recorded in virtually all voting. A Select Committee on Committees more recently criticized these "sunshine" provisions, complaining that they inhibit candid discussion of controversial issues, discourage changes of opinion, hamper efforts to reach compromises, and subject members to greater pressures from lobbyists.[66]

Some of these effects could subvert the requirements of generality and autonomy, and could therefore provide justifications for limiting publicity.[67] But why not present such justifications in open session, where they can be vigorously debated and precisely formulated to fit each type of case? This approach neither the committee nor other critics of publicity seem to have seriously explored. Another important distinction is overlooked by the advocates of secrecy. They tend to blur the difference between a need to keep proceedings closed, and a need to keep the records of the proceedings confidential. The argument for closed sessions is more compelling than the argument for confidential records. But the former is often mistakenly assumed to fulfill the function of the latter, thereby extending indefinitely into the future the secrecy that may be warranted only in the present. Citizens may reasonably refuse to accept a justification for closed sessions unless they can inspect records of the sessions at some future time. Even when secrecy is warranted now, the further question should always be asked: *when* may citizens learn what happened?[68]

Secrecy does not always take the form of closed meetings or concealed records. Even in so open an institution as the Congress, public policy can be made without the public knowing much about it. Sometimes the ignorance is the fault of citizens themselves; their representatives are only accessories, guilty of failing to enlighten their constituents. But at other times, legislators deliberately prevent an issue from receiving wide public discussion, and enact laws without the benefit of the reactions that such discussion might bring. This strategy is especially tempting when the motives of representatives are genuinely benevolent.

A case in point is the policy on public financing of treatment for kidney disease. According to one account, the debate on this policy in the early 1970s was conducted "sotto voce." The discussions were "carried out mainly within the inner councils of the medical-scientific community and the political-governmental system . . . Both opponents and proponents were reluctant to have this issue fully considered in public debate, fearing that it was too divisive for the polity to handle."[69] Some political scientists would endorse this reluctance, arguing that policies that put a value on life, especially some of those that allocate scarce medical resources, should not be fully explained in public. One writer imagines the "perfectly 'rational' congressman" trying to justify the legislature's decision to limit expenditures for medical care: "Mrs. Jones, I share your grief about the plight of your husband, but we simply cannot afford to spend $30,000 per year to keep him alive when people are dying elsewhere who could be saved for much less."[70] Such candor threatens the "life-preserving norm that decent societies should respect."[71] Another scholar similarly would encourage policy makers to pretend that they are not putting a price on life even though they are in fact doing so: "the polite fiction might just be enough to protect people's self-respect."[72]

These arguments posit a gap between legislators and citizens that is neither plausible nor desirable in legislative ethics. Why should we assume that legislators are any more capable than citizens in rationally deciding questions about the value of life? In the case of kidney disease, legislators did not in fact act like rational economists. Congress committed far too many resources to one kind of disease and one group of victims, in effect diverting funds from programs that could help more people who suffered from other kinds of diseases.

But even if legislators could in secret strike the right balance between an efficient allocation of resources and the respect for the "life-preserving norm," they would on this view still have to make sure that citizens did not understand their real reasons for the balance they struck. Perhaps Mrs. Jones would not at this moment want to hear a cost-benefit analysis of her dying husband's treatment, but neither would she choose to hear lies from her congressman. The rational legislator may exhibit a lack of sensitivity, but the benevolent legislator exhibits a fault more dangerous in the character of a public official—a lack of candor. If citizens cannot know the principles on which legislators act, they cannot judge the ethics to which legislators aspire—or the ethics to which they fail to aspire.

Similarly troublesome is the argument that legislators should quietly suppress consideration of certain controversial questions. Some political scientists look back nostalgically to the late-nineteenth-century Congress where legislative leaders "put the lid on" the discussion of many issues of intense concern to their constituents, such as the controversy over bilingual education. They praise the Rules Committee for keeping the question of aid to parochial schools off the congressional agenda in the early 1960s, and they wish legislative leaders now would do the same with the question of abortion funding.[73]

There may be good reasons for legislatures to avoid such issues, but they are not the reasons of legislative ethics. More precisely, we should say that the publicity requirement demands that legislators give reasons for refusing to consider these issues. Nothing in the legislative process is more important than the agenda of legislation, and therefore nothing is more important in legislative ethics than the principles by which legislators set that agenda. If leaders can keep the agenda clear of questions that should not be discussed, they can also keep it clear of questions that *should* be discussed. The leaders of the Democratic party abused the power to control the agenda when for more than a century they kept Congress from seriously confronting the question of racism.[74] Legislators today stand guilty of similar abuses insofar as they refuse to consider, or to explain why they refuse to consider, pressing questions of welfare and justice, however divisive such questions may be.

A third kind of secrecy is structural. The dramatic growth in the size of congressional staffs and the fragmentation of power in the committee system create conditions that resist the requirement of publicity.[75] An unintended flood of information can have the same result as deliberate denial of information. When dozens of staffs issue numerous reports and dozens of subcommittees hold frequent meetings, the sheer quantity of information frustrates the efforts of citizens to learn what their legislators are doing. Even journalists find difficulty in distinguishing the significant from the trivial in the overwhelming stream of facts that issue forth from Congress each day of the session. They are also less likely to notice when significant information is missing. In face of the informational deluge, journalists fall back on familiar formulas. When the financial disclosure forms appear, the press reliably runs a list of the ten wealthiest senators.[76] The press tend to concentrate on the particular incident or type of incident, rather than on the general practice or institutional pattern. They report on legislators' junketing, but not on legislative provincialism.[77]

Efforts to remedy these problems should not reduce the flow of information but should seek better ways of filtering it. The ultimate responsibility for any such selection lies with citizens and journalists outside of government, but Congress could take more initiative on this problem than it has in the past. An Office of Public Affairs, if granted at least the independence enjoyed by the Library of Congress or the Congressional Budget Office, could facilitate the selective scrutiny of congressional activities. Whatever institutional devices we devise, they should provide not simply more information but more information of significance about the decisions legislators make and the conditions under which they make them.

Legislative ethics is possible if its requirements are interpreted in the context of the legislative process. The requirements constrain the conduct of legislators, but not in a way that prevents them from performing their proper roles as representatives. The tension between these ethical and political demands, though both may be rooted in a common ethics, is never fully resolved. The ethical legislator is constantly tempted—and often obligated—to satisfy particular claims, to defer to reasons irrelevant to the merits of legislation, and to conceal personal and political activity that citizens may wish to know. How these conflicts should be resolved at any political moment is best decided in a legislative process that itself observes the requirements of legislative ethics. In a process in which legislators act publicly and autonomously on general principles, both legislators and citizens stand a better chance of finding a resolution that, however temporary, respects the fundamental values that they share.

5

The Private Lives of
Public Officials

While demanding more privacy for themselves, citizens are granting public officials less.[1] Candidates and officeholders have been forced to disclose
their financial affairs and medical histories more than ever before, and
the press has more extensively publicized their drinking habits, sexual
conduct, and family life.[2] Some of the legal protections against libel and
invasion of privacy of public figures have eroded.[3] The privacy of public
officials *should* receive less respect than the privacy of ordinary citizens,
but the reasons for this difference have not received careful consideration.
As a result, the boundaries of the private lives of public officials are often
misconceived, and the content of democratic discussion misdirected.

The question of privacy arises for public officials when they decide
what to disclose about themselves, and to whom to disclose it.[4] The
question also confronts the many officials who have occasion to decide
what to reveal about other officials, and to whom to divulge it. Personnel
officers, in particular, must often decide whether to probe into the personal affairs of a prospective or current employee of the government.
Members of the press, too, encounter the question in deciding what to
print about an official, and so do voters in determining what to consider
in assessing a candidate for office. The secrecy or confidentiality that
officials claim for some governmental business, however, should not be
treated as an issue of privacy or as a part of private life even by analogy.
When officials legitimately keep governmental business secret from other
officials or the public, the reasons must relate exclusively to the nature
of the policy, institutional effectiveness, or the privacy of other citizens—
not to the rights of privacy of the public officials themselves.[5]

Although the law gives some guidance in understanding the claims of privacy of officials, it does not settle the question. Privacy law remains relatively undeveloped as it applies to public officials, and in any event legal rights and duties do not exhaust moral ones.[6] Moreover, defending a right of privacy in court can be self-defeating. Even while winning the legal contest, an official is likely to sacrifice his or her privacy in the publicity that attends the court proceedings.[7] Yet where the law is silent or inconclusive, political ethics does not wholly fill the void. The pertinent ethical principles are often in conflict, and the variables affecting the conclusion are numerous. It is therefore not possible to discover a set of rules that would determine in advance the kinds of activities that should constitute the private life of a public official. It may be possible, however, to establish a basis for the privacy of public officials, and then to formulate the factors that should (and those that should not) be considered in deciding to what extent that privacy may be overridden.

Private life consists of those activities that may be known, observed, or intruded upon only with a person's consent.[8] The dimensions of the sphere of privacy are not always clear, since they partly depend on conventions that are neither absolute nor stable. But within this sphere, however it is defined at any particular time in a particular society, citizens have a right to control information about themselves.[9]

Respect for the privacy of anyone makes sense only within a theory that assumes that everyone's private life deserves at least prima facie priority over the claims of public life. Theories that do not accept this assumption conceive of the problem in very different terms. Plato's *Republic,* for example, abolishes the foundations of any private life for the guardians who rule the ideal state—eliminating the family and private property in order to create unity in the state. Socrates considers the objection that the guardians will not be happy if they have to give up the pleasures of private life. Such happiness, he replies, is "senseless and childish"; the guardians, after all, will enjoy a better and more honorable life than other citizens. Anyhow, the aim should be to make the whole society good, not to make one section of it happy.[10] One reason that Plato does not lament the eclipse of a private life is that he shared with many classical thinkers the view that private life is inferior; it connoted, as its etymological origins suggest, a deprivation.[11] Even Aristotle, who thought that Plato had gone too far in his quest for social unity, still conceived of private life as deficient. The private realm of the family and household could satisfy needs of the body, but not the distinctively human quality of reason, which could be actualized only in the public activity of the polis.[12]

The primacy of the public remains prominent in some modern political thought—in Rousseau's vision of a society where "every citizen will feel himself to be incessantly under the public eye,"[13] in Hegel's exaltation of the ethical superiority of the state where "public and private ends are identical,"[14] in Marx's critique of the class bias of bourgeois claims for private life.[15] From none of these perspectives can the privacy of public officials or rulers be readily justified as an extension of the privacy of citizens. If the privacy of the latter is suspect, so a fortiori is the privacy of the former. Furthermore, privacy in the form that liberals seek usually becomes an issue only in a large and diverse society. Such privacy is not possible in small, closely knit communities. It might not be necessary in a more homogeneous or in a more tolerant and humane society.

Although early liberals did not explicitly discuss the modern notion of individual privacy, their theories supplied a framework that could comfortably accommodate it. Beginning with a concept of a relatively asocial individual or small family, they demanded justification for any social intervention into the natural liberty or the private sphere of individuals.[16] As later liberal theorists and liberal societies, sometimes reluctantly and sometimes unwittingly, circumscribed this private sphere, it became less and less clear that anything was left of it.[17] It became increasingly important to maintain a sanctuary for the more intimate and personal relations of citizens—privacy in the narrower sense defined above. The hope was (and is) that at least this kind of privacy could be preserved.

It is not the aim here either to defend or attack these views about the privacy of citizens, but rather to see what implications follow for the privacy of public officials if we accept, as many theories and many societies do, a presumption in favor of the privacy of citizens. Since officials are citizens too, the presumption quite naturally implies that the private lives of officials and citizens should be equally respected. This may be called the principle of uniform privacy. But there are also good reasons for granting officials less privacy than citizens. These reasons give rise to a principle of diminished privacy. The problem is to discover the kinds of considerations that would permit the second principle to prevail over the first: when should what would otherwise count as the private life of a public official be open to public scrutiny?

The Value of Privacy

The principle of uniform privacy depends on showing that privacy has value for public officials for the same reasons, or for reasons just as strong, as it does for ordinary citizens. Privacy has two kinds of value for the individual—instrumental and intrinsic. Instrumentally, privacy contributes to liberty by ensuring that individuals can engage in certain activities free from observation, intrusion, or inhibiting threats.[18] Public officials need such protection, sometimes even more than citizens, because if their privacy is violated, the exposure is likely to be greater. Privacy also supports fairness and equal opportunity by ensuring that private activities that are irrelevant to public duties do not affect an individual's chances for gaining public employment.[19]

The instrumental justification, though important, does not fully capture the distinctive value of privacy, and some philosophers have therefore sought a justification in the nature of the human relations in which privacy plays an intrinsic role. These relations include love, friendship, and trust, which presuppose a certain degree of privacy.[20] More generally, they are relations that take on a different character when other people observe or know about them.[21] Viewed intrinsically, privacy is justified even if none of the usual harmful consequences (such as loss of a job) is likely to ensue. Because many public officials live in the glare of publicity, the moments alone and with their family and friends are precious, and stand in special need of protection. Furthermore, if officials are to sustain a conception of their own character that is at all independent of their public reputation, they need to be able to escape the public eye from time to time. Without such escape, an official may suffer what Erving Goffman calls stigmatization: "The figure the individual cuts in daily life before those with whom he has routine dealings is likely to be dwarfed and spoiled by virtual demands (whether favorable or unfavorable) created by his public image."[22]

Most of the arguments for the value of privacy to the individual may also be reformulated as arguments for the value of privacy to society. If privacy protects the liberty and opportunities of individual officials, it also can increase the pool of available talent for public positions. Without some assurance of privacy, the unorthodox and the sensitive person is less likely to seek and hold public office, and government loses the competence and diversity that such people may bring. Also, by respecting the privacy of public officials, we may also encourage greater respect for the privacy of citizens. Officials who are in the habit of honoring the privacy of other officials may be more likely to respect that of ordinary citizens. By their own example, officials demonstrate the importance of individual privacy in society. Finally, the titillating details of private lives tend to divert our attention from the larger issues of public life. The quality of deliberation in a democracy is debased when sensationalist exposés of private activities displace discussion of substantial questions of public policy.

The principle of uniform privacy affirms the value of the private lives of public officials, but the principle cannot always be sustained. Public officials are not simply ordinary citizens. They have power over us, and they represent us in other ways. From these differences follows the principle of diminished privacy for public officials. That principle takes precedence over the principle of uniform privacy when the needs of democratic accountability cannot otherwise be met. Because officials make decisions that affect our lives, we want to make sure that they are at least physically and mentally competent; that they do not abuse their power for private ends and are not vulnerable to the improper influence of others; and that they are likely to pursue policies of which we would approve.[23] Their public conduct may reveal much of what we need to know, but in many instances, if we are to hold officials accountable for the power they exercise, we need to learn something about their private lives. (Many officials outside of government also exercise power over us, and insofar as they do, the principle of diminished privacy applies to them too.)

It is sometimes suggested that some officials, especially presidents, ambassadors, and congressmen, represent us not only in their public decisions but also in their private conduct.[24] They stand as symbols for personal values that we share. On this view, political leaders are usually expected to observe higher standards of personal morality than expressed in the "least common denominator of society's . . . standards."[25] Leaders represent our aspirations, not necessarily our behavior. Beyond the symbolism, the way officials conduct their private lives can affect for good or ill the way citizens conduct theirs. Public figures who deal gracefully and courageously with personal difficulties—marital problems, an errant offspring, alcoholism, breast cancer, death of a loved one—not only excite admiration but invite imitation. To be sure, these benefits of diminished privacy might be achieved, and no doubt sometimes are, simply through hypocrisy; it is the appearances that are effective. But since for other reasons (those relating to accountability) citizens will already know something about the private lives of officials, the strategy of hypocrisy cannot be prudently recommended either to society or to officials.

Nevertheless, probity in one's personal life is not a sufficient condition for making moral decisions in public office (many of the major Watergate conspirators evidently led impeccable private lives). It is probably not even a necessary condition (some of the most laudable policies have been made by officials whose personal behavior was hardly exemplary). Indeed, in some cultures flouting private morality may enhance the stature of a public leader. In Indonesia, President Sukarno's "massive preoccupation with sex" was said to be "a matter of admiration rather than disapproval—a demonstration, perhaps, of [his] continuing virility and thus of his political potency as well."[26] Preoccupation with the private virtue of officials may lead us to neglect (or even mistakenly excuse) the public vice they perpetrate through the decisions they make in office. Accountability for these decisions thus may sometimes actually require that citizens know less about the private lives of officials, or at least pay less attention to them. An official may choose, for prudential or for superogatory reasons, to disclose his or her private affairs, but the principle of diminished privacy does not cogently extend beyond what is directly relevant to holding an official accountable for the duties of public office (in ways to be explained below).

Although everyone's privacy deserves respect, public officials must sacrifice some of their privacy for the good of society, including the protection of the privacy of ordinary citizens. One form of an argument for the priority of the principle of diminished privacy is largely utilitarian in character—that the interests of the larger number of citizens take precedence over those of the smaller number—and hence does not fully respect the individual rights of officials. If we could assume that officials consent to the limitation of their privacy, we would have a more satisfactory basis for diminished privacy, and indeed many writers have maintained that the act of seeking or holding public office constitutes such consent.[27] Such an act involves more of a real choice than the status of simply being a citizen, which is sometimes (dubiously) counted as proof of consent.

But while some degree of consent to less privacy does seem to follow from holding some kinds of public office, such consent is not sufficient to negate all claims of privacy for officials. In the first place, the vast majority of public officials (postal employees, clerks, schoolteachers) do not, and should not be expected to, consent to relinquishing rights that an ordinary citizen enjoys simply because they hold a state-supported job, which is otherwise like any other job in society. The Supreme Court has generally rejected the "privilege" doctrine that once warranted the government's denying constitutional rights to public employees.[28] In the second place, even for those officials at higher levels who might be presumed to accept some diminished privacy, the argument from consent does not by itself suggest *what* these officials should consent to. The appeal to consent does not eliminate the need to specify the scope of diminished privacy.

The rationale for diminished privacy provides reasons that any citizen, including a public official, should be able to accept insofar as he or she accepts general principles of democracy. They invoke the necessity of accountability. But the rationale does not justify an unrestrained or general exposure of the private lives of anyone. It implies that private lives should become public only to the extent necessary for certain limited purposes, specifically to ensure democratic accountability. This implication yields two kinds of criteria that should govern any potential intrusion into the private life of an official: substantive criteria, which refer to types of positions and activities; and procedural criteria, which refer to methods of inquiry. The substantive criteria indicate (more or less determinate) boundaries of private life, while the procedural criteria proscribe certain ways of investigating private life, whatever its boundaries may be.

The Scope of Privacy: Substantive Criteria

It is commonly said that the private life of a public official should not be disclosed unless it is relevant to his or her official duties.[29] This view is, at best, a shorthand statement of the substantive criteria for diminished privacy. The ways in which private lives may be relevant are complex. How much privacy a public official should sacrifice depends not only on the nature of the position he or she holds, and the nature of the (presumed) private activities, but also on the relationship between them. For example, the more influential the position, the less are more intimate activities protected. Moreover, the nature of the position and nature of the activity are themselves complex terms, and each needs to be analyzed separately.

The most important feature of the nature of the position is the level of authority or influence that the official exercises. Consistent with the aim of accountability, we assume that we need to know more about officials who wield more authority over us. The authority need be neither formal nor direct. Typically, top White House aides, as much because of their close association with the president as because of their actual authority, invite more inspection than other officials of similar rank in other offices. It is doubtful that someone less close to President Carter than Hamilton Jordan should have had to endure such public scrutiny of conduct at Sarsfield's Bar, or comments about the wife of an ambassador at a private party.[30]

We should consider not only the level of the position but also the kind of issues with which an official deals. Griffin Bell's confirmation as attorney general ran into opposition when it was revealed that he belonged to several private clubs that excluded women and blacks. Although Bell should have disclosed this information himself, he did resign his memberships, conceding that they were incompatible with the office of attorney general, which he saw as a "symbol of equality before the law."[31] Secretary of State Cyrus Vance and Defense Secretary Harold Brown also belonged to discriminatory private clubs, but no similar objections were raised against them. This suggests that most people regard the close connection between the issues with which the attorney general deals and his club memberships as a significantly distinct factor in such cases. It would be better of course if no cabinet members belonged to discriminatory clubs (and still better if no such clubs existed). But the reasons for denying privacy in these matters to the attorney general are even more compelling than the reasons for denying it to other officials at roughly the same level.

When the connection between memberships and the issues dealt with on the job is more tenuous (and the job is at lower levels of government), we encounter claims of "associational privacy" that would protect the privacy of the memberships. Courts have held, for example, that a policeman's membership in a nudist society is his "private life," and not "his employer's concern." Nudism, the court solemnly observed, is not the only recreational activity for which policemen must remove their weapons.[32] The connection between nudism and law enforcement seems remote enough, but some kinds of political activity may raise problems. In several cities, policemen have won the right to belong to the John Birch Society, secretly if they wish.[33] Such a right should not prevail if we have reason to believe that membership in organizations of this kind adversely affect the fair enforcement of the law.

Another aspect of the nature of the position is the form of the appointment—whether, for example, the official is an elected representative, a political appointee, or a career civil servant. This aspect makes much less difference than is usually thought. Once we take into account the level of the position and the kinds of issues dealt with, most of the differences between the various forms of appointment disappear. We are entitled to know more about a congressman than an analyst in the Office of Management and Budget because the congressman usually has more influence and deals with a more general range of issues. How much we should know about congressmen depends partly on our theory of representation (whether we assess, for example, their character or only their public positions on issues),[34] and more specifically on our theory of legislative ethics (whether we examine their role in the legislative process or only their financial affairs).[35]

But whatever theories we adopt, the privacy of legislators should be determined by much the same criteria that we use for political appointees. The press and the public generally ignored the excessive drinking of Hugh Johnson, the head of Roosevelt's National Recovery Administration, just as they later overlooked the drinking habits of many senators and congressmen.[36] We should want to object to the tacit protection from public comment that these men enjoyed since their drinking evidently had a significant effect on the performance of their public duties. But we would not distinguish the cases on the ground that one is a political appointee and the others are elected representatives.

The traditional distinction between political appointees and career civil servants, prominent in Max Weber's theory of bureaucracy, justified granting more of a "private life" to administrators (who were seen as politically neutral) than to politicians (who were politically committed).[37] But the distinction has now lost most of its significance in the higher levels of the American federal bureaucracy. For most of the top executives, the line between political appointment and career service no longer clearly divides politicians and generalists who make policy from administrators and specialists who implement it.[38] How much of the private life of high-level executives should be known, therefore, ought to depend more on their influence and the kinds of decisions they make than on the form of their appointments.

The form of appointment, however, affects privacy in one important respect—not what is known but who should know it. Without completely accepting Weber's theory of bureaucracy, we can assume that civil servants are at least initially responsible to their superiors and the norms of the professional service. If so, the circle of persons who know about the private lives of civil servants should be smaller and more specific than the wider public who should know about political appointees and representatives. It is essential for some officials to know perhaps even more about the private life of an intelligence agent or a Strategic Air Command employee than about the private life of a congressman or an assistant secretary, but it is not necessary for so many people to know.

How much an official's privacy should be diminished also depends on the nature of the activity in question—its character and its effects. Although the content of what should be private is largely conventional, a general feature of many private activities is intimacy. We usually expect privacy for our physical condition and our personal relations with family, friends, and certain associates (those with whom we have "privileged" relationships), and for activities carried on "in private" at home. The boundaries of what is intimate are neither precise nor absolute, and even the most intimate facts about public officials may not be protected if the facts are highly relevant to the performance of their duties. But we should be inclined to say that the more intimate the activity, the more compelling must be the connection with the official's position; and, conversely, the less intimate, the less compelling the connection has to be. Consider the legal requirements for financial disclosure that now apply to legislators and high officials in the executive and judiciary.[39] The chief purpose of the requirements is to expose potential conflicts of interest—a purpose obviously related to holding officials accountable. But the relevance would not be strong enough to overcome privacy objections if private financial affairs were not at the edge of intimacy. Our attitude would be very different toward a requirement, for example, that officials list all their friends and the frequency of meetings with them.

Even though the relevance of financial disclosure outweighs the claim of privacy, it should not be an excuse for publicizing all other personal information that may pertain in some way to an official's financial affairs.

It is a legitimate concern of the public if, as a Massachusetts judge stated, Senator Edward Brooke deliberately overstated by a relatively small amount his financial liabilities.[40] If Brooke misrepresented his financial worth in these proceedings, he may also have done so in his financial statement to the Senate Ethics Committee, and in either case, the public is entitled to know about it. Brooke complained that the public has no right to intrude into "every bureau drawer, every clothes closet, every item in my checkbook, every personal agreement" with members of his family.[41] Insofar as the press went beyond reporting the financial facts and others necessary to make sense of them, however, Brooke's complaint has merit. Even some of the proponents of the requirement for financial disclosure concede that medical bills, church contributions, and many other items on personal tax returns should not have to be disclosed.[42] A California court struck down, on privacy grounds, a state law that required all public officials to disclose major financial investments.[43] A less broadly drawn statute—requiring fewer officials who must disclose, and specifying what must be reported and to whom—probably would have passed judicial scrutiny.

If otherwise intimate activities are carried on in a way that risks the violation of public duty, they lose the protection of privacy. In the past, members of Congress usually connived at the sexual improprieties of their colleagues, and even when they did not (as when they forced House Speaker David Henderson to resign in 1903 because he was sexually involved with a daughter of a senator), the press did not report them.[44] But beginning in the summer of 1976, the public was treated to an orgy of sex exposés: no less than seven congressmen were reported to have engaged in illicit sex, or to have attempted to do so. Six of the episodes involved misuse of public funds (for example, Wayne Hays kept a mistress on the House payroll) or encounters with the law (for example, Allen Howe allegedly solicited two policewomen posing as prostitutes), and therefore could hardly be considered private matters.[45]

But the seventh case, which was not always distinguished from the others, could be considered an invasion of privacy. In the middle of the 1976 campaign for a Michigan Senate seat, the *Detroit News* reported that one of the candidates, an incumbent Congressman, had carried on an affair with an unpaid woman member of his staff seven years earlier. The claim that the incident reflected badly on his judgment and maturity did not receive much credence (a church official remarked, "Remember, he's not running for bishop").[46] But the reports of the incident distracted the candidates from further discussion of the more substantial issues in the campaign, such as school busing and criminal law. Apart from the effect on the privacy of the candidate, the quality of public debate generally suffers if such scandals become an issue, unless they involve abuse of office or violations of the law.

A public official can properly claim that much of his or her family life is private. At stake is not only the official's privacy but that of other people. An example of a practice that violates such privacy is what has been called the "transfer technique."[47] This typically involved an investigation into an official's family circumstances to see if he could be persuaded to resign by reassigning him to a location his family would resist. This kind of investigation would be no more acceptable if its aim were to reward the official with an assignment his family liked.

Some facts about family life (such as marriage and divorce) are of course a matter of public record.[48] It is surely proper that these facts be considered when assessing a public official if they are relevant to the office, according to the other criteria we have been using. But the official has no obligation to reveal the details of life behind the public facts, and often an obligation to other parties not to do so. New York Governor Nelson Rockefeller quite properly resisted pleas to explain the reasons for his divorce and remarriage in 1963. Some family members of public officials become, formally or informally, officials themselves (such as the first lady, or the spouse of an ambassador), and they should expect no more privacy than other officials with similar influence and similar functions. In other cases, facts about a family member of an official—a spouse's health, a son's delinquency, or marital problems—might bear on the capacity of the official to do his or her job. But even here, it would seem better to publicize the effects (if and when they occur), rather than the causes.

However, when a candidate for public office makes his family life a campaign issue (for example, by portraying himself as a "good family man"), he opens to public inspection what might otherwise be private. The candidate can hardly complain if the press looks into his family life to verify his boasts. For similar reasons, we may "want to know if there is a big split in someone's life—if he is a professed feminist and at the same time a womanizer."[49] But again there are limits. Because Spiro Agnew was piously lecturing America on parenthood at the time, Jack

Anderson and Brit Hume reported that his son had left his wife and was living with a male hairdresser. Anderson and Hume now say they regret the story because it was "going after the son to expose the father."[50] But the real objection is not that Agnew's statements could not legitimately be said to invite scrutiny of his family (arguably, they could). Rather, the objection should be that the effect of the story depended on exploiting readers' prejudices against unconventional styles of life.

We should distinguish two different ways in which an otherwise private activity may affect an official's capacity to perform the duties of public office: the direct effects that come from the official's own attitudes or actions in private life; and the indirect effects that result from other people's attitudes or actions toward the official's private life. In general, it would be better if neither kind of effect were publicized until it showed up in official performance. To probe possible causes before they have produced public consequences usually is to risk exposing affairs that are legitimately private. But often we cannot follow this principle, especially when we are evaluating a candidate for high office.

The direct effects constitute the stronger basis for diminished privacy. When the evidence is compelling, they may override even claims based on intimacy. Although a person's physical condition is conventionally regarded as particularly private in our society, some writers have argued that candidates for public office should have physical examinations, the results of which should be publicly announced.[51] Publicity about serious health problems of high-ranking officials, whether elected or appointed, is now more generally expected. Difficulties still arise when officials and their doctors, believing that a health problem is not serious, decline to disclose the information, and the public and the press become suspicious. Justice Rehnquist's doctors refused to identify the drug that caused an adverse reaction for which he was hospitalized in 1981, saying only that it was one of several used to treat his chronic low back pain.[52] Since the justice had been repeatedly slurring his speech and stumbling over words in court, some observers (including physicians) suspected that he was suffering from delirium tremens as a withdrawal effect of alcohol. A more complete disclosure could have avoided this conclusion.

Proposals for psychiatric examinations of candidates for high public office are more problematic, chiefly because we have less confidence about the validity or objectivity of such examinations.[53] But a candidate or official who has experienced severe mental or physical problems in the past should not conceal this history. As an aspiring candidate for the vice-presidency, Senator Thomas Eagleton should have told not only George McGovern in July 1972 but also the public about his three hospitalizations for mental problems. No intimate details perhaps were necessary; a statement such as the one he was eventually forced to issue would have been sufficient, had he volunteered it earlier.[54] Since mental illness still carries a stigma in our society, the decision to disclose it can never be easy. Eagleton may have been correct that his past mental and physical problems would not affect his capacity to do the job. But a public official cannot be permitted to make that determination alone— at least not one who aspires to high office.

Officials at lower levels of influence and with less serious mental and physical problems do not have the same obligation to divulge such information, certainly not to the general public. Dr. Peter Bourne, a close aide to President Carter until he was forced to resign, recognized this difference in his efforts to protect the privacy of his administrative assistant by using a fictitious name on her prescription for methaqualone (a powerful and controversial sedative). Defending himself, Bourne cited the Code of Ethics of the American Medical Association, which prevents a doctor from revealing confidences about a patient.[55] The code does not countenance violating the law, however, and using fictitious names on prescriptions infringes federal regulations on the dispensing of controlled drugs—regulations to which the president's chief adviser on drug abuse should be especially sensitive. That Bourne's conduct may have violated the law would not necessarily settle the issue, however, since many believe the law to be too rigid in this area. (The practice of using fictitious names for prescriptions is said to be prevalent in Washington, and seldom prosecuted.) But the rationale for the law itself is cogent, and there are alternative means for protecting the privacy of officials without defeating the general purpose of the law. For example, pharmacists and others who divulge the identity of patients to unauthorized persons could be made subject to stiff penalties.

The indirect effects of private life on public duties raise further problems. The problems typically arise when an official is alleged to have engaged in controversial activities that are commonly classed as matters of private morality.[56] Adultery and homosexuality are the most familiar examples. Since the evidence that such activities directly affect anyone's ability to do a job is usually nonexistent, the objection turns on the reaction of other people to the knowledge that an official engages in the activity. Public reaction, it is said, undermines confidence in the agency in which the official works, and could impair the ability of the agency to win support for its policies. Merely the possibility of publicity about the conduct can weaken an official's political position. Some critics think that President Kennedy and his brother hesitated to challenge FBI Director Hoover because of their fear that Hoover might leak what he knew about the president's extramarital liaisons.[57]

Indirect effects may count against privacy if an official could reasonably have avoided making his conduct public. When Walter Jenkins, a close aide to President Johnson, was charged with homosexual activity in the men's room of a Washington YMCA in 1964, the incident received wide publicity and Jenkins promptly resigned.[58] Even if Jenkins had not suffered a nervous collapse at the same time, and even if the press had not learned of the homosexual incident, the president and his staff probably would have concluded that the risk of serious political effect justified their setting aside any claim that Jenkins' sexual conduct was no one else's business. But the responsibility for the political effects should not be the decisive factor. We also need to consider the nature of the official's position and the importance of the decisions and policies that are likely to be affected. When a budget analyst in NASA was dismissed for allegedly making homosexual advances near Lafayette Square in Washington in 1963, the press properly did not publicize the incident, and the D.C. Court of Appeals ordered him reinstated.[59]

The objection from indirect effects is often a disingenuous way of expressing moral disapproval since there is usually little reason to believe that disclosure of the conduct will cause much political damage. This is all the more true when public attitudes toward sexual conduct are shifting. In many parts of the country, homosexuality is no longer politically fatal and in some places it may even count in favor of a politician. In the early 1980s two conservative Republicans were arrested for homosexual solicitation. Although both were from conservative districts, only one was defeated for reelection. (The other won reelection, but later resigned after a subsequent arrest on a morals charge.) In 1984 Representative Gerry E. Studds, a Massachusetts Democrat, won reelection despite his confession of an affair with a male page. His constituents could reasonably have objected to the intimate involvement with a young person employed by Congress, quite apart from its homosexual character.

(Another Congressman was defeated in the same year after disclosure of his sexual relationship with a female page.) But Studds's strong record of constituency service and his open acknowledgment of his homosexuality convinced enough of his Cape Cod constituents to support him; some may have seen a vote for him as a political statement in favor of sexual liberation.

But even if we expect the political reaction to be unfavorable, we should still want to protect an official's right of privacy with respect to the conduct in question. Indirect effects resulting from misconceived moral principles and prejudices ought to be disregarded. Strict liberals, following John Stuart Mill, would argue that activities like homosexuality are self-regarding and should be free from any kind of social intrusion.[60] We cannot apply the distinction between self- and other-regarding activities to public officials in exactly the same way that liberals apply the distinction to citizens. Publicity about an official's sexual conduct may very well harm other people, even those who do not disapprove of the conduct, because performance in office often depends on maintaining public confidence. But the distinction between self- and other-regarding activities could be applied indirectly. We could insist that, if the only effects on an official's performance in office spring from the reaction of people who fail to respect the distinction, the effects should be disregarded.

Critics have argued that the liberal distinction is impossible to maintain, and, further, that society should seek a public morality that does not in principle treat any activities as always self-regarding or private.[61] Although the distinction certainly suffers from many problems, it is worth trying to preserve it in some form. The alternative conceptions of public morality, insofar as the critics offer any, seem to assume a communal consensus that could be achieved only through eliminating moral diversity. Nevertheless, an adequate standard of privacy for public officials does not necessarily depend on accepting the distinction. We could instead adopt a distinction between moral principles and mere prejudices. With such a distinction, we might be able to show that disapproval of homosexuality and similar practices is a prejudice, not a proper part of either a public or a private morality.[62]

In any case, the question of whether we count indirect effects as sufficient to override claims of privacy cannot be settled without judging the status of the attitudes that create the indirect effects. Such a judgment must ultimately rest on a conception of morality and a theory of political liberty, which must be to some extent independent of the attitudes being judged. Even if the attitudes express sincere and intense beliefs, they should not outweigh privacy unless they refer to conduct that would be regarded as a serious wrong from a wide variety of moral perspectives in society. Public attitudes toward otherwise private conduct should by themselves warrant neither disclosure of the conduct nor sanctions for the conduct if it is disclosed.[63]

The most difficult cases concern conduct that should properly be regarded as immoral but that does not directly affect an official's performance on the job. Wife abuse, now treated more seriously than it used to be, is a case in point. The chief of the Securities and Exchange Commission's enforcement division resigned in 1985 within a week of a newspaper report that he had repeatedly beaten his wife. Although his wife's charges had appeared in the public record at the start of the divorce proceedings nearly a year and a half earlier, virtually no one had taken notice until the *Wall Street Journal* reported them in the front-page story that prompted his resignation.[64] By all accounts, the official's performance on the job had been exemplary. But White House officials immediately decided that once he became publicly known as a wife abuser he could not remain in office.

The managing editor of the *Journal* set aside the paper's "general rule" protecting the private life of public officials because of the whole set of facts surrounding the case: that the official "admitted in public the charges of wife-beating . . . that he is one of the most important law enforcement officials in the country . . . that the White House was aware of the issue of family violence and seemed to be concerned about it . . . that he had indicated that he would resign his position at the SEC if that would get his wife to take him back . . . and the questions raised about his indebtedness and . . . the issues in the Southland case [in which not he but a former law client had been charged with a cover-up of a bribery scheme]."[65] Although this editor's justification may seem too much like a laundry list of factors, it comes closer to recognizing the complexity of the case than the responses that other journalists gave. Some seemed to assume that the fact that the conduct appeared in the court record was sufficient reason to print it, or the fact that the official had to spend some time in court was enough to show that the conduct was affecting his job performance.[66]

The official's own admission on the court record is probably a necessary condition for justifying the publicity because without it (or some independent proceeding to establish guilt) we cannot have a reasonable basis for believing the charges. Although not explicitly mentioned by any of the journalists, the most important necessary condition is that the official's conduct is a serious moral wrong. None of the other factors the *Journal* editor cited seems to qualify as a necessary condition. But combined with the admission of guilt and the seriousness of the moral wrong, any one of several of these other factors probably would be sufficient to justify the publicity.

Among the other factors, those connected with the nature of the office are the most significant. Citizens should know if an official responsible for supervising the enforcement of laws repeatedly commits wrongful acts of violence. Such conduct may reveal a disregard for important moral principles underlying the legal system, including those laws that the official is charged with enforcing. The conduct may raise reasonable doubts about future performance on the job even if the official's past performance has been faultless. More specifically, citizens may reasonably expect to know about domestic violence if it provides evidence about the seriousness of the personal financial difficulties of an official whose job involves investigating the finances of other people. In this case, according to the court record, the violence was occasioned by anxieties and arguments about the worsening financial condition of the family.

But whatever factors may be sufficient to justify publicity about what would otherwise be the private life of an official, they do not include the indirect effects from the reaction of the public. It is not enough (even when it is relevant) to point to the public scandal that an official's conduct may cause. The question must always be asked: *should* the public be scandalized?

The Scope of Privacy: Procedural Criteria

Some procedural criteria protect private activities not because the activities are private but because the method of intrusion would be wrong even if the activity were public. These criteria follow from prohibitions against force and fraud, and often, but not always, involve violation of the law. The break-in at the office of Dr. Henry Fielding to collect psychiatric information to discredit Daniel Ellsberg or the planting of a spy on McGovern's campaign staff to look for "dirty stuff . . . who was sleeping with whom . . . who was smoking pot,"[67] a newspaper reporter's posing as a friend to extract confidences from a newly elected politician[68]— all of these may be challenged as improperly forceful or fraudulent, quite apart from whatever invasion of privacy may have occurred. Other criteria, however, derive more specifically from the value of privacy, and it is these on which this section concentrates.

It is often not possible to tell in advance what private activities may be relevant to our assessment of official performance, but this fact should not warrant unlimited inquiry into private lives in the hope that something relevant may turn up. This is not to say that an investigation, prompted by independent evidence and seeking further specific evidence relevant to official performance, should be proscribed merely because it is likely to uncover some purely private information in the process. But even if the boundaries of private life cannot be precisely delineated, we presume that *some* beliefs and activities are protected (as the principle of uniform privacy stressed). We should therefore object to methods that intrude into potentially private conduct in a way that by their nature cannot discriminate among activities that are legitimately a matter of public concern and those that are not. We should seek, among available alternatives, the method that is likely to intrude to the minimum degree necessary; and we should prefer methods that give officials some control over what personal information about themselves is disclosed. A brief analysis of cases in three different areas will illustrate what these procedural criteria imply.

Surveillance of an official at home generally runs afoul of the procedural criteria. Some surveillance of this sort may be illegal, such as the wiretaps that in 1969 were placed on the phones of Morton Halperin and other aides of Henry Kissinger, evidently for the purposes of discovering the source of leaks that supposedly had damaged national security.[69] But whether legal or not, such surveillance should provoke ethical qualms. When a reporter asked Kissinger in 1974 if he had any doubts about the "ethicality" of these wiretaps, he replied that if any of his subordinates had been found guilty of security leaks, it would have "reflected badly on [his] own judgment." The implication is that because the taps involved risks to his own reputation, they were not morally objectionable.[70] Showing that a practice is not in your self-interest, however, does not dispose of other, often more important, ethical objections, including those based on privacy.

Officials who bring their personal activities and possessions into public space should expect less privacy, but they should still not be subjected to unlimited observation. Surely an official should be able to have a family picnic at a park without worrying, for example, whether a photograph displaying his slovenly table manners will appear in the morning paper.[71] Nor should it be impossible for an official to hold a family funeral in a church without his every reaction being photographed or commented upon. That Henry Kissinger's garbage may betray some information of public concern should not license members of the press or anyone else to rummage around in it, whether or not it is in a public place.

It is sometimes supposed, however, that once an official arrives at his office, all privacy protections disappear. The legal counsel for the Los Angeles County Office in Pomona defended the continuous monitoring of conversations in that office, maintaining that public officials "have no reasonable expectation of privacy" on the job.[72] To be sure, most of what goes on in a government office is public business, but even here a preserve of privacy might be staked out. The importance of such a preserve, as well as the difficulties of defining it, can be illustrated by the case of Otto Otepka.

Otepka was an official in the State Department's Office of Security until he was dismissed in 1963.[73] His critics charged that he had improperly supplied the Senate Internal Security Subcommittee with classified information, and had in other ways demonstrated disloyalty to his superiors within the department. His defenders maintained that he had been ousted merely because of his zealous security checks on prospective appointees (especially Democrats), and his denial of security clearances to some of them. Quite apart from the merits of these arguments, the methods that Otepka's superiors used to accumulate evidence against him raise some problems of privacy. Not only did his superiors conduct surveillance of his home and tap his telephone, but they also gathered the trash he discarded in his wastebasket and burn-bag, attempted to search his desk at night, drilled open his office safe where he kept private papers, and instructed a secretary to report on his conversations. It could be argued that the surveillance at the office, because it took place on government premises and involved government property, did not violate Otepka's privacy. Moreover, the information the investigators were seeking was part of the political process, and, though it might be protected by norms of confidentiality, could not be considered part of Otepka's private life.

Yet officials should still be able to claim control over some information or activities even on the job. They should be able to determine to some extent when their private thoughts (even if in writing) become a part of the political process. Some unofficial conversations with secretaries or colleagues deserve similar protection. The line between the official and the personal on the job is hard to draw, and probably need not be drawn at all if investigators have good reason to believe, for example, that a governmental employee is passing secrets to enemy agents. But a general warrant to engage in indiscriminate searches and surveillance on the job ought not to be conceded. Whatever methods are used, they should permit a significant area of private life to persist, however it might be defined.[74]

Employment tests and interviews are a second area where questionable methods are sometimes used. One objection to some of these tests and interviews is that the questions asked are not relevant to the job—questions, for example, that delve into driving habits, religious affiliation, birth control methods, dating relationships, or the marital and financial status of parents.[75] Such questions would usually be disallowed (except perhaps for sensitive intelligence positions) by the substantive criteria we have already discussed. But tests often seek information that is arguably relevant to the job and nevertheless violate the procedural criteria because they intrude indiscriminately into private lives.

Personality tests probe characteristics—reliability, self-confidence, general psychological stability—that may significantly affect a person's capacity to do a job. (Whether such tests accurately identify these characteristics is a separate issue.) Congress directed the Peace Corps to select volunteers of sound mental health, and the corps implemented this directive by administering the Minnesota Multiphasic Personality Inventory, which asked volunteers for "true" or "false" responses to statements such as these: "Once in a while I laugh at a dirty joke," "I loved my mother," and "During one period when I was a youngster I engaged in petty thievery." Other tests required federal employees to complete these sentences: "I feel ashamed when——" and "I secretly ——" and "My childhood——".[76] Such indiscriminate rummaging in the minds of individuals would in general infringe the procedural constraints on diminished privacy.

Although surprisingly few employees objected (even in the Peace Corps), personality tests can hardly be regarded as fully voluntary. The individuals taking such tests nevertheless retain some control over the information they disclose, even if they must resort to wile to protect themselves. In this respect, the polygraph test is even more objectionable because the individuals at least theoretically relinquish even that degree of control over information about themselves. The test procedure sometimes involves other objectionable practices as well: the reactions of the subject, who is encouraged to read pro-polygraph literature planted in the waiting room, are observed by a "receptionist" and reported to the examiner, who includes the observations as part of his evaluation.[77] The Civil Service Commission has sharply restricted the use of polygraph tests, but the government continues to administer a substantial number to employees each year, and proposals for their more extensive use still regularly surface.[78]

Interviews themselves may also threaten privacy. The case of Ed Morley illustrates how this can happen, as well as how the issue of privacy can become entangled with other ethical questions.[79] An army officer who had served in Vietnam, Morley sought a post as assistant administrator for program analysis in the Environmental Protection Agency in the Lindsay administration in 1971. The head of the agency was about to hire Morley when members of the staff raised questions about Morley's moral character; they objected to his previous support of the war, and doubted the sincerity of his more recent opposition to it. Morley accepted a series of further interviews with the staff, but objected to the last one, with Mike Ash and Randy Parker, as an "invasion of privacy." The interview, Morley thought, took the form of "an inquisition," in which Ash and Parker pried into his "views on some very fundamental things."

Morley could not very well complain that his participation in the conduct of the war was a private matter, though he could (and did) object to the ways in which the EPA staff took into account his war record. Among the objections were: (1) that the members of the agency were not competent and did not have the authority to decide whether or not he was a war criminal; (2) that to disqualify him because of his earlier views on the war would be to apply a political test for public office in a way that resembled the tactics of McCarthyism; and (3) that his earlier views on the war were not relevant to an administrator's position and would have no significant impact on staff harmony and morale unless members of the staff improperly ignored (1) and (2).

None of these objections is, strictly speaking, based completely or mainly on privacy, but Morley was not mistaken in claiming an "invasion of privacy." Although privacy is not the only important issue in this case and Morley may not himself always have distinguished it from other issues, the objection from privacy has some merit. In principle, Morley might have maintained that his conversion to an antiwar view was a private matter, but he felt that he had to disclose his current beliefs, in part to avoid misinterpretations of his military service.[80] Some staff members doubted that his conversion was genuine or complete; they wondered, for example, to what extent his opposition to the war was based on merely pragmatic rather than moral grounds. Ash and Parker suspected that if they asked him only about the war, he was clever enough to give the "right" answers. They wanted him to "reveal what kind of person he was." To test the sincerity and depth of his conversion, they attempted to conduct an interview that probed his personal views on a whole range of "basic values."

The result was an interview that evidently proceeded indiscriminately, violating the procedural criteria of privacy. That the interview also covered some topics relevant to his performance in the agency or may have raised some doubts about his general reliability does not remove the objection to undertaking such an interview in the first place. An interview that tests sincerity and searches for the "whole person" in this way is not likely to respect any boundaries of the private life of a candidate, however narrowly those boundaries may be drawn. Even if the sincerity of Morley's views on environmental reform had been the primary issue, such an inquisitory interview would have been inappropriate. His past public record, and his responses to questions of obvious pertinence to the job, should have given agency officials sufficient information to decide whether to hire him.

How extensive an interview or an employment test should be depends partly on the nature of the position to be filled. A candidate for Congress, for example, who seeks to represent citizens on a wide range of issues, may be less entitled to object to probing interviews. (A large part of the reason may be merely that a more diverse public can assess the propriety of the questions and the adequacy of responses better in the case of the congressional candidate than in the case of an administrative candidate such as Morley.) Yet current practice often seems to be the reverse of what would be called for by the nature of the position. Lower-level, more specialized, public employees have been more often subjected to personality and polygraph tests and probably also to improper interviews. Few officials are likely to be so effective as Secretary of State George Shultz was in convincing their superiors to drop the idea of conducting lie-detector tests.[81]

Many of the recent efforts at both the federal and state levels to test public employees for evidence of drug use are questionable for similar reasons.[82] Drug use is not necessarily a private matter for persons in many kinds of public positions, but the methods by which the use is discovered and deterred should not intrude into matters that are private. When employees are given no notice at all that tests may be conducted, are required to provide urine samples taken in the presence of others, and are granted no right to appeal the findings or disciplinary action taken on the basis of the findings, the tests violate privacy. So do tests conducted without any reason to suspect significant drug use among the targeted group, or without any attempt to define that group narrowly. More carefully designed tests that did not have these objectionable features could be justified, but the justification would still have to show that drug use could significantly affect the work of the employees to be tested.

A third area to which procedural criteria apply concerns the personnel records of public employees. Here too, methods should be selective and give officials some control over information about themselves. Even if we optimistically assume that the records contain only relevant or necessary information, we have not disposed of the privacy problem. First, like any employer, the government properly collects a great deal of personal information about all employees (for example, facts about medical insurance, life insurance beneficiaries, and home mortgages). Although personnel officers need access to this data, other officials, including the employees' superiors, and the press and the public, do not. The method of record keeping, therefore, should distinguish between such personal information, which could be kept in completely separate files, and job-related information, which would be available to an employee's superior or in some circumstances to a wider public.[83]

Second, individual officials should have some control over all of the records about themselves, specifically the right to see what is in their own files, to determine who else sees them, and what is included or excluded from them. The Privacy Act of 1974 gave federal employees the right to examine their personnel files. But legal provisions are not likely to solve the problem completely, since officials have been known to maintain "ghost files" containing confidential information unknown and unavailable to their subordinates. The State Department kept such a file on Murray C. Smith III, a young foreign service officer who was "selected out" in 1971, evidently partly on the basis of this file.[84] In this case, the information concerned his public antiwar activity, but the same procedure could well be used to collect private information, and even if the employee knew about it, he would be unlikely to challenge the abuse formally, for fear of publicizing the sensitive information more widely.

The private lives of public officials deserve protection because the privacy of all citizens has value. However, because officials must be held accountable in a democracy (in part to safeguard the privacy of others), officials should not expect to enjoy the same protection as ordinary citizens do. What the scope of the private life of officials should be depends on a manifold set of criteria that do not by themselves yield precise boundaries. The criteria are best conceived as a framework of factors about which citizens and officials should deliberate when questions of privacy arise, and to which citizens and officials should refer to decide when such questions ought to arise.

In democracies, especially the imperfect ones we know, it is important to seek justifiable boundaries between public and private life. The purpose of such boundaries is not only to secure the privacy of officials and citizens; it is also to ensure the publicity of affairs of public import. Spurious claims of privacy shield officials from needful scrutiny by a democratic public, and thereby subvert the democratic processes of deliberation and accountability. The private lives of public officials are as important for what they exclude as for what they include.

6

Paternalistic Power

Like parents, public officials sometimes make us act against our own will for our own good. They do wrong in order to do good: they interfere with liberty in order to promote welfare. Unlike the wrongs of dirty-handed politicians, those that parental politicians commit typically fall on the same persons whose good is served. Such actions create a direct conflict between liberty and welfare, and pose what should perhaps be called the problem of parentalism but has traditionally been known as the problem of paternalism.[1]

The simple liberal solution resolves the conflict completely in favor of liberty: it rejects paternalism absolutely. This is the position that John Stuart Mill explicitly defends. "Because it would be better for him" or "Because it will make him happier" can never, in Mill's view, justify restricting the liberty of a sane adult.[2] The general benefits of liberty, he argues, far outweigh any gains in welfare that paternalism might offer. But this absolutist opposition to paternalism is difficult to maintain, and in fact Mill himself does not maintain it consistently. Confronted with cases where someone acting in ignorance is likely to harm himself, Mill approves of trying to stop him.[3] Many later liberals emphasize, more explicitly than Mill, that some adults always, and all adults sometimes, are incapable of exercising liberty. The growing complexity of modern society and increasing knowledge about the human psyche give greater reason to doubt the capacity of individuals to exercise liberty for their own good. But these later liberals do not abandon the presumption in favor of liberty.

The problem of paternalism, then, is best conceived not as a question of choosing between liberty and paternalism but as a question of reconciling paternalism with liberty. More specifically, we should try to formulate criteria of justifiable paternalism so that they are consistent with the principle of liberty. If a paternalistic intervention restricts only decisions that are already unfree, if it is limited in scope, and if the person whose decisions are restricted accepts its purpose, the intervention does not violate the principle of liberty. Liberty is preserved insofar as persons are not prevented from acting according to their own conception of the good.

Although this approach remains faithful to liberal aims, we cannot accept it without substantial revision. In many important instances of paternalism, the meaning of the criteria—the sense in which a decision is unfree, an intervention limited, and an acceptance of its purpose valid—is problematic. It is so because the paternalism involves the exercise of political power in ways that Mill as well as modern liberals neglect.

The liberal paradigm of paternalism usually presents a relationship between two individuals, who interact personally and for a specific purpose. On this view, the paternalist may be seen as exercising power over the person whose welfare is being promoted, but the power is assumed to be directed toward ends that both parties can be known to share, and the unequal power between the parties is assumed to be limited to the specific purposes of the intervention. These individualistic assumptions carry over to the discussion of governmental paternalism. The government takes on the character of a benevolent individual, using its power for agreed-upon ends and intervening only from time to time to promote those ends.

What the paradigm obscures are two features of the power that inheres in paternalism—its contestable and systematic character. The power is contestable in the sense that there often is fundamental and reasonable disagreement about the ends it should serve. It is systematic in the sense that its effects (including the inequalities it reinforces) reach beyond the scope of the intervention itself. Recognizing these political dimensions should affect the way we understand paternalism.

This recognition should affect, first, the concept of paternalism—what we count as a paternalistic intervention. Relations that are ostensibly voluntary transactions between individuals—relations between professionals and clients, for example—turn out to be more paternalistic than usually assumed. It should also affect the justification of paternalism—how we interpret the criteria that warrant an intervention. The criteria must provide for the possibility of resolving the disagreement about interventions and for controlling their structural consequences. Finally, a more political understanding should influence the application of the concept and criteria—how we judge instances of paternalism. Our judgments about the paternalism in particular cases should depend partly on the kinds of political institutions in which the paternalism takes place. Justifying some kinds of paternalism may call for establishing processes that give its beneficiaries (and citizens more generally) some democratic control over those institutions.

The Concept of Paternalism

A paternalistic decision or policy places constraints on the liberty of persons for the purpose of protecting and promoting their own good.[4] This definition points to three elements of paternalism, each of which may be problematic: the locus of the constraints, their form, and their purpose.

The locus of paternalism refers to the relationship between those whose liberty is restricted and those who impose the restriction. Even into that most original of paternalistic relations—between parent and child—politics intrudes. Political power and parental power cannot be kept so sharply separate as Locke and many modern liberals assume. They presuppose that we can distinguish a class of persons, defined only by their chronological age, whose liberty may be legitimately constrained for their own good. This presupposition begs the question not only of how to justify the criterion of chronological age, but also of how to determine who has the right to restrict a child's liberty—parents, guardians, the state, or no one?[5]

More commonly in the literature, paternalism refers to relationships between two adults. It is important—but not so common—to distinguish between relationships in which the paternalists and the persons they would help are more or less equal in status, and relationships in which paternalists, by virtue of their social role or institutional position, have greater status. What constitutes a restriction on liberty in the latter kind of relationship (such as that between a professional and his client) may, as we shall see, differ from what counts as a restriction in the former kind of relationship. Inequalities that are initially quite independent of the paternalistic intervention may come to affect its character, and it may in turn reinforce the inequalities. Even if itself isolated or sporadic, the intervention can generate paternalistic effects that persist in time and spread in social space, extending well beyond the encounter of the two individuals. Paternalism in these contexts is misrepresented if described as only a relationship between individuals.

The other important locus of paternalism is the relationship between citizens and the state.[6] Here what seems like the opposite mistake commonly occurs: paternalism is confused with certain kinds of state power, such as undemocratic policies. But the mistake is essentially the same. Paternalism is given no political identity of its own; its political character is completely drawn from the other political concepts with which it is associated. If we identify the paternalistic with the undemocratic, for example, we cannot distinguish paternalistic restrictions that are not sanctioned by democratic procedures from those that are so sanctioned. A president who deceives citizens for what he believes to be their own good acts undemocratically as well as paternalistically if his action violates constitutional norms, but he acts only paternalistically if his action conforms to such norms. Only the latter kind of action poses the distinctive problem of paternalism, since any objection to the former kind rests on a general argument for democratic government. Failing to respect these distinctions militates against criticizing democratic officials for paternalistic decisions, and against establishing democratic processes to control justifiable paternalism.

Certain kinds of legislation are also often mistakenly called paternalistic. Examples are laws that require contributions to some cooperative scheme (such as medical care) or laws that regulate working conditions (such as minimum wages or maximum hours of work). These should not be considered paternalistic, so long as their purpose is to give effect to the desires of a democratic majority, rather than simply to coerce a minority who do not want the benefits of the legislation.[7] Legislation is paternalistic with respect to the minority only if the majority could promote their own good in some other (fair) way without coercing the minority, and if the justification for the legislation depends in part on an appeal to the good of the minority. Legislation that does not meet these conditions may still count as paternalistic toward the majority. A law prohibiting the use of certain drugs is paternalistic with respect to anyone in the majority, including legislators themselves, who might want to use the drug. Even if persons in some way consent to a restriction of their liberty for their own good, the restriction remains paternalistic if they wish to perform the proscribed action while the restriction is in effect. The classical example is Odysseus' request to be bound to the mast so that he could not succumb to the Sirens' song.

The second element of the concept raises the question of whether paternalism always involves a restriction of liberty. It is not helpful to broaden the concept of paternalism, as some writers propose, to include all cases in which a moral rule is violated to promote an individual's good.[8] Violations of moral principles other than liberty are at most incomplete instances of paternalism, since they do not alone prevent persons from choosing or acting on their own conception of the good. If for your own good I break a promise to you, but do not restrict your liberty in any way, then I do not actually impose my conception of good on you.[9] Furthermore, the instances that these writers wish to count as paternalism—for example, a doctor deceiving a patient—not only can but should be regarded as involving a restriction of liberty. Although deception is not necessarily coercive,[10] it is likely to constrain action when practiced by persons or institutions who act from positions of superior power or prestige.

The concept of paternalism should recognize that restrictions on liberty may take the form not only of physical or legal coercion, but also of more subtle impediments that arise from unequal power in some kinds of relationship. In this and similar instances, the paternalist imposes a conception of the good by limiting, in some way, actions that a person may wish to perform. A patient's liberty may be restricted when a doctor fails to provide information that would be likely to incline the patient to choose a different course of action.[11] Similarly, the choices of citizens are constrained when governments decline to disclose significant information. Yet it is also important to avoid construing the concept of liberty so broadly that the problem of paternalism dissolves. The so-called positive concept of liberty (the liberty to do what is good or worthwhile) would not, at least in its stronger forms, serve to clarify the nature of paternalism. With such a concept, paternalistic intervention would never conflict with liberty. Restrictions on individuals for the purpose of making them better off could not count as constraints on their liberty at all.[12]

The purpose of paternalism (the protection or promotion of a person's own good) is also subject to reasonable disagreement. Although the concept of paternalism includes goods ranging from prevention of immediate physical harm to the promotion of a whole style of life, the goods to which paternalism refers must be limited to those experienced by the specific person whose liberty is restricted. Paternalism should not encompass the benefits or harms that the person may bring to others or to society in general. Otherwise, we could not distinguish paternalism from what is called moralism (the legal enforcement of morality). This distinction is needed to keep open the possibility of agreeing with Mill that morality should not be legally enforced, but disagreeing with him that paternalism is never justified.[13] The justifiability of the goods with which paternalism deals, to be sure, cannot be determined without invoking a moral theory or at least some standards of evaluation, but the conceptual distinction between paternalism and moralism does not depend on accepting any particular theory or standards.

Nor does the concept of paternalism presuppose a radical individualism in which the good or harm done to each citizen has no effect on other citizens. Contrary to what some theorists assume, paternalism remains a distinctive problem even if Mill's dichotomy between self-regarding and other-regarding actions cannot be sustained.[14] Even if it is impossible to say of any particular action that it affects only one person in the way that for Mill makes the action self-regarding, we can still offer, among the reasons for restricting a person's liberty, the claim that the restriction promotes his or her own good. In this way, paternalism refers not to a distinct class of *actions,* but to a class of *reasons* that we may use to justify or condemn restrictions even on actions that affect other people as well as the person being helped. This way of understanding paternalism is especially important in political ethics, which deals with the effects on large numbers of people interacting over time. Paternalistic reasons for actions can usually be distinguished even when the actions themselves cannot be classified as paternalistic because their aims and effects are too complex and extensive.

The problem of paternalism becomes more salient when the claim that an action harms other people turns out on inspection to be tenuous, and a constraint on liberty cannot be defended without showing harm to the person whose liberty is being restricted.[15] Absolute opponents of paternalism typically try to invoke every possible kind of social harm, however remote or speculative, to justify an intervention that would otherwise have to be supported on paternalistic grounds. But even if we can plausibly show social harm, we may wish to invoke paternalistic reasons to strengthen the justification for an intervention, and often we may need to call upon these reasons to establish any adequate justification at all.

The Justification of Paternalism

It is difficult to maintain that a person's own good is never a justification for the restriction of his or her liberty.[16] The law, for example, does not permit anyone to agree to being killed or mutilated, to engage in dueling or other forms of mutual combat, or to conclude a contract to sell oneself into slavery. No one is allowed to take certain drugs without a doctor's prescription. Those few writers who have held that paternalism is never justified either have limited their claim to certain kinds of paternalism (such as that enforced by the criminal law), or have narrowed the definition of paternalism so that a restriction of liberty that may appear to be paternalistic is not.[17] More commonly (and more clearly), qualms about paternalism can be acknowledged by establishing stringent criteria for its justification.

Despite his express opposition to paternalism under all conditions, Mill describes a case that we may take as exemplifying the criteria for justifiable paternalism. "If either a public officer or anyone else saw a person attempting to cross a bridge which had been ascertained to be unsafe, and there were not time to warn him of his danger, they might seize him and turn him back, without any real infringement of his liberty; for liberty consists in doing what one desires, and he does not desire to fall into the river."[18] Mill seeks to preserve his antipaternalism by denying that this is a case of paternalism at all. But though the person who is restrained does not desire to fall into the water and drown, he does desire to cross the bridge. Anyone who intervenes to protect him thwarts this desire, and restricts his liberty for paternalistic reasons. The intervention is justified because of special features of this case, and they suggest the criteria that must be satisfied if paternalism is to be justified in other cases.[19]

First, the decision of the person who is to be constrained must be *impaired*. In this case, the would-be bridge-crosser is ignorant of a crucial fact about the situation in which he acts. We assume that his desire would be different if his decision were fully free or voluntary. Second, the restriction is *limited*. The intervention is temporary and reversible; the person could, after learning that the bridge is unsafe, continue across it.

Third, the restriction prevents a serious and irreversible *harm*. We may have good reason to believe that the harm is one that the person wishes to avoid more than he wishes to cross the bridge.

It is tempting to view these criteria as a way of founding the justification of paternalism on the idea of consent, and up to a point this view can be helpful.[20] The three criteria, taken together, can be seen as justifying paternalistic constraints at a particular time by appealing to consent at some other time. Any objection to a current interference with liberty may in this way be overcome by the providing of a free choice in the future. That a decision is impaired justifies our not securing consent when we impose the restriction; that the intervention is limited creates an opportunity for consent in the future; and that the harm is serious provides a good reason for expecting the consent to be given at some other time. Paternalism is thus justified insofar as the criteria establish that the person whose liberty is restricted will or could consent to the restriction. For Mill's case, this kind of justification seems plausible enough, but when we try to extend it to political cases, we run into difficulties. The three criteria do not apply in any simple way to many instances of paternalism that involve the exercise of contestable or systematic power.

Many decisions that we may wish to restrict are not impaired in so temporary and easily correctable a way as is the decision of the person who does not know that the bridge is unsafe. The variety of possible impairments is great, including not only ignorance, but also psychological compulsion.[21] Even ignorance may go beyond lack of knowledge of a specific fact; people may be unaware of a general body of knowledge that substantially affects their decisions (such as medical or legal doctrine or the procedures of a governmental agency). They may be incapable of appreciating what facts are relevant to their decisions because they weigh evidence incorrectly, do not recognize what counts as evidence at all, or are totally devoid of reason (as is, for example, a comatose patient). Psychological compulsions range from physiological necessity (such as drug addiction), which may be irresistible in most circumstances, to mere temptation (such as a conflict of interest in politics), which may be compelling only under unusual circumstances.[22]

Some of these impairments seem sufficient to count as part of a justification for paternalism and some do not, but there does not appear to be any categorical difference between them that would distinguish those that warrant intervention from those that do not. Most writers refer to degrees of impairment (whether it is "severe" or "serious"), thus deliberately leaving the distinction indeterminate. Because of this indeterminacy, paternalists often mistake a disagreement about values for impairment of judgment: they treat as incompetent anyone who acts on ends that they regard irrational.

To avoid this mistake, we should try to keep the criterion of impairment separate from judgments about the ends of actions. However difficult it may be to identify the impairments that would justify intervention, we should not say that a decision is impaired simply because an individual chooses a course of action that appears to us irrational (for example, refusal of life-saving surgery, or profligate expenditure of a trust fund). To justify paternalism, we must identify some impairment that can be described independently of the end or good an individual chooses. This interpretation of the first criterion is important in many individual cases, but it is crucial in most collective cases, as in the decisions and policies of government, where citizens and officials disagree fundamentally about the ends to be promoted by paternalistic intervention. Also, in these collective cases, we should look for impairments that arise from social structures or affect large numbers of people in similar ways, and we should seek institutional protections, such as hearings and appeals procedures, that in particular cases could partially override general prohibitions in professional practices or governmental legislation.

The difficulty of distinguishing kinds of impairment also carries implications for the second criterion (the requirement that the intervention be limited). Especially when faced with doubtful cases of impairment and contestable ends of intervention, we should seek restrictions on liberty that, like those in Mill's bridge example, are temporary or easily reversible. But it is not always possible to limit the restrictions in this way. In the first place, if the impairment is not temporary, the restriction, to be effective, cannot be temporary either. A senile or comatose person may never be able to decide voluntarily whether a constraint on his liberty was warranted. Even a perfectly normal person's ignorance of medical or legal knowledge is, for all practical purposes, permanent. All the more so is this true for the deficiencies from which whole classes of citizens may suffer. Overcoming the deficiencies of this kind may require paternalistic interventions—job training or remedial education, for example—that continue indefinitely.

In the second place, an intervention itself can change people so that their future choices, though unimpaired, differ substantially from what they would have chosen if the intervention had not taken place. Citizens might subsequently consent to an intervention, but only because the intervention itself caused them to approve of the restriction on their liberty. Extreme examples of this self-justifying kind of paternalism are brainwashing and hypnosis, but milder and sometimes desirable forms, such as drug-education programs or compulsory counseling in welfare programs, also change a person's fundamental attitudes, and create difficulties for any attempt to justify paternalism by appealing to subsequent consent. Paternalistic power spreads systematically through time.

Nevertheless, the requirement that the constraint on liberty be limited at least entails that society should choose the least restrictive alternative consistent with the purposes of the intervention. This implies, first, a presumption in favor of regulation rather than prohibition. Public officials and others who exercise power over us should discourage rather than proscribe harmful activities. The requirement also suggests that the constraint should not extend, in scope or time, beyond the action specifically affected by the impairment in question. If the intervention must be continuous or systematic, we should insist that the opportunity for consent is continuous and systematic as well. A one-time review, focusing on individuals one by one, would not be sufficient.

If prior or current consent is not possible, we should provide the possibility of future consent—for example, by requiring a waiting period instead of establishing a permanent prohibition. The waiting period could include an opportunity for citizens to discuss and protest the restraints placed on them. Such an institution would function less as an enforcer of legislation and more as a forum for deliberation about fundamental ends. If the intervention involves continuing and extensive intrusion into the liberty of citizens and its justification cannot be reviewed in any of these ways, it would not satisfy the second criterion.

We should also seek a restrictive formulation of the purpose of paternalism as stated in the third criterion. But the formulation suggested by Mill's example (which would permit only the prevention of serious and irreversible harm) seems too restrictive.[23] It would rule out, without sufficient reason, some of the most plausible candidates for justifiable paternalism among social practices and political policies. Often paternalism is meant to prevent persons from choosing a course of action that risks harm instead of pursuing a safer course that they might not at the moment prefer. When the harm or benefit is not certain, we can be less confident that all persons would or should accept the imposition of the same degree of risk.

Furthermore, the comparative seriousness of the harm or benefit itself may be contestable. Even so obvious a harm as death is not one that everyone should always want to avoid. Surely one ought to be able to choose to shorten or end one's life rather than indefinitely to endure a humiliating and painful illness. In a pluralist society, judgments about the quality of life, and about the acceptability of means necessary to preserve life, are bound to differ. A Jehovah's Witness, for example, should be able to reject a blood transfusion even if it is necessary to save his life. Neither can we clearly identify a class of harmful actions that should be restricted simply because they prevent the exercise of free choice in the future. Mill thought that a contract to sell oneself into slavery should be absolutely prohibited on these grounds, but almost any kind of contract involves a sacrifice of future liberty.[24] A slavery contract is simply an extreme case, and could not be prohibited, at least on paternalistic grounds, without also proscribing many other kinds of contracts. (Society of course may regulate contracts to make sure they are freely entered into, and may wish for nonpaternalistic reasons to ban some kinds of contracts completely.)

The problem of determining the kind of harm or benefit that would justify paternalism becomes most acute when the impairment is relatively permanent, and the restriction on liberty relatively unlimited. In such cases, the person whose liberty is constrained may never have a chance, even in the future, to accept or reject the appraisal of the harms or benefits that supposedly justifies the paternalism. If future consent is impossible, we should insist that paternalists have compelling grounds for believing that the intended beneficiaries of an intervention would, if their judgment were not impaired, accept the benefit that the intervention is supposed to achieve.

To satisfy this criterion, we need criteria to specify what harms persons would wish to avoid, or what benefits they would wish to enjoy, if their judgment were not impaired. These criteria sometimes can be based quite firmly on a person's own settled preferences or plan of life revealed by previous actions. If we know the persons well, if we can consult their family and friends, or if they have declared their wishes in advance (as, for example, in a "living will"[25]), we may have a well-founded idea of what harms they would want to avoid. However, even in individual cases where the parties can interact personally, it is often difficult to determine what a particular person would want. Friends and family may not be reliable sources, and previous declarations may not be relevant to current circumstances. The problem is all the more difficult when the task is to determine what would serve the welfare of large numbers of persons. Paternalistic legislation, which applies to an entire society, cannot easily be tailored to the settled preferences or life plans of particular individuals. We are thus driven to search for a theory of the good that, insofar as possible, invokes only values that all rational persons can accept.[26]

John Rawls offers a theory of primary goods that can be enlisted to help with this problem. "As we know less and less about a person," Rawls writes, "we act for him as we would act for ourselves from the standpoint of the original position. We try to get for him the things he presumably wants whatever else he wants."[27] Primary goods are "things that every rational man is presumed to want. These goods normally have a use whatever a person's rational plan of life." They include rights and liberties, powers and opportunities, income and wealth, and self-respect.[28] Although Rawls provides the most promising basis for the criteria that liberal paternalism needs to identify primary goods, his theory does not supply a completely neutral perspective that anyone, whatever his or her conception of the good, could accept. Rawls's primary goods, as critics have pointed out, are not equally valuable for all life plans. These goods are less obviously valuable for persons who would create a society in which some kinds of religious ideals predominate, or a society in which certain kinds of economic relations prevail.[29]

To escape this objection completely, we would have to step outside of liberal theory altogether. Marxist theory offers one way around the objection. Here the notion of "false consciousness" plays a role formally analogous to the impaired judgment that justifies paternalism in liberal thought. As liberal individuals do not always know their own best interests and must be guided by paternalistic measures, so Marxist classes do not always know their own good and must be moved by a vanguard, a revolution, or some other means of transforming their consciousness.

As the liberal seeks an objective standpoint from which to identify a good for individuals, so the Marxist attempts "to infer the thoughts and feelings which men would have in a particular situation if they were *able* to assess both it and the interests arising from it in their impact on immediate action and on the whole structure of society."[30] With Marxist theory it becomes possible to transcend the conception of primary goods that Rawls and other theorists attribute to individuals in a liberal society. But Marxism attains this transcendence at a cost. It severs the conception of the good completely from "what men *in fact* . . . [want] at any moment in history,"[31] even when their choices are not impaired in the specific ways that we have already noted. It therefore places almost no limit on the extent to which the choices of citizens may be overridden, and thus radically discounts the value of individual liberty.

A more satisfactory way of dealing with the objection to a Rawlsian interpretation of the third criterion would follow more closely the actual conceptions of the good that persons hold. When the good of the particular person can be determined, it should be decisive. When it cannot or when the good of many persons is involved, the conception of the good should be one that is generally acceptable. Its general acceptability should not be merely assumed or determined hypothetically. It should be tested through actual deliberation in the political process or other appropriate institutions.[32] Because citizens legitimately disagree about the ends of paternalistic intervention, they should have the chance, regularly and openly, to choose and review the ends that paternalistic policies and practices impute to them and their fellow citizens. The ends that citizens choose in such a process, however, should make room for as many life plans as possible, at least among those that are actually pursued, or likely to be pursued, in that society.

The implications of interpreting the criteria of justifiable paternalism in these ways can be further developed by examining several areas in which paternalism appears in public life. When we take account of the contestable and systematic power that resides in the public practices of paternalism, we are led to view those practices in a somewhat different light and to seek institutional reforms of a somewhat different form than the traditional views of paternalism suggest. Paternalism in the professions is an instructive place to begin because the power of professionals in our society increasingly resembles that exercised by public officials, and because many public offices are increasingly populated by professionals.

The Paternalism of the Professions

It is widely assumed that the relationship between professionals and the persons they serve is justifiable paternalism if it is paternalism at all. By enlisting the help of professionals, clients implicitly admit the lack of some essential knowledge that professionals can provide; the professionals intervene in limited and foreseeable ways, and promote a good, such as health or legal redress, that the clients obviously accept. Since the clients choose their professionals, can refuse their advice, and can go to a different professional, we may suppose that clients, in effect, consent to whatever restrictions on their liberty the professionals impose.

This voluntaristic portrait of the relationship between clients and professionals neglects some features of professionalism that give rise to paternalistic power. A profession is characterized, inter alia, by claims to a body of knowledge and specialized training; a monopoly over the training and practice of the profession (including self-regulation); and social prestige that further enhances the authority of its members.[33] The ignorance of clients that sometimes justifies paternalism also restricts their ability to choose among professionals, and to decide whether to follow professional advice. Abetted by the profession's claim to superior knowledge, professionals may be inclined to intervene in ways less limited than are actually called for by their clients' circumstances. For what they believe to be their clients' own good, professionals may, for example, withhold information, prescribe treatment, or provide services without the client's knowledge.[34]

Although the client usually agrees with the general goal promoted by the profession (health, justice, welfare), professionals pursue these goals in many different ways, some of which a particular client may not accept but is powerless to defy. To seek a second opinion, to engage another professional, or to charge malpractice is often difficult. The client must challenge not merely an individual professional, but an institutionalized profession that in principle claims to be the exclusive arbiter of the competence of its members, and in practice rallies to protect its members from criticism. The client encounters the professional in a setting of systematic power.

Given the unequal roles of the professional and the client, it is not surprising that professionals sometimes restrict their clients' liberty in ways that transgress the limits of justifiable paternalism. This excessive paternalism is not a logically necessary consequence of professionalism, however, and in recent years many people, including professionals themselves, have urged changes in the relationship between professionals and their clients, to reduce or eliminate paternalism. The changes not only require new attitudes on the part of both the professionals and their clients but also call for new institutions, including some that would democratize the relationship between professionals and clients. A brief look at three professions illustrates the implications of recognizing paternalistic power in the relationship between professionals and clients.

The salient feature of the traditional model of the relationship between doctor and patient is, according to many writers, "paternalistic benevolence."[35] The doctor's superior medical knowledge and altruistic intentions, on this view, warrant acting in a patient's interest without fully informing the patient of the nature of the diagnosis or the treatment, if the doctor believes that the health of the patient is best served in this way. In extreme cases, the doctor may use deception and even subtle forms of coercion to secure a patient's compliance.

The traditional model may be challenged on both normative and empirical grounds.[36] Doctors who adopt a paternalistic attitude may violate the liberty of patients by restricting the range of choices that they can make. Although doctors may know best what treatment is most appropriate for a specific pathology, they do not necessarily know best how information or treatment will affect the whole well-being of a patient. Although doctors may find it difficult to explain to patients the diagnosis and the options for treatment, they can usually give much more complete and honest explanations than the traditional model demands.[37] The contractual theory of the doctor-patient relationship that is associated with the traditional model is suspect for similar reasons. The notion that the relationship rests on a contract in which the patient at least temporarily surrenders his autonomy to the doctor has been criticized for, among other things, implying that doctors are accountable to no one but themselves and the standards of their profession.[38] Furthermore, several empirical studies have shown that the more fully a doctor explains a diagnosis and treatment, the more likely a patient is to comply with the doctor's instructions, and to be satisfied with the treatment.[39]

Proponents of a more participatory model of the doctor-patient relationship propose measures such as a Patient's Bill of Rights and a system of Patients' Rights Advocates. They urge changes in professional standards and education to encourage doctors to consult more openly with their patients, and to regard their professional ethics as part of a universal ethics that creates a presumption against paternalism.[40] It has also been suggested that the traditional interpretation of "informed consent" should be altered. Instead of appealing to the "professional standard of care" (what would a reasonable doctor in this community have told the patient?), we should employ a layman's standard (what would a reasonable patient need to know in order to make an intelligent decision?).[41] With the latter standard, patients and more generally citizens could begin to exercise more control, similar to that which they would exercise in a genuine democratic process, over their own and their society's welfare. All of these proposals seek to foster a doctor-patient relationship in which a patient's ignorance and a doctor's unilateral action are limited—in short, a relationship that minimizes paternalistic power.

The relationship between lawyers and their clients also manifests paternalistic tendencies.[42] One survey of the attitudes of lawyers found that many "seem to need and gain pleasure from being paternalistic and dominating."[43] A manual entitled "How to Handle a New Client" advises the lawyer to give some clients what they want—"the calm reassurance of a good, wise parent."[44] It might be supposed that the conduct of a paternalistic lawyer is less pernicious than that of a paternalistic doctor. The needs of clients may seem less urgent than those of patients, clients usually can more easily change lawyers than patients can change doctors, and clients can more readily understand legal options than patients can comprehend medical alternatives. But if we attend to some of the more subtle forms of power that infuse the lawyer-client relation, we will be less tempted to depreciate its paternalistic dangers. In many circumstances, the lawyer is the client's last hope of protection against severe deprivations of liberty, and often the client, especially if indigent, is fortunate to have a lawyer at all, let alone any choice among lawyers.[45] The law can appear as mysterious as medical doctrine, and the criterion for what should count as a successful outcome of a legal dispute can be less clear than that for an outcome of medical treatment. Moreover, insofar as paternalism warrants professionals' favoring their own patients or clients over other citizens, the social consequences of lawyers' paternalism may be more harmful than those of doctors'. Winning a client's case, unlike curing a patient, is not an intrinsic good.[46]

The paternalistic model of legal practice not only can have undesirable social consequences, but it also may not serve the best interests of clients. A study of sixty New York lawyers litigating personal-injury claims found that "clients who actively seek information about their problems and participate in and share responsibility for dealing with them" are likely to get better results than "clients who trustingly and passively delegate responsibility."[47] Reform-minded lawyers and citizens have urged changes that would discourage paternalism in the lawyer-client relation, including simplification of legal language, and training in more participatory styles of legal practice. Some have also proposed guidelines, perhaps enforced by law, that would require lawyers to consult more extensively with their clients. Specifically, such guidelines stipulate that a lawyer should discuss with the client any delegation of responsibility for the case to another lawyer, the terms offered or accepted in any out-of-court settlement, how much time should be devoted to the case, whether to go to trial, and some decisions about courtroom tactics (such as the use of expert witnesses).[48] Some have suggested that lawyers should be required to secure the client's written approval every time they make an important decision in the case.[49]

Yet another kind of professional relationship—between social worker and client—may be criticized for excessive paternalism.[50] Added to the paternalistic tendencies of professionalism are further effects that flow from the position of social workers as agents of the government. Because social workers must follow general policies set by government, they may not be able to define a client's good exclusively as the client might. In the process of helping the client, the social worker may also change "the client's attitudes and conduct so that he conforms more closely to expected and accepted patterns of behavior."[51] The process bristles with the dangers of self-justifying paternalism. Furthermore, because clients are typically poor, and members of minority groups, the inequalities of class and race exacerbate the inequalities of professionalism. The professionals act from a position of systematic power, which they may in turn reinforce.

To counter what has been called "welfare paternalism," reformers have urged greater participation by clients in the agencies that social workers and other professionals now dominate, stronger statements of the rights of clients, various legal protections (including the appointment of welfare rights advocates), and the separation of income maintenance from the other services, so that a citizen may obtain the former without the latter.[52] Many have welcomed the growth of self-help organizations, such as the Mobilization for Youth, which can improve counseling and other social services for the needy while avoiding the paternalism that professional social workers might foster.[53] One writer has even proposed that social workers serve clients on a fee-for-service basis, subsidized by the government, but otherwise independent of government authority, so that the social worker may, without conflict, pursue the good of the client.[54]

The participatory approach guiding many of these reforms in all three of the professions is not itself without problems. In their efforts to exorcise the baleful aspect of paternalism, the reformers sometimes forget that paternalism has a benign side. At least ideally, doctors, lawyers, and social workers bring professional skills and a sense of caring that can genuinely benefit their clients—most successfully when the relationship is not adversarial.[55] Carried too far, the participatory approach could absolve professionals of responsibility for the advice they give, and could restrict the liberty of clients who, will full knowledge, wish to delegate authority for some major decisions to their doctor, lawyer, or caseworker. Professionals themselves, furthermore, may legitimately claim certain rights to control how they do their jobs.[56] But to satisfy the criteria of justifiable paternalism, some participatory institutions are likely to prove necessary. Within such institutions, professionals are more likely to exercise their power to correct genuine impairments in limited ways in the pursuit of ends their clients share.

Compulsory Medical Treatment

The paternalism that inheres in the professional-client relationship usually takes the form of granting clients little control over decisions made in their behalf, rather than forcing them to act in certain ways for their own good. Typically, the professional restricts opportunities for choice by withholding information, rather than by compelling action. The constraint seems more direct when the government is the paternalist, using the law to prohibit specific actions either by forcing benefits on people, or by imposing sanctions if they act contrary to what others consider to be their own good. But as we move from the cases of professional paternalism to those of state paternalism, many of the essential features of paternalistic power remain the same. In many cases, the government in effect institutionalizes the interventions of professionals. In other cases, officials of government act as professionals themselves, using the law or the administrative process to enforce their expert judgments about the welfare of citizens. In all cases, the presence of contestable and systematic power can affect the justifiability of the paternalistic intervention.

Courts have generally held that adults of sound mind have the right to decide what is done to their body, and have therefore, in principle, rejected the paternalistic imposition of medical treatment.[57] The courts recognize the right of patients to decline lifesaving treatment under emergency and nonemergency conditions, both where the prognosis is poor and where it would be favorable if the treatment were administered. A patient can be compelled to accept medical care if it is necessary to protect public health or to prevent harm to other people, especially children.[58] But the patient's own harm cannot justify interference, even on grounds that the patient has contracted with the doctor, or that the doctor has a legal and ethical obligation to do everything within his power to save the patient's life.[59] The patient's liberty takes precedence over both of these claims.

Although the general principle is strongly antipaternalist, it has been eroded by exceptions of three kinds. First, the doctrine of "therapeutic privilege" permits doctors to withhold information if they think that the information would harm a patient, and thus may allow them to administer treatment without the patient's full knowledge. We have already seen that most instances of the withholding of information cannot be considered justifiable paternalism. Similar objections often apply to the use of placebos, which is, in effect, a form of compulsory nontreatment.[60]

More difficult to judge is the second kind of exception: cases in which the patient does not simply reject treatment, or even request that treatment be discontinued, but asks the doctor to administer a treatment that is likely to bring death. A doctor may refuse to take such an active role, not purely for paternalistic reasons, but for other moral reasons: the doctor may claim that he or she ought not to be directly responsible for the death of another person.[61] The question of whether agreeing to administer treatment that causes death differs fundamentally from not agreeing to administer treatment that would preserve life partly depends on how one resolves some controversial problems in the theory of action and ethics more generally (such as the status of the distinction between acts and omissions).[62] It cannot be resolved by medical criteria alone, such as the supposedly technical distinction between "ordinary" and "extraordinary" measures. That distinction is no less dependent on contestable judgments of value than is the distinction between acts and omissions.[63]

The question is also political. Our judgment about the moral difference between administering and withholding treatment should depend partly on the differences in the discretionary power they require in institutional settings. Where we cannot personally judge the character of the paternalists and where we cannot easily monitor their routines, we may be wary of granting them much discretion in matters of life and death. On the one hand, directly bringing about death seems the more dangerous power. Anyone who is willing to override the moral constraints against killing when it is justified may be more likely to violate these and other constraints when it is not justified. Some such notion may be at the root of the common tendency to regard such persons with more moral suspicion than those who merely fail to save a life. On the other hand, in an institutional setting there are more opportunities for failing to prevent death (justifiably as well as unjustifiably), and there are greater difficulties in identifying a failure itself (which is rarely a specific act done at a particular time). In these circumstances, rules to prevent unjustified omissions may be at least as important as rules against unjustified acts. To sustain rules of the former kind, prevailing moral views could not place great weight on the difference between direct and indirect ways of bringing about the death of patients who wish to die. Institutional procedures would have to provide for review of actions that were not taken as well as those that were.

The third class of exceptions to the principle against compulsory medical treatment—the most expansive—covers cases in which the patient is assumed to be mentally incompetent. It is often difficult to determine whether a patient is, in fact, incompetent. Doctors may disagree, and, in any case, they should not have the last word.[64] Paternalism cannot be justified, as we have seen, if the chief criterion for mental incompetency is that the patient prefers an end (even death) that the doctor regards as irrational. We may also wish to claim that mere ignorance should not be sufficient. But cases of "false belief" should give us pause. Should we accept the decision of an otherwise rational patient who refuses to have the surgery necessary to stop the spread of cancer simply because she believes that she does not have cancer?[65] False beliefs alone do not warrant compulsory treatment, but they may call for extraordinary techniques of persuasion that would not otherwise be justified. If we license such techniques, we must also establish institutional safeguards to ensure that they are not abused.

When there is no doubt that a patient is incompetent (when the patient is comatose, for example), there is still a question about what criteria of harm or benefit should apply. We have seen that if possible the criteria should refer to what the patient desires or would desire if competent.[66] In the case of Karen Ann Quinlan, the young woman who suddenly lapsed into "a chronic persistent vegetative state," the New Jersey Supreme Court seemed to invoke such a criterion. The justices appealed to what the patient herself would desire if she were "miraculously lucid for an interval . . . and perceptive of her irreversible condition."[67] But the judgment in such cases is overdetermined: we assume that the particular patient would not wish to continue to live in this condition because we assume generally that no patient would. When the prognosis is less certain or when the treatment is more controversial, what one patient would desire is more likely to diverge from what patients generally would desire.[68] In these circumstances, we need institutions in which to resolve disagreements about contestable ends, whether the criterion refers exclusively to the ends of a particular patient or to the ends that all patients share.

Even in circumstances like that of the Quinlan case, such institutions are desirable. Although no one may disagree that the patient would wish to die, some of the other parties involved may have legitimate reasons for wanting the patient to live. The key question then becomes: who should decide? We are rightly reluctant to give the parents or family full authority to decide because their interests may differ from the patient's. But we should also be hesitant to delegate responsibility solely to doctors, or to agents of the state. They too may have different interests, and also may understandably not wish to give professional or public sanction to the termination of life. In the Quinlan case, the New Jersey Supreme Court resolved—or evaded—this problem by requiring the consent of the parents, the attending physicians, and an ethics committee (the nature of which was left vague).

Since then, ethics committees have proliferated in hospitals in this country. Although their role is mostly advisory, their influence has steadily increased. They have encouraged more extensive discussion of the moral issues raised by the treatment of incompetent patients, as well as other kinds of cases.[69] In this way, they provide a forum for more legitimate judgments about the exercise of contestable paternalistic power in such cases. But since we also seek general standards that reflect values that all citizens share, these committees cannot replace legislatures in this area. The committees should work within a framework established by legislation, though they should also have a voice in the legislative deliberations.

The Law of Involuntary Guardianship

The law of most states provides that courts may appoint guardians to manage the estate and the personal affairs of persons who are not capable of doing so themselves. The chief rationale is paternalistic: guardianship is necessary to protect individuals from themselves. Typically, wards may not, without the approval of their guardian, dispose of property, enter valid contracts, marry, change domicile, or choose agents to act for them (doctors, lawyers, or even a different guardian).[70] The practice of guardianship seems justified in many cases where the mental deficiency is clear (for example, severely retarded adults). But the courts and the state have also appointed guardians for persons who were deemed "improvident," "physically incapacitated," "excessive drinkers," "aged," "idlers," or "spendthrifts."[71] An Ohio court placed an eighty-five-year-old man, otherwise perfectly sane, under guardianship at the request of one of his potential heirs because he had given away a large portion of his estate (though he still had a trust fund that fully provided for all his own future needs).[72]

The broad reach of guardianship law, as it has often been applied, runs afoul of the criteria for justifiable paternalism—not only by invoking overly broad criteria of impairment, but also by restricting liberty beyond what would be necessary to protect wards. Commitment to a hospital is often taken as a sufficient reason for appointing a guardian, though the ward may still be perfectly competent to manage his or her affairs in most respects. Courts and the state rarely monitor guardianships closely, and the procedure for terminating a guardianship is difficult and seldom invoked by wards themselves.[73] Even when a guardianship is initially justified, the grant of such extensive discretionary power should not continue indefinitely without regular and independent review. The dangers of the institutionalized power of guardianships cannot be checked without institutionalized protections that permit challenges to the potentially controversial values that guardians impose on their wards.

Some of the dangers of guardianship might be alleviated if more states adopted the so-called Minnesota Plan, more generally appointing state officials to serve as guardians.[74] To be sure, state paternalism brings problems of its own—the potential indifference and rigidity of an impersonal bureaucracy. But state officials are less likely to have any financial stake in the guardianship and their decisions are more likely to be open to public scrutiny. Legal provisions for prior consent (for example, designating guardians and specifying their authority in advance), and better procedures for hearings, reviews, and appeals in guardianship cases might also help. Whatever institutions are established, they should track the criteria of justifiable paternalism. They should permit guardianship only if the impairment, the extent and duration of the guardianship, and the potential self-harm not only initially satisfy but *continue* to satisfy the criteria. As the paternalistic power of guardians is systematic, so should be the process of its review.

The Distribution of Public Welfare

The general question of whether the government should redistribute income to the poor depends on the theory of social justice, not on an account of paternalism. Any restrictions on liberty that the government imposes to obtain the resources for redistribution do not fall on the recipients of welfare, but on the other members of society.[75] Even Mill would countenance such restrictions ("acts done for the benefit of others than the person concerned") as a legitimate exception to his presumption against governmental interference with individual liberty.[76] Once we accept a system of public welfare, however, the form in which the government distributes benefits can give rise to paternalism.

While granting citizens a right to certain benefits, a welfare system may require that recipients satisfy certain conditions, or use the benefits in certain ways. Such requirements can be defended in some circumstances on grounds of administrative efficiency and social justice. But when they are primarily intended to promote the good of the recipients, they constitute paternalism because they prevent recipients from using the welfare payments as they might otherwise like to do. One kind of requirement—that recipients accept any available job for which they are qualified—is sometimes proposed for paternalistic reasons, but it is also supposed to ensure that welfare goes only to those who most need it, and to keep the welfare rolls as small as possible.[77] Another requirement—that recipients accept counseling by social workers or welfare officials—encourages a paternalistic relationship of the kind that we have already considered.

The distinctive problem of paternalism in welfare policy arises when the government requires that the welfare payments be used in certain ways by providing in-kind benefits instead of income—food stamps, clothing, or housing.[78] Such a policy is sometimes defended on grounds of administrative efficiency: in-kind aid avoids the problem of regional differences in the prices of goods, and reduces opportunities for corruption. But since administrative arguments cut the other way too (in-kind payments entail a more elaborate bureaucracy), the justification of in-kind aid must rest to a great extent on a paternalistic basis.

The "underlying assumption" of such a policy, critics say, is that "the poor need assistance because, unlike the rest of the population, they are unable to make the relevant choices by themselves."[79] If the government does not force recipients to use the benefits for purposes that will do them the most good, the recipients, more inclined to satisfy present than future desires, are not likely to act in their own best interests. The trouble with this rationale and the policy it promotes is that rarely do legislators and administrators have good evidence that the decisions of all or most recipients are impaired in the way required to justify paternalism. Moreover, in-kind aid is not, among practicable welfare policies, the one that interferes least with the liberty of recipients.

Some defenders of in-kind aid may still point out that the purpose of a welfare system is to provide for basic needs, not to offer a certain level of income. In-kind aid gives recipients greater liberty than they would have without such aid, and perhaps even greater liberty than they would have with cash aid if they use it imprudently. But though there may be agreement on the general purpose of welfare, there is likely to be legitimate disagreement about the levels of goods necessary to satisfy basic needs and the relative priorities among them. Unlike income payments, in-kind aid would impose contestable ends on the recipients. Also, when imposing these ends, the state deprives recipients of the responsibility of making choices about their basic needs. They become more dependent on the state, and more vulnerable to its systematic power in other areas of their lives.

A policy of a guaranteed income or a negative income tax seems a more promising approach. It could serve the generally acceptable aims of a welfare system, while avoiding the more contestable judgments inherent in a policy of in-kind aid.[80] A guaranteed-income policy gives recipients more opportunity to learn to manage their own affairs better, and eventually to become less dependent on the direction of other people and the state. The methods for distributing welfare range on a continuum, from the provision of cash through cash with advice, cash with compulsory advice, vouchers, in-kind payments, and dictated expenditures.[81] Any welfare system based on a paternalistic rationale should begin with the least restrictive policy on the continuum, and move to more restrictive ones only if they are necessary to make the system just, and only if they are consistent with the other criteria for justifiable paternalism. This approach could minimize the stultifying effects of the paternalistic power that the providers of welfare exercise over its recipients.

The Regulation of Drugs

No paternalistic arguments need be marshaled to justify a large dose of regulation, or even prohibition, of harmful drugs. An argument from social harm is often sufficient. Mill prescribes the labeling of drugs "with some word expressive of [their] dangerous character," stringent controls on drugs that contribute to crime, and prohibition of the use of drugs by persons who while under the influence of drugs have previously committed crimes or otherwise harmed other members of society. On Mill's principles, still more restrictions would be warranted to reduce the opportunities for fraud, and undue pressure on potential buyers of drugs.[82]

It is true that some forms of the argument from social harm tread precariously close to paternalism—for example, those that deny drugs to children and persons in a "delirious state." Also, much of the crime associated with certain drugs occurs in black-market operations, which would not exist if the drugs were legal. Furthermore, the decision that a drug is harmful involves a judgment about the degree of risk that a rational person should accept. Since no drug is completely safe, the government determines for citizens the various trade-offs between risks and benefits of drugs, and in the process may rely on paternalistic assumptions.[83]

Nevertheless, in recent years it has been relatively harmless drugs that have generated the most controversy.[84] A 1962 amendment to the Food, Drug, and Cosmetics Act mandated that the Food and Drug Administration require manufacturers to show that a new drug is not only safe, but also effective.[85] Some political critics have assailed this amendment as opening the door to paternalism: "Freedom is the issue. The American people should be allowed to make their own decisions. They shouldn't have the bureaucrats in Washington, D.C. trying to decide for them what's good and what's bad, as long as it's safe."[86] If the government may prohibit the use of drugs because they are relatively ineffective, so the argument goes, the government on the same grounds could also proscribe many other products and activities. They could ban, for example, sugared cereals or frivolous games, which do not benefit citizens so much as some other products or activities.[87]

In a controversy with curious political overtones, many of these arguments have been directed against the FDA's ban on Laetrile. Also known as Vitamin B-17 or Amygdalin, Laetrile has long been touted as a cure or treatment for cancer. Studies show that the substance is not effective in the treatment of cancer.[88] But since 1970 at least fifteen states have legalized Laetrile, and several courts have overruled the FDA ban, implying that it constitutes unjustified paternalism.[89]

For its own part, the FDA has not claimed unqualified paternalistic authority, but rather has sought to show that the decision to use Laetrile is usually impaired. FDA officials argue that the cancer victim's choice between Laetrile and alternative therapies, which are likely to be more effective, cannot be free. The victim decides in a "climate of anxiety and fear" created by the morbid nature of the disease and exacerbated by pecuniary and political pressures that the pro-Laetrile movement itself has produced.[90] Labeling Laetrile ineffective would not be sufficient because most people who want the drug already know that medical opinion considers it ineffective.[91] Some of them simply do not trust the medical establishment, and others no longer have the strength of will to follow medical advice. By pointing to a serious impairment and a harm that any rational person wants to avoid, FDA officials, in effect, seek to meet the criteria for justifiable paternalism. Their argument may also be seen as an effort to justify their own use of contestable and systematic power by pointing to less desirable and accountable forms of such power exercised by the promoters of Laetrile.

Insofar as the opponents of Laetrile can in this way show that the decision to use the drug is substantially impaired, paternalistic prohibition of its use would be justified. However, the justification still assumes that the cancer victims accept the goal of saving their own lives, and this assumption obviously does not apply to terminal patients. The FDA argues that we have no useful and reliable criterion to identify terminal patients, and that, even if we did, permitting them to use Laetrile would create enforcement difficulties, and tend to legitimize the drug for other patients.[92]

The FDA argument on this point should not be dismissed as a mere bureaucratic quibble. The moral validity of public policy depends partly on its effective and fair enforcement. Yet surely a person's considered decision to risk death, if it is ever to be respected, should not be abridged in the face of a prognosis of virtually certain death. The administrative objections raised by the FDA therefore should not settle the question.[93] The government may regulate and in certain circumstances proscribe Laetrile on paternalistic grounds, but an unqualified ban on the drug would not be consistent with the criteria of paternalism.[94] The institutions for implementing paternalism that is justified should also be designed to inhibit paternalism that is not. Institutional procedures should recognize and protect the legitimate claims of terminal patients and others who may seek exemption from general prohibitions.

The Regulation of Safety

Like drug regulation, some safety legislation can be justified as necessary to prevent harm to others, or to pursue social goals efficiently. The Department of Transportation has not been charged with paternalism for recalling defective trucks and cars, or for mandating head restraints and other safety features on vehicles. The courts have generally upheld such regulations as a legitimate exercise of the police power of the state.[95]

Most of these measures, however, leave the consumer free not to use the safety devices, and thus differ from laws requiring ignition interlock systems or passive restraints in all cars, or laws fining drivers and passengers for failing to use seat belts. Laws that directly constrain drivers in these ways have met with some judicial resistance and legislative reversal, partly on grounds that they constitute "an infringement on . . . personal freedom," thus raising the specter of paternalism.[96] If such laws cannot be defended on grounds of social harm, they may not be justifiable at all, for their paternalistic rationale does not seem compelling. It is difficult to identify, independently of the refusal to use safety devices, any specific impairment that consumers suffer, and to show that they do not really want to accept the risks entailed by this refusal. As paternalistic measures, the laws, then, fail to meet the criteria of justification; they subject citizens to an illegitimate exercise of contestable and systematic power.

Yet the argument from social harm appears even more tenuous—so much so that despite their intention its proponents end up making paternalistic appeals. Laws requiring motorcyclists to wear protective helmets illustrate this lapse into paternalism. In defending the helmet laws as necessary to protect society, many of their proponents stretch the concept of social harm to the point where it merges with paternalism.[97] A leading advocate of such laws maintains that "a society has a right to protect itself and its individual members from clear and present danger, and . . . requiring motorcyclists to protect themselves and all of us from this damage and this cost is completely within the right . . . and indeed the duty . . . of a compassionate community."[98]

What is the social cost? No good evidence supports the claim that helmetless riders are more likely to injure others in accidents.[99] Society (including insurance companies) could in principle avoid increased costs by refusing to compensate helmetless victims. If motorcyclists were willing, for their folly, to forgo making claims on society's medical resources, what further reason could society have to compel them to wear helmets? Even the courts, which have been willing to accept almost any legislative definition of social harm in these cases, usually reject the view that "the State has an interest in the 'viability' of its citizens and can legislate to keep them healthy and self-supporting."[100] "This logic," a Michigan justice declared, "would lead to unlimited paternalism."[101] The proponents of helmet laws could still insist that, strictly speaking, they are not paternalists. Their aim is to further social utility, not the good of individuals as such. But then their "compassionate community" begins to look more like a manipulative state. Its power would promote the good of citizens only as a means to the ends of the state.

Neither the paternalistic nor the social-harm argument, then, satisfactorily supports the helmet laws. Both fail not merely because of what they say about helmet laws, but because of what they imply about the conception of power in society. Each in its way neglects the dangers of power in paternalistic policies. Must we therefore simply accept the antipaternalist argument against policies like helmet laws?

The antipaternalist argument also expresses a conception of power, and it is no more attractive. To resist so resolutely any paternalism in regulation is to reinforce a conception of society in which each member owes nothing to others, except not to harm them. On this conception, society could, and perhaps should, refuse to come to the aid of citizens who hurt themselves as a result of taking risks that most other citizens regard as irrational. Victims of accidents who take foolish chances would be left to fend for themselves; injured motorcyclists who shun helmets would be left unattended on the streets and highways.[102] (If they were not, the social-harm argument would come into play again.) Such radical individualism would leave little room for the realization of the mutual concern of all citizens for the welfare of each. It would eliminate paternalistic power at the cost of social responsibility.

The antipaternalism of current policy toward motorcyclists does not follow this logic to such ruthless conclusions. Since 1976, when Congress told the Department of Transportation to stop withholding highway funds from states that had no mandatory helmet laws, many states have relaxed or repealed their laws. But no state has taken steps to deny care to helmetless victims, or otherwise to treat them differently from other victims. While rejecting paternalism, these states nevertheless sustain the social obligation of citizens to help others who harm themselves. The way that this policy combines antipaternalism and public benevolence may lack theoretical elegance, but the way that it steers between the dangers of both commends it as a practical compromise.

It is an acceptable compromise, however, only so long as the costs of the benevolence do not impose a substantial or unfair burden on other members of society. Helmetless motorcyclists evidently do not create such a burden, but drivers and passengers who refuse to use seat belts probably do. Seat belt laws could in this way be defended as necessary to prevent social harm. But they may be better justified as a form of self-paternalism. Through the democratic process, citizens may decide that they wish to protect themselves from their own foolishness by creating an additional and more certain incentive to use seat belts. Their decision would provide grounds for supposing that they do not really accept the risk of beltless travel. Also, much more than helmet laws, seat belt laws apply generally to all citizens since nearly everyone sometimes travels by car. These laws can therefore be more plausibly seen as constraints imposed by the majority on itself for its own good, rather than on a minority for its good.

In this and other cases, our aim, practically as well as theoretically, should be to respect the value of paternalism while keeping its interventions within bounds set by the value of liberty. The point is not to embrace or eradicate paternalism totally, but to locate its justifiable limits. The criteria of justifiable paternalism serve that purpose. At least they can do so if they take account of the contestable and systematic power that inheres in institutionalized paternalism as practiced by public officials and by professionals in and out of public office.

7

The Ethics of Social Experiments

Experiments on citizens—the very idea conjures up the image of an authoritarian regime using citizens as means for its own ends. But in recent years, it has been democratic governments that appear to have undertaken the most deliberate and systematic social experiments on their citizens. Benign in intent, the experiments have tested public policies on a small number of citizens before deciding whether to propose the policies for all citizens. With staffs and subjects often numbering in the thousands and budgets in the millions, the experiments have studied housing allowances, education vouchers, educational performance contracts, health insurance plans, and guaranteed income programs.[1]

Like any experiments with human beings, these projects raise serious ethical problems concerning the risk of harm to the subjects. Governments have benefited from many years of experience with medical experimentation and have established reasonably effective guidelines to protect subjects in such research. The history of social experimentation is shorter, however, and public knowledge of it thinner. Public officials, researchers, and moral philosophers have only begun to attend to the special ethical problems that social experimentation creates.[2] The general issue concerns the conditions under which governments may expose some citizens to risks in order to benefit other citizens and society as a whole, but special complications arise in the initiation and termination of social experiments. The problems are well illustrated in one of the most important of the recent investigations, the Denver Income Maintenance Experiment (DIME). By understanding the ethical criteria that officials used and those they should have used in this experiment, we should be in a better position to judge other social experiments in the future.

The Story of the DIME

The DIME was part of the last in a series of four government-sponsored studies designed to discover to what extent (if any) recipients of a guaranteed income would change their behavior. The most prominent question was whether they would work less. Each of the experiments attempted to isolate the effects of income maintenance from various other factors that might affect the work behavior of families who received the guaranteed income. A predetermined number of families who met the requirements for enrollment for each experiment were selected randomly and assigned to experimental or control groups. The experimental groups received income payments under one of several plans, which differed in the amount of income guaranteed to the families.[3]

Policy makers hoped to use the results of the research to assess various income maintenance programs that the government might adopt, including proposals for a negative income tax. Critics of the earlier experiments, as well as some of the researchers who conducted them, suspected that the short duration (three and five years) had biased the results. Since participants had known that the experiment would end in a few years, they were not likely to quit their jobs, or make any drastic changes in their habits of work—at least they may have been less inclined to do so than if they had expected the income guarantee to continue indefinitely. Also, in a temporary experiment, especially one in which increased earnings reduced the benefits, some participants (for example, women who worked part-time) might have attempted to reduce the amount of time they worked during the experiment, postponing until the experiment ended employment they might have otherwise accepted.

Initiating the Experiment

To meet the objections to the shorter-term experiments, one of the subcontractors for the income maintenance project, the Stanford Research Institute (SRI), proposed the creation of a new experimental group that would continue for twenty years. When compared with the five-year group, the new group would give a better indication of the "true long-run responses" of families in actual governmental programs, which citizens perceive as relatively permanent. In March 1974 William Morrill, assistant secretary of Health, Education, and Welfare for planning and evaluation, recommended approval of a twenty-year sample in the DIME. He explained the experimental need for such a sample, and then added:

> While we plan to tell the families that the program will continue for 20 years, it is not necessary to run this experiment for the full 20 years to obtain the required information we desire. The true long run response of these families, who will expect the program to last for 20 years, can be observed by comparing their responses over a 5-year period with the responses of families participating in the shorter term experiments, who will expect their guarantee to last only 3–5 years.
>
> Hence . . . we tentatively plan to terminate this new treatment group at the end of five years . . .
>
> In order to eliminate any ethical issues relating to the early termination of the 20-year sample, families would be given a choice at that time as to whether to accept the lump sum payment or to continue receiving their regular benefits.[4]

Other officials still saw problems with the proposal. One criticized the plan to end the experiment after five years and provide lump-sum payments. He argued that some of the families would almost certainly find out that the experiment would end in the fifth year, and would then adjust their behavior so that they could remain eligible for the monthly payments in that year and thus for the lump-sum payment. Even if officials managed to keep the plan secret, to give lump-sum payments to those who happened to remain eligible in the fifth year would be arbitrary and unfair.

Another official put forward a more explicitly ethical objection. He believed that the proposal raised "serious questions about the ethics of using people as guinea pigs in research experiments without fully disclosing possible consequences."[6] He pointed out that if the families really expected the program to last for twenty years, they might take on long-range debt commitments, decide to have more children than otherwise, choose to retire early, decide to forgo savings, or give up life insurance. But if the experimenters "emphasized that the transfer payments might be stopped at any time, the effect of the experiment might be negated."

After taking account of these and other criticisms within the department, Morrill again recommended establishing a twenty-year group, but this time—"in order to eliminate any possible ethical issues"—he omitted the termination option.[7] He now proposed to continue the program for the full twenty years. The undersecretary approved the proposal, and enrollment of the twenty-year group began in July 1974.

Initially, the experimental group included about 110 families—both black and white, some with one and some with two parents, nearly all with earnings below $5,000 annually. The sample soon had to be expanded, first, to include more families whose level of income would make them eligible for DIME payments, and then, in response to protests from the Mexican-American Legal Defense and Education Fund (MALDEF), to include some Mexican-American families. Under the supervision of Mathemathica Policy Research (MPR), another subcontractor, "enrollers" made personal contact with each family, presenting a package of materials, which included a letter inviting the family to join the experiment, and an agreement stipulating the terms of their participation. To enhance the credibility of the invitation and especially the twenty-year guarantee, the letter carried the signature of an official of the Colorado state government. That families believe this guarantee is "of crucial importance to the success of the experiment."[8] About the guarantee, the letter said: "It is the intent of the Federal government to continue your family's income guarantee for a period of twenty years. Should it be necessary for the government to terminate this program before twenty years have elapsed, the government's plan is to make a cash settlement with your family to help cover the unused portion of your income guarantee period."[9] The enrollment agreement, which the enrollers asked the head of each household to sign, included this provision: "Finally, I understand that . . . while it is the intention of the Government to continue the program for twenty years, both the operation of the program and the duration of the payments are subject to modification as determined by the Secretary of Health, Education, and Welfare, or his designee."[10]

Terminating the Experiment

In November 1978, staff from HEW, SRI, the state government of Washington and Colorado, and MPR's Denver office met to discuss the conclusion of SRI's "most recent study of the data from DIME."[11] One of the chief conclusions, though expressed in cautious technical language, surprised the assembled group: "The nonrandom assignment of families to the twenty-year program (particularly among those who previously received financial treatments) makes it extremely difficult to interpret any responses estimated for this group." Among other differences, the participants in the experimental group had worked significantly less in the year before the experiment than had those in the control group. Various statistical attempts to correct for this difference proved unsatisfactory. Everyone at the meeting reluctantly but unequivocally agreed that the experiment now had no research value. They concluded that families should be disenrolled as soon as suitable arrangments could be made, but left unresolved the question of what compensations should be provided to the families. Also unanswered—now as well as then—was the question of who had been initially responsible for the error in the design of the sample that had brought the DIME to this unhappy impasse.

R. G. Spiegelman, the project director at SRI, outlined the major issues that HEW officials considered at this point.[12] Any decision would have to recognize HEW's "obligations to the public": taxpayers could reasonably object to continuing a program that yielded absolutely no research value. Spiegelman mentioned two kinds of "obligations to the families," legal and moral. It was generally agreed that the government had no legal obligation at all to continue the income payments or even to offer any significant lump-sum settlement, though some officials in HEW thought that some of the families, encouraged by welfare rights lawyers, might decide to sue.

The discussion of the moral obligations owed to the families seemed to take for granted that early termination was justified, and concentrated on the criteria that the procedures for terminations should satisfy. First, safeguards should be provided to protect the families from exploitation in any negotiations with the government about the amount of a settlement. Second, any settlement should recognize the fact that families may have made personal decisions on the assumption that the program would continue, and would suffer serious losses when the income payments ceased. The program has "a moral, if not legal, obligation to assure the families they they will be no worse off as a result of DIME participation than if they had not participated at all." SRI staff "felt intuitively" that continuing the support to the families for twenty-four to thirty months would fulfill this moral obligation.

John Palmer, who became acting assistant secretary in November 1979, was inclined to agree with his predecessor's view that the government owed the families at most three years' worth of benefits. Palmer argued that "there is an implicit *quid pro quo* involved in participation in such an experiment, and that since there is no longer any benefit to taxpayers and the Federal government in continuing the experiment, there is no reason for taxpayers to continue funding benefit payments that exceed AFDC plus Food Stamps and the added administrative costs."[13]

Palmer also evidently feared that to request from Congress the large appropriation necessary to continue the program or to provide large lump-sum payments would create adverse publicity and jeopardize support for policy research in the future. Already Senator William Armstrong of Colorado had publicly condemned the experiment as a waste of governmental funds. Officials in HEW's legislative liaison office talked informally to members of the staffs of some of the others in the Colorado delegation who usually could be counted on to support HEW's liberal programs. But the officials found little enthusiasm for the additional appropriations that would be necessary to give the DIME families a large settlement. Generally, the mood in Congress that spring, effectively expressed in several unusual budget-cutting resolutions, threatened many of HEW's most important programs.

The Director of MPR and some of his staff had argued vigorously with HEW officials, insisting that the government had a moral commitment to carry on the program for twenty years, or at least to provide a cash settlement that would be equivalent to what families would have received if the program had lasted for twenty years. Like Spiegelman, they pointed out that the families may have relied on the government's promise, perhaps making irreversible decisions (for example, having another child or retiring early) that they would not have otherwise made. Palmer rejected this line of argument, maintaining that the families were probably made better off by participation in the experiment than they would have been if they had stayed in the regular welfare system. With a reasonable period of notice, they should now be able to adjust quite easily to life without the experiment, and find themselves at least no worse off than before.

Nevertheless, Palmer still had some doubts. He was not completely sure that the government did not have an "inviolable commitment" to these families. He was also troubled by the fact that he himself had been officially though not actually responsible for initiating the twenty-year sample in 1974. Furthermore, his deputy assistant secretary for income security policy, Michael Barth, had come to the conclusion that the decision was wrong. Although Barth had earlier endorsed the decision, he began to have second thoughts while preparing the materials to implement the decision. He now believed that it did not adequately fulfill the government's commitment to the families. Palmer agreed to postpone implementation at least until Barth could conduct a review of the "options for termination."

Barth outlined the following options: (1) continue the payments for fifteen years as originally intended (cost: $9.7 million, or $5.31 million discounted at a rate of 10 percent); (2) continue the payments but without varying them when a family's income changed (cost: $8.27 million, or $4.7 million discounted); (3) terminate with lump-sum payments equivalent to present discounted value of fifteen years' worth of payments (cost: $1.47 million); (4) terminate with transition payments for three years based on each family's average payment in the previous year (cost: $1.47 million); or (5) terminate immediately, phasing out payments over six months (on the model of unemployment compensation) (cost $300,000). Only options (4) and (5) could be funded from resources HEW expected to have available; options (1), (2), and (3) would require congressional approval.[14]

Barth presented these (and some other) options to three outside consultants whom he asked to recommend "the soundest course of action," specifically taking into account "moral/ethical" factors. The consultants' recommendations ranged from a modified version of (5) to a variation of (3). Barth reported that the officials in Colorado's Department of Social Services and HEW's regional office in Denver with whom he had talked favored some version of (4). So apparently did some staff members of key congressional delegations. The staff of Senator Gary Hart, who might have been expected to support a more generous settlement for the families, never responded to Barth's inquiries. From Senator Armstrong's previous public statements, HEW officials inferred that he would oppose continuing the payments for more than a few months.

In June 1980 Palmer decided in favor of a plan that, like (4), continued payments to the families for three years but at a declining rate so that families would realize that the payments were ending. In addition, Palmer instituted a program of counseling and support to help the families during the period of transition. In July he sent Secretary Patricia Harris a memorandum informing her of his decision. In September 1980 the department announced the death of the DIME.

The Ethics of the DIME

An analysis of the ethical issues raised in the twenty-year program of the DIME is best conducted in two parts—the first centering on the decision to initiate the twenty-year experiment; the second, on the decision to terminate it. For each decision, we should consider the ethical criteria officials used, and insofar as they were inadequate, to suggest how the criteria should be modified.

Initiating the Experiment

Officials decided to begin the twenty-year experiment in the context of a series of income maintenance experiments that had been widely regarded as not only successful but also ethically unobjectionable. As Peter Rossi and his associates wrote in 1978, the income maintenance project is "an excellent example of a class of intrinsically benign interventions." They found it "difficult to imagine that providing households with more money of the magnitudes involved can do anything but affect them marginally for the better."[15] It is not surprising, then, that before initiating the twenty-year sample officials did not review the ethics of the whole income maintenance project.

However, they should have considered—and to some extent did consider—whether the twenty-year experiment satisfied ethical criteria that should govern any such social experiment. These criteria are of two general types: those concerned with the consequences of the experiment, principally the risk of harm to the subjects; and those concerned with the conditions under which subjects and other citizens voluntarily participate in the experiment, principally the existence of informed consent.[16] The first set of criteria on its face seems utilitarian and sometimes officials so interpreted it, aggregating the benefits and harms for the experimental participants and for society as a whole.[17] But, as we shall see, some interpretations of the criteria gave greater weight to harms that subjects might incur, and would thus disallow some experiments that promised great benefits to society.

Officials believed that the social benefits of the income maintenance experiments could be substantial, including perhaps the alleviation of poverty in the United States. The twenty-year program in the DIME seemed an essential extension of the research, necessary to respond to what otherwise might be fatal objections to the earlier experiments. The program satisfied the standards that respected researchers use to assess the experimental value of such studies. For example, the central hypothesis of the experiment was of "compelling policy importance," and the desired information could not be obtained in any other "cheaper or simpler way."[18] Furthermore, officials believed that the income maintenance experiments could encourage other social experiments that would improve the design of other public policies such as health care and housing. In general, many people, taxpayers as well as future clients of governmental programs, stood to benefit if officials tested various programs in an experimental setting before embarking on a full-scale program for the entire society.

That the twenty-year sample in the DIME might positively contribute, at least in a small way, to these social goals was not implausible. But officials neglected the possibility that if the experiment went awry the effects on future research and on welfare policy could be negative. Furthermore, in their enthusiasm for the social knowledge the experiment could produce, officials did not distinguish between the benefits that would come from greater knowledge for whatever purpose it might be used, and the benefits that could come from knowledge that would favor some kind of income maintenance program for the poor. They evidently discounted the possibility that the findings of the experiments could strengthen the political hand of opponents of guaranteed-income programs and similar policies. Insofar as officials estimated social benefits on the assumption that the results of the experiments would be favorable to income maintenance programs, they risked biasing not only the conduct of the experiment but also the decision whether to start the experiment in the first place.

The benefits to the participants in the experiment were more immediate. The participants would enjoy a higher standard of living and a greater sense of security during the experiment than they had before—probably higher and greater than they would have had in the absence of the experiment. The most serious risk to the participants was the possibility that some might quit their jobs, retire early, or distance themselves from the labor market in other ways that would jeopardize the livelihood of their families after the experiment ended. The twenty-year program plainly increased this risk and added others that participants in the shorter experiments usually did not encounter at all (for example, those that resulted from having more children or taking on long-range debts.) HEW officials were certainly aware of these risks, as some of the objections to Morrill's first proposal indicated. But when Morrill revised the plan, he concentrated more on the objections to early termination, assuming that if the experiment ran the full twenty years the risks to the participants would not be serious.

Because the calculation of many of these harms and benefits of the experiments is so speculative, some researchers would simply exclude the long-term effects in evaluating the acceptability of the experiments. They propose a "short-term" criterion that would "require the experimenter to restore the *status quo ante*—to assure that . . . subjects are left after the experiment as if it had never existed."[19] The criterion cannot mean that we should restore subjects to their condition prior to the experiment (which in most cases would be much worse). Nor can it require that we actually erase all the effects of the experiment. Presumably what it implies is that the government should compensate subjects for any harm attributable to the experiment, the degree of harm being determined by comparing their condition immediately after the experiment with what their condition would have been had they not participated. It may be possible to use some such test of "short-term" harm in assessing (say) a three-year experiment, but it is extremely difficult to make the required comparisons after a twenty-year experiment. Further, even if it is possible to do so, it may not be desirable. In many social experiments (including the DIME), to eliminate the risk of harm would be to undermine the point of the experiment. The aim of such experiments is precisely to learn how people behave in response to risks.

Despite its difficulties, the "short-term" criterion points in the right direction. Unlike criteria of harm and benefit that many others propose (for example, the "ratio of benefit to harm" in HEW's guidelines), the "short-term" criterion goes beyond the calculation of general costs and benefits and seeks some independent protection of participants themselves. We can adopt this (substantially modified) version of the criterion: an acceptable experiment must be likely not only to yield social benefits at least as great as the harms that it causes participants; but also to impose a degree of risk of irreversible harm on participants no greater than that to which they would have been exposed if they had not participated. Even without invoking the notion of the rights of participants, these constraints thus would proscribe some experiments, no matter how beneficial they might be for society as a whole.

In contrast, a standard utilitarian criterion would leave participants more vulnerable, justifying much inconvenience and significant harm to them when the social value of the experiments is, or can plausibly be described as, great ("alleviating poverty in our society"). To be sure, we can imagine instances where an experiment might be so important that substantial risks to the participants would be warranted. Suppose the government must urgently design some administrative procedure for coping with a shortage of flu vaccine, or with terrorist threats to pollute water supplies. The risks of not conducting some preliminary tests could very well be much greater than any harm the participants would experience.[20] Such experiments should still have to satisfy the second criterion mentioned above, however.

Even on a nonutilitarian criterion, the nature of the harm itself may be problematic. It is not always clear what should count as a harm to participants in social experiments. Some people may object to an experiment because they do not agree with its objectives or with the ways they anticipate its findings may be used. Some opponents of income maintenance policies claimed that they would be harmed by the experiment because it increased the chances that the government would adopt such policies in the future. One reply is that the experimental findings might also have the opposite effect. But this reply does not reach the more fundamental question of whether participants who disagree with the aims or eventual uses of an experiment can legitimately complain that they are thereby suffering harm. The harm that comes from the discovery of knowledge or the discussion of controversial policies may be quite real. But just as we do not let such harm count as a reason to restrict free speech, we should not permit it to weigh against a decision to conduct an otherwise socially beneficial experiment.

Another problem about the nature of harm arises when what some participants see as a harm others may see as a benefit. In the DIME, one husband believed he had been harmed because his wife divorced him. The experiment had given her the financial independence she needed to leave him. Not surprisingly, she regarded this outcome as a benefit of the experiment.

In other instances, protecting participants from certain harms—by scrupulously respecting certain rights—may turn out to have undesirable consequences for the participants, more undesirable than the harms that the protections are supposed to prevent. The protection of the right of privacy is a case in point. Officials in all of the income maintenance experiments took great care to protect the confidentiality of the information about income and family composition that interviewers collected from participants. They successfully resisted repeated requests from legal authorities who sought the information. The president of MPR had vowed that he would go to jail rather than divulge even the list of names and addresses of the families enrolled in the program.

The experiments thus respected the privacy of the participants quite well. The problem was that it may have respected that privacy too well. Because no official in HEW knew the identities or particular circumstances of the participants, officials tended to think of the families in abstract terms. They could not easily tailor any of the changes in the programs to suit the needs of particular individuals or groups. Nor could they consult participants about any of the effects of the experiment. Their distance from the participants may have made the risks seem less vivid and easier to disregard. Also, officials who wished to know more about participants in order to design measures to help them during the experiment and its termination could not obtain the information they needed.

Even if we agree on what should count as a harm, we still must determine what degree of risk of harm should be accepted in any experiment. Since people differ in their willingness to accept risk (of even the same harm), a key question in social experimentation is political: who should decide what degrees of risk are acceptable? Experimenters may often favor a higher degree of risk than participants would choose, but participants may not be in a good position to judge for themselves since they often do not understand the experiment as well as the experimenters do.

These differing perspectives point to the need for an independent body, which could be composed of social scientists and others knowledgeable about social experiments, citizens who are representative of groups likely to be participants in the experiments, and officials of government. Such a body would make recommendations to the officials charged with deciding whether to conduct social experiments, and the recommendations would normally be available for public discussion. This kind of political process certainly would not resolve all the problems of assessing risks in experiments, but it could encourage wider discussion of the conflicting attitudes that citizens, experimenters, and officials may take toward such risks.

However beneficial or harmless an experiment may be, officials must still make sure that participation in the experiment is voluntary. Criteria that refer only to benefit and harm are not sufficient. Experimental subjects participate in a governmental project that is not intended for their benefit (though it may benefit them incidentally). The purpose of an experiment is to provide information that may benefit other citizens in the future. Unless the participants freely agree to take part, they are being treated only as means, not as ends in themselves. Since their role in an experiment differs in this way from the role of citizens in an ordinary program of government, the form of consent should also differ. We cannot assume that indirect agreement or tacit consent (expressed through the normal democratic process) establishes the consent of the participants in an experiment, even if it confers legitimacy on the decision to undertake the experiment. As in medical experimentation, so too in social experimentation we need the express consent of the subjects—what is usually called "informed consent."[21]

The requirements for informed consent stated in HEW's own guidelines are sensible as far as they go. They stipulate that experimenters should tell subjects about the procedures, explain the possible risks and benefits, and present alternative procedures. Experimenters should also offer to answer any questions, and inform the subjects that they may withdraw at any time. Looking over this list, we might conclude that the DIME satisfied the criterion of informed consent as well as could be expected. But behind the list lurk a number of serious problems.

First, how much should experimenters have told participants about the experiment and its possible effects? HEW officials rejected the proposal for a five-year experiment in which participants would be told that the experiment would continue for twenty years. Although their reasons for rejecting it may have been partly practical, officials correctly saw that this deception was inconsistent with informed consent. But officials did not take seriously the question of whether the needs of the experiment could be reconciled at all with any adequate requirement of disclosure, even if officials avoided deliberate deception.

For the experiment to work, participants had to believe that the program would continue for twenty years. The experimenters made special efforts to encourage this belief. But they also realized that they had to warn participants that the experiment could end at any time, and insofar as the participants took the warning seriously, their expectations about the program were no longer those the experiment presupposed. Experimenters, therefore, probably did not communicate this warning adequately. Enrollers were instructed to tell participants, if they asked about termination, that the government could "cancel the program at any time, as it could do with any program."[22] Such a statement surely underestimates the probability of the DIME's termination. Participants were not told that the usefulness of continuing the experiment itself would cease after five years (no further data were needed once the comparison with the regular five-year groups was completed). Had the participants been given such information, some might have realized that the pressures to end the income payments after five years would grow even if nothing happened to go wrong with the experiment.

There is yet another problem in determining what should be disclosed to participants. More often than medical experiments, social experiments take place in an environment over which researchers have little control, and consequently it is much harder to inform the participants fully about what might happen during the course of the experiment. After one participant appeared on a television program about the experiment, his foreman and several of his coworkers taunted him about thinking he was "somebody special" and pretending to be "poor." He punched the foreman, and was fired. His wife divorced him and sued him for child support payments he could not afford; he narrowly avoided imprisonment.[23] Officials could hardly have foreseen this sequence of events, but they should have informed participants that unforeseen harms were likely to occur, and could have given some examples of those that had occurred in similar experiments in the past.

Even when we have determined what participants should be told, we have not disposed of the problem of informed consent. The income maintenance experiments, like most social experiments, enrolled persons with lower income and less education than average, persons who may have difficulty in fully understanding the nature of the experiment and its possible effects on them. It is therefore questionable whether their consent can be regarded as sufficiently informed. Because of this problem, some writers favor a principle of "inverse selection," which would require experimenters to choose as subjects those most likely to understand the

191

experiment.[24] This principle, however, could prohibit many of the experiments that government should be most interested in conducting. It could discourage experiments intended to benefit the most disadvantaged citizens, whose participation may be needed but who may not be the most likely to understand the experiment.

A more constructive approach would be to require not only that experimenters provide the participants with certain information but also that the participants demonstrate that they understand the information before the experiment can continue. We might distinguish between information that would help subjects gain the most benefit from the experiment, and information that would help enable subjects to avoid serious harm. With respect to the latter kind of information, we should require demonstrated understanding, not only disclosure. The DIME probably met this requirement. Many of the participants apparently did not know how the program's marginal tax rate worked, and therefore may not have used the program to full advantage. But they did seem to know when the experiment was supposed to end, whom they could call if they had questions or complaints, and that they could withdraw at any time.[25] As far as this aspect of consent goes, the DIME participants understood enough to be said to have consented.

The inducements that experiments offer to subjects are also sometimes alleged to undermine informed consent. Some families in the DIME received as much as $9,000 in benefits from the program in 1978, arguably a strong incentive to participate. Unlike an earlier experiment where participants continued to receive payments even if they refused to talk to the interviewers, the DIME required that subjects submit to periodic interviews and mail in various forms if they wanted to receive their monthly checks. We should be concerned about the danger of exploitation through such "bribes" in social experiments, but it seems hard to argue that the benefits the DIME offered participants were unreasonably or inappropriately high. They did not exceed what the government would offer any citizen in similar circumstances if an income maintenance program like the DIME were actually adopted. Moreover, as Thomas Schelling has argued, keeping compensation low in order to protect subjects may be paternalistic. "People who deprecate 'undue enticement' are somewhat like those who explain that paying household help too much spoils them. People incur risks of life and health and sell away their privacy and dignity every day . . . maybe it isn't up to [the designers of the experiment] to decide that in the interest of their potential subjects they should keep the compensation down."[26]

Besides the requirements that refer to the agreement to join the experiment (such as disclosure and reasonable inducement), informed consent should stipulate that participants consent while the experiment continues. At a minimum, this means that they should have a genuine option of withdrawing at any time. The families in the DIME certainly could have quit the experiment at any time, and they knew they could. Not surprisingly, very few of them did, fewer than in the earlier experiments. The benefits of the program must have seemed too good to give up. Even if one member of a family began to have doubts about participation (perhaps resenting the intrusion of interviewers), that member might not have been able to persuade the other members to quit. Nevertheless, we cannot expect experimenters to ensure that the decision to withdraw is as easy in all respects as the decision to join. If we were to insist that remaining in an experiment provide no net advantage over leaving it, we could justify only experiments that would, on other reasonable criteria, be unacceptable. The right of withdrawal would become more genuine the more unpleasant or harmful the experiment. It seems enough to require that subjects be able to withdraw without any substantial penalty or any other harm about which they have not been forewarned.

Who should consent? This is usually a straightforward question in medical experiments, but in social experiments people who are not actually participants may be significantly affected by the experiment. In "saturation" experiments (such as those designed to evaluate housing allowances), many citizens who are not participants may suffer harm (such as a loss in their competitive position in the housing market). The income maintenance experiments could have had only a negligible effect on the market in the communities in which they were conducted. But nonparticipants (especially those who were in other ways similar to the participants) might understandably complain that the government unfairly denied them benefits that the participants received. MALDEF's appeal on behalf of the Mexican-Americans was just such a claim. Officials eventually accepted MALDEF's claim that some Mexican-Americans should be added to the sample, and they did so apparently more for political than experimental reasons. The additional sample was no more useful experimentally at the time when officials decided to include it than when they had earlier decided to exclude it.[27]

To accept a general claim based on distributive justice that all groups deserve to be represented in an experimental sample (as if it were a regular governmental policy) would be to render most social experiments impossibly expensive and cumbersome. Even when experiments significantly affect nonparticipants, as the DIME affected the Mexican-Americans in Denver, we cannot demand that nonparticipants consent in the same way that participants consent. The interests of nonparticipants can usually be sufficiently protected by requiring only that an experiment be approved by the duly elected and appointed officials in the community where the nonparticipants live. In this respect, an experiment may be thought of as if it were a normal program of government, even though it must meet more stringent standards of consent with respect to participants.[28]

Terminating the Experiment

Once officials had concluded that the twenty-year program in the DIME had no research value, the key ethical question became: what kind of commitment does the government have to the families in the program? Officials first concentrated on the question of whether the government had made an "inviolable promise" to provide the benefits for fifteen years (or an equivalent settlement). We should first understand what the foundation for such a commitment might be.

The class of moral obligations into which the commitment to the DIME families most naturally fits is that of fidelity or promise-keeping.[29] Beyond the general reasons for keeping promises, two features of the commitment to the families provide especially strong support for this obligation. Both derive from the fact that the families risked harm by relying on the government's commitment.[30]

First, the potential harm was not trivial: families may have made irreversible decisions that affected their lives in major ways. We might be tempted to suggest that the government should have tried to find out whether individuals did in fact make such decisions. Useful though this information would have been, collecting it was certain to be problematic. The problem is not merely one of administrative ethics: could officials justify intruding in this way into the private lives of the families? It is also one of what might be called administrative epistemology: how could any official ever know to what extent decisions such as having another child were influenced by the security the experiment seemed to provide? Remember also that the privacy protections built into the experiment prevented officials from knowing the identities of the families. In the absence of an acceptable procedure for ascertaining whether the experiment harmed any family, the government probably should have assumed the worst, and offered a settlement to satisfy the expectations of any family who believed the program would continue.

To sustain an obligation to the families, it is not sufficient that they suffered harm from relying on a promise; it is necessary that they had good reason for relying on it.[31] But, as some officials emphasized, all the communications to the families in the twenty-year DIME program contained an "escape clause." The families should have realized that the government's commitment could not be relied on absolutely—indeed, given the vagaries of politics, could not be relied on very much at all. If the families did not realize this, that is their fault; and the government and taxpayers should not have to bear the cost of such folly. There are three objections to this line of argument.

First, the experiment could not work unless the subjects believed the commitment, and all those administering the experiment therefore had strong incentives to make the commitment as credible as possible to the families. (This is another way in which the experiment differs from an ordinary "entitlement" program like Social Security, the terms of which the government may change from time to time without being guilty of reneging on a commitment.) The record in the DIME case gives ample indication of the efforts of officials to enhance the credibility of the commitment. In addition, there were many unrecorded encounters between the staff and the participants, providing opportunities for the staff (especially the enrollers) to exaggerate the strength of the commitment.

A second objection centers on a message communicated to the families *after* the meeting when officials had come to the conclusion that the experiment should be terminated. In a letter to the families in early 1979, Thomas Harper (of MPR's subsidiary, the Council for Grants to Families) reported that, among other changes in the program, data would no longer be collected from the families. He wrote that "although the interviews are ending, the payment program continues under revised Rules of Operation," adding in a reassuring tone that the DIME is a "successful study which has supplied significant information to the government" and that the changes in the rules "will not diminish that success."[32] Families could reasonably have interpreted this letter as an up-to-date reaffirmation of the government's commitment, further strengthening their reliance on the government's original promise. That officials approved such a further commitment even after they knew the twenty-year sample in the DIME was not a "successful study" and after they had begun to discuss ending the payments may warrant a charge of deception, beyond the allegation of promise-breaking.

A third objection to the view that the families did not have good reason to rely on the government's promise must be treated more cautiously. One consultant put the objection this way: because the families are poor and many are members of minorities, they probably could not fully appreciate the "escape clauses" the government attached to its original promise. This characterization of the families may be accurate. After all, many people surviving in poverty may quite rationally learn to trust nobody, least of all the government. However, in the absence of evidence about what people actually believed, the argument may carry elitist if not racist connotations. In any case, the first two objections alone ought to be enough to defeat any attempt to deny that the government had a commitment to the families.

That the government made a commitment to the families does not necessarily imply that it should be fulfilled. Like promises, commitments may sometimes be overridden. Of the various ways philosophers suggest that promises can be overridden, only one seems relevant in this case: a promise may be set aside if the circumstances that obtain when it is to be fulfilled differ significantly from what both parties understood when they made it.[33] Notice that this principle does not sanction releasing either party from an obligation if the circumstances change in ways that both parties should have foreseen. The point of a promise is often to ensure performance in the future when changes in circumstances will quite predictably tempt one of the parties not to perform.

The change in circumstances that officials cited in this episode was that the DIME was no longer serving its original purpose. They argued that therefore the government should not have to carry out the terms of the original agreement. But the fact that the twenty-year sample in the DIME had lost its experimental reason for existence was not only foreseeable, it had been foreseen and rejected as grounds for terminating the payments. The uselessness of any data collected after the fifth year was the reason that Morrill in his first proposal suggested offering participants a lump-sum payment if they would leave the program in that year. But Morrill quickly abandoned this proposal, and neither he nor anyone else had then proposed actually terminating the payments in the fifth year.

It is true that no one anticipated that the twenty-year experiment would become useless in the specific way that it did—that it would yield no results at all. But this additional way in which continuing the experiment lost its point does not relieve officials of their obligation. On the contrary, this further uselessness counts against the officials since the government and their contractors, not the families, were responsible for the errors that caused it. Had they designed the experiment properly, they would have been able to cite only the fact (which they did foresee) that continuing the experiment would yield no more data, rather than the fact (which they did not foresee) that the experiment could produce no results at all. Although these considerations do not necessarily show that the government owed the families fifteen years' worth of benefits, they do establish that the uselessness of the experiment cannot be a relevant reason for overriding the government's obligation to the families.

Palmer's quid pro quo argument (that since the families were no longer providing the government any service, the government owed them no more benefits) in effect appeals to changed circumstances, but in a way that requires a somewhat different response. On this argument, the new circumstances brought into play another more compelling obligation: the government's duty to all taxpayers. This is properly a moral consideration in the sense that the government's settlement with the families should satisfy general standards of fairness or justice. Not all such charges of injustice that taxpayers could put forward are legitimate, however. It seems a tenuous basis for such a charge to claim, as some taxpayers do, that social experiments are a waste of money, or that people should not be given guaranteed income anyhow. Arguments of this sort are pertinent at the stage of making a decision to initiate the experiment, and if they do not carry the day in deliberations at that stage, they should not be given any weight later when officials are trying to arrive at a fair settlement for ending an experiment.

The political climate was another kind of changed circumstance that some officials evoked to override the government's commitment to the families. Political factors certainly might count as moral reasons under some conditions. We should distinguish between (1) political factors that refer to only the interest of the officials or the department (for example, the possibility that a large settlement for the families would draw more public attention to the failure of the DIME and expose officials to criticism or loss of their jobs); and (2) political factors that refer to the interests of citizens more generally, at least indirectly (for example, the likelihood that the settlement would generate more political pressure against any welfare programs for the poor). It is only the latter kind of political factor to which we should give any moral weight.

No doubt there are many such factors in this case, but the effects of most of them are quite speculative. For every political factor of this kind telling against a large settlement with the DIME families is another one arguing for the settlement. Public support for welfare programs may be eroded if the government carries out the original plans for the settlement, but trust in government, especially among the poor and minority groups, may be undermined if government is perceived as reneging on the commitment. Similarly, future experiments may be jeopardized if the costs of the DIME are increased by a large settlement, but social scientists and citizens are less likely to participate in any such experiments in the future if the government cannot be depended on to honor the commitments it makes in experiments.

In contrast to these speculative considerations, officials faced one set of political factors that seemed quite immediate and certain. In its budget-cutting mood that spring, Congress would not have been likely to appropriate the funds that any large settlement required. If HEW officials could have morally justified one of the settlements they could have funded on their own (the fourth or fifth options mentioned above), possible congressional opposition would have created no further problem, moral or otherwise. But suppose officials believed that the government had a greater commitment to the families than HEW alone could fund (for example, the fifteen-year annuity proposed by one of the consultants). Officials then faced a serious (and quite characteristic) moral dilemma of administration.

Officials might have taken what some would regard as the more noble approach. As Kant would have counseled, they could have ignored all the serpentine calculations about what politicians might do, and simply presented Congress with the proposal they believed to be morally right.[34] If Congress rejected it, congressmen would bear the moral responsibility for whatever happened to the families. There is a lot to be said for this approach. Officials cannot be certain that Congress will actually reject the proposal they believe to be morally required. It may be argued, furthermore, that as the representative body in a democracy Congress should ultimately make such decisions anyhow. At the least, this approach seems to provide the appropriate perspective for administrative deliberations. HEW officials should have decided, independently of any appraisal of what Congress was likely to do, what settlement was morally right. Then (if necessary) they could have considered how politically to persuade Congress to accept it.

But the "leave-it-to-Congress" approach has a flaw that is probably fatal in this case. Senator Armstrong's public comments and other information gathered from congressional sources gave officials reason to believe that Congress might do worse than simply decline to fund a larger settlement for the families. Congress might take the occasion to instruct HEW to offer less than the maximum that the department could fund on its own. By going to Congress to get more for the families, HEW officials could have ended up with less than if they had never gone at all. A Kantian administrator might derive some comfort from believing that the moral blame for such a result would rest with Congress. But other officials surely ought to recognize that they share the responsibility for what happens to the families. They cannot escape blame by letting Congress decide, when they believe that Congress is likely to provide a settlement that is less than what is morally justified and less than what HEW could have offered on its own.

Evaluations and Implications of the DIME

No one can take much satisfaction in the way the twenty-year program in the DIME turned out. Not only did this part of the experiment yield few if any usable results, it also breached some important ethical principles. The government exposed families in the program to risks about which it did not provide full information, and in the end failed to honor a commitment on which the families had good reason to rely. Yet (except for the error in drawing the sample for the experiment) none of the decisions made at each stage of this episode looks so bad as does the final outcome.

On the first set of criteria—those concerned with benefits and harms—the decision to initiate the twenty-year sample in the DIME seems reasonable in light of what officials knew at the time. The significance of the experiment for social policy was great, and the design of the experiment satisfied the standards of respected professionals in the field. Moreover, many participants could expect to secure substantial material benefits from the experiment. Not only did the likely benefits of the experiment exceed its likely risks, but also the risks were no greater than those to which subjects would have been exposed if they had not participated.

However, the most serious risk—even from the viewpoint of 1974— was that for various reasons the program might have to be terminated after five years. Officials did not make adequate provision for this possibility, either in their calculations about whether to start the experiment or in their plans to implement it. Furthermore, officials may have underestimated the risks in the experiment simply because the variety of harms that social experiments can produce are often complex and controversial. In general, the appraisal of risks in an experiment probably should not be left exclusively to officials and experimenters, who may tend to exaggerate the benefits and slight the risks.

Officials gave less explicit attention to the other set of criteria—those stipulating that participation in the experiment be voluntary. But officials and experimenters certainly made a good-faith effort to secure the informed consent of the families. With some criterion of disclosure evidently in mind, officials rejected the plan that would have deceived the participants. They designed an enrollment procedure that, for the most part, provided participants with essential information about the experiment, and they established a monitoring procedure that could detect gross misunderstandings that participants may have had about the experiment. Officials did not disclose some incidental risks of the experiment (such as divorces, which had occurred in earlier experiments), and did not stress one quite central risk—the possibility of premature termination. Officials could not emphasize this possibility too much without undermining the purpose of the experiment, but they could have described the possibility in more detail and with more accuracy than they did. If officials believe that they cannot provide reasonably accurate descriptions of such risks, they should not undertake an experiment of this kind.

The other elements of the criterion of voluntary participation that involved the families posed no serious problems in the DIME. The government did not offer undue enticement to the families to persuade them to take part, and did not place any obstacles in the way of any participants who wished to withdraw. Neither federal nor state officials, however, made any systematic effort to secure even indirect consent of nonparticipants who might be affected by the experiment. Nonparticipants expressed themselves only in unofficial and adventitious ways (as in MALDEF's campaign to place Mexican-American families in the program).

The decision to terminate the experiment raised different ethical questions: the basis of commitments governments make and the conditions under which they can be overridden. The government did make a moral commitment to the families in the DIME. Because officials and experimenters had a strong incentive to convince the participants that the experiment would continue for twenty years, the government should have presumed that the families relied on the commitment, some to their detriment. The commitment could have been overridden if either the participants freely agreed to relieve the government of it, or if circumstances had changed significantly from what both parties had originally expected. But for various reasons (such as the protections of privacy built into the experiment), the government could not try to persuade the families to give up the benefits the program had promised. The circumstances had certainly changed: the experiment had become useless. But since officials had foreseen that continuing the payments after the fifth year would serve no experimental purpose, the further uselessness for which officials were responsible could not be grounds for repudiating the government's commitment.

The change in the political climate, however, may count as a reason for not fulfilling the commitment in its original form. Insofar as officials had good reason to believe that asking Congress for funds to carry out the original commitment would actually produce a more unfavorable settlement for the families, officials could justify offering the families less than they had been promised. But notice how limited this justification is. It does not license giving the families less than the maximum available from HEW's own funds—for example, reducing the payments for reasons of paternalism or responsibility to taxpayers.

The justification, moreover, does not imply that the more modest settlement actually fulfills the government's commitment to the families, and absolves the government of moral blame. The "government" here includes not only the officials who originally made the commitment, but also the members of Congress who could have supported the appropriation necessary for a settlement equivalent to the remaining fifteen years of the program. That Congress did not make the original commitment does not let its members off the moral hook. Some of the same considerations that sustain the moral obligation of HEW officials also imposes one on members of Congress.

The story of the twenty-year program in the DIME is not a chronicle of moral depravity or even moral insensitivity. The characters in the drama of the DIME not only discussed the ethics of what they were doing, but also manifested good intentions in what they did. Yet officials erred, both in the criteria they used and in the way they applied the criteria. Although most of the errors seemed rather small at the time they were made, their cumulative effect was great.

Because seemingly minor mistakes become magnified in this way, officials in charge of social experiments in the future should avoid even apparently trivial transgressions of the ethical criteria that govern the conduct of such experiments. Officials should formulate these criteria more explicitly than the officials did in the DIME, and they should seek advice about whether the criteria are satisfied from citizens who do not themselves initiate or conduct the experiment. We need not abandon social experimentation as an instrument of government simply because the DIME went awry. But we should learn from the experience of the DIME to make sure that future social experiments meet stringent standards, ethical as well as experimental.

Notes

Credits

Index

Notes

Introduction

1. Immanuel Kant, *Eternal Peace*, in *The Philosophy of Kant*, ed. C. J. Friedrich (New York: Random House, 1949), Appendix I, pp. 457–458 (translation somewhat modified). Cf. Matthew 10:16.

2. Cf. Isaiah 11:6; and Woody Allen, *Without Feathers* (New York: Warner Books, 1976), p. 28.

3. Dean Acheson, "Ethics in International Relations Today: Our Standard of Conduct," *Vital Speeches of the Day*, 31 (Pelham, N.Y.: City News Publishing Co., 1965), p. 228.

4. John Rawls, *A Theory of Justice* (Cambridge, Mass.: Harvard University Press, 1971), pp. 20–22, 48–51.

5. Immanuel Kant, *Critique of Judgment*, trans. James Meredith (Oxford: Oxford University Press, 1961), Introduction, sec. 4, p. 18. See Hannah Arendt, *Lectures on Kant's Political Philosophy*, ed. Ronald Beiner (Chicago: University of Chicago Press, 1982), pp. 7–77.

6. Arendt, p. 76.

7. Immanuel Kant, *The Critique of Pure Reason*, trans. Norman Kemp Smith (London: Macmillan, 1961), A134/B173–174.

8. State of Tennessee, Senate Resolution no. 41 (May 18, 1977).

9. In a subsequent revision of the code (Senate Resolution no. 2, Jan. 28, 1985), the Ten Commandments quietly disappeared.

1. Democratic Dirty Hands

1. Jean-Paul Sartre, *Dirty Hands*, in *No Exit and Three Other Plays*, trans. Lionel Abel (New York: Vintage, 1960), p. 224.

2. Niccolò Machiavelli, *The Prince*, trans. Robert Adams (New York: Norton, 1977), chap. 15, p. 45.

3. Niccolò Machiavelli, *The Discourses*, in *The Prince and The Discourses*, trans. Christian Detmold (New York: Random House, 1950), bk. I, chap. 9, p. 139. Also see bk. I, chap. 26, p. 184.

4. On the possibility of conflict in moral systems more generally (not only

political morality), see Alan Donagan, "Consistency in Rationalist Moral Systems," *Journal of Philosophy,* 81 (June 1984), pp. 291–309; and Ruth Marcus, "Moral Dilemmas and Consistency," *Journal of Philosophy,* 77 (March 1980), pp. 121–136.

    5. *The Prince,* chap. 8, p. 27.

    6. *The Prince,* chap. 15, p. 44.

    7. Michael Walzer, "Political Action: The Problem of Dirty Hands," *Philosophy and Public Affairs,* 2 (Winter 1973), p. 161. Other contemporary discussions of the problem include: Stuart Hampshire, "Public and Private Morality," in *Public and Private Morality,* ed. Stuart Hampshire et al. (Cambridge: Cambridge University Press, 1978), pp. 23–54; Bernard Williams, "Politics and Moral Character," in Hampshire, pp. 55–74; Thomas Nagel, "Ruthlessness in Public Life," in Hampshire, pp. 75–92; and Stanley Benn, "Private and Public Morality: Clean Living and Dirty Hands," in *Public and Private in Social Life,* ed. S. I. Benn and G. F. Gauss (New York: St. Martin's, 1983), pp. 155–181; and W. Kenneth Howard, "Must Public Hands be Dirty?" *Journal of Value Inquiry,* 11 (Spring 1977), pp. 29–40.

    8. For more precise statements of this contrast, see Samuel Scheffler, *The Rejection of Consequentialism* (Oxford: Clarendon Press, 1984), pp. 1–13; and Thomas Nagel, *The View from Nowhere* (New York: Oxford University Press, 1986), pp. 164–188. Although both present balanced and in some respects similar analyses of the contrast, Scheffler is somewhat more sympathetic to consequentialism; and Nagel, to deontology.

    9. Walzer, p. 162.

    10. Ibid., p. 171.

    11. Ibid., p. 177–178.

    12. Alan Donagan suggests both approaches, though he places greater weight on the second (*The Theory of Morality* [Chicago: University of Chicago Press, 1977] pp. 180–189.) Also, see the discussion by Alan H. Goldman, *The Moral Foundations of Professional Ethics* (Totowa, N.J.: Rowman and Littlefield, 1980), pp. 62–76.

    13. Georg Wilhelm Hegel, *The Philosophy of World History,* trans. H. B. Nisbet (Cambridge: Cambridge University Press, 1975), pp. 85–93.

    14. Donagan, p. 186, 189.

    15. Ibid., p. 186.

    16. Ibid., pp. 66–74.

    17. Donagan (p. 184) seems to suggest a similar reason for denying the paradox, though he does not attempt to explain how such a reason could be thought to follow from common morality or any deontological principles.

    18. Walzer, pp. 171–172.

    19. See, for example, Henry Sidgwick, *The Methods of Ethics,* 7th ed. (London: Macmillan, 1907), p. 413. A recent critic of this separation is Bernard Williams, in *Utilitarianism: for and against,* ed. J. J. C. Smart and Bernard Williams (Cambridge: Cambridge University Press, 1973), pp. 118–135; and Bernard Williams, *Ethics and the Limits of Philosophy* (Cambridge, Mass.: Har-

vard University Press, 1985), pp. 101–102; 108–110. For a recent defense of the consequentialist position on this question, see Scheffler, pp. 43–53.

20. Walzer, p. 179.

21. The assumption is William Safire's (see "Lying in State," *New York Times,* May 1, 1980, p. A31). Vance offers a plausible alternative account in *Hard Choices* (New York: Simon and Schuster, 1983), pp. 373–413.

22. A thoughtful attempt to make some sense of a notion of moral distance is Lawrence Becker, "The Neglect of Virtue," *Ethics,* 85 (January 1975), pp. 110–122. Also see Jonathan Glover, *Causing Death and Saving Lives* (New York: Penguin, 1977), pp. 286–297.

23. See the selections in Bonnie Steinbock, ed. *Killing and Letting Die* (Englewood Cliffs, N.J.: Prentice-Hall, 1980).

24. Michael Walzer, *Just and Unjust Wars* (New York: Basic Books, 1977), p. 324.

25. Bill Keller, "Essential, They Say, but 'Repugnant'," *New York Times,* January 20, 1986, p. A24.

26. To hold the top officials culpable when they meet the criteria of personal responsibility does not imply that the lower-level officials are excused. See pp. 47–64.

27. Although this argument is more naturally made by consequentialists, it has a nonconsequentialist version: see Williams, "Politics and Moral Character," p. 64.

28. David Halberstam, *The Best and the Brightest* (New York: Random House, 1972), pp. 520–521. Also see William C. Westmoreland, *A Soldier Reports* (Garden City, N.Y.: Doubleday, 1976), pp. 115–116. Bundy himself (according to one scholar who has interviewed him) does not recall the incident in these terms.

29. Westmoreland, pp. 116–118.

30. Halberstam, p. 521.

31. "Like numbers of civilians in positions of some governmental authority, once [Bundy] smelled a little gunpowder he developed a field marshal psychosis" (Westmoreland, p. 146).

32. For an example, see the Report of the Commission on Wartime Relocation and Internment of Civilians, *Personal Justice Denied* (Washington, D.C.: Government Printing Office, 1982). More generally, see Robert Amdur, "Compensatory Justice: The Question of Costs," *Political Theory,* 7 (May 1979), pp. 229–244.

33. The judgments are normally more contestable than those required in the arguments where hypothetical consent has (somewhat) greater plausibility— the defense of a social contract and the justification of paternalism. In the former, the posited end is sufficiently broad and its alternative sufficiently unattractive that we are inclined to believe that all reasonable persons would accept it. In the latter, the end seems acceptable because it refers (or should refer) specifically to the conditions of the person or class of persons subject to the paternalistic intervention, as well as to generally accepted goals. See pp. 157–160.

34. Graham Allison and Lance Liebman, "Lying in Office," in *Ethics and Politics,* ed. Amy Gutmann and Dennis Thompson (Chicago: Nelson Hall, 1984), pp. 38–39. Also, Graham Allison, *Essence of Decision: Explaining the Cuban Missile Crisis* (Boston: Little, Brown, 1971), pp. 226–229.

35. Although within a few years the basic facts of the negotiation had become known to many people outside of government and could be inferred from careful reading of Robert Kennedy's *Thirteen Days,* the first public statement by those who participated in the decision making during the crisis was in "The Lessons of the Cuban Missile Crisis," *Time,* Sept. 27, 1982, pp. 85–86.

36. Generally on undercover police work, Gary Marx, "The New Police Undercover Work," *Urban Life,* 8 (January 1980), pp. 399–446; and James Q. Wilson, "The Changing FBI—The Road to ABSCAM," *Public Interest,* 59 (Spring 1980), pp. 3–14. Also see Gerald Kaplan, ed., *ABSCAM Ethics: Moral and Ethical Issues in Deceptive Investigations* (Washington, D.C.: The Police Foundation, 1982).

37. A balanced assessment of the legitimacy of the investigations is Sissela Bok, *Secrecy* (New York: Pantheon, 1982), pp. 265–280.

38. Cf. Andrew Altman and Steven Lee, "Legal Entrapment," *Philosophy and Public Affairs* (Winter 1983), pp. 51–69.

39. Thomas Powers, *The Man Who Kept the Secrets: Richard Helms and the CIA* (New York: Pocket Books, 1981), pp. 159–164, 189–200, 368–377.

40. Ibid., p. 438.

41. Assassination is currently prohibited by an Executive Order. For a discussion of one (abortive) proposal to regulate the use of such methods in the CIA, see Lance Liebman, "Legislating Morality," in *Public Duties: The Moral Obligation of Government Officials,* ed. Joel Fleishman et al. (Cambridge, Mass.: Harvard University Press, 1981), pp. 260–261.

42. U.S. Senate Select Committee to Study Government Operations, *Alleged Assassination Plots Involving Foreign Leaders,* 94th Cong., 1st sess. (Washington, D.C.: Government Printing Office, 1975), pp. 195–215.

43. Immanuel Kant, *Eternal Peace,* ed. Carl J. Friedrich (New York: Modern Library, 1949), p. 470. Cf. John Rawls, *A Theory of Justice* (Cambridge, Mass.: Harvard University Press, 1971), pp. 133–134. Also see John Stuart Mill, *Considerations on Representative Government,* in *Essays on Politics and Society,* ed. John Robson (Toronto: University of Toronto Press, 1977), 2:493, 432–433.

44. Mill, *Representative Government,* p. 493.

45. Interview with Richard Helms, Faculty Study Group on the Moral Obligations of Public Officials, Harvard University, March 8, 1978. Helms also invoked in his own defense his oath to the CIA, and he challenged the jurisdiction of the committees that asked him the questions.

46. Arthur Maass, *Congress and the Common Good* (New York: Basic Books, 1983), pp. 234–235.

47. Ibid., pp. 240–242.

48. Maass (ibid.) also objects to the tactics that Gravel and Dellums used. They acted unilaterally before Congress as a whole had a chance to decide whether

to release the information. If they had reason to believe that Congress would decide in favor of disclosure in a relatively short time, they could be criticized for ignoring their responsibility to their colleagues. But in fact they probably had better grounds to doubt that Congress would so act.

49. The principle is of course valid under some circumstances. An official should be considered (at least partly) morally responsible for the wrongs others commit as a result of his doing right if the wrongs are reasonably foreseeable and avoidable without causing greater harm to innocent citizens. Arguably, the HEW officials acted on this principle when they decided not to go to Congress to seek more funds for the families in the Denver Income Maintenance Experiment because they believed Congress might (wrongly) deny the families any funds at all. See pp. 197–199.

50. A useful selection of relevant articles as well as a short bibliography is in James P. Sterba, *The Ethics of War and Nuclear Deterrence* (Belmont, Calif.: Wadsworth, 1985). Also see Douglas MacLean, ed., *The Security Gamble: Deterrence Dilemmas in the Nuclear Age* (Totowa, N.J.: Rowman and Allanheld, 1984); Douglas P. Lackey, *Moral Principles and Nuclear Weapons* (Totowa, N.J.: Rowman and Allanheld, 1984); and Walzer, *Just and Unjust Wars,* chap. 17.

51. The Bishops' Letter (*Challenge of Peace: God's Promise and Our Response*) is defended in *The Security Gamble* by the Rev. J. Bryan Hehir, "Moral Issues in Deterrence Policy," pp. 53–71; and criticized by George Sher, "The U.S. Bishops' Position on Nuclear Deterrence," pp. 72–81. The text of the letter is in the *National Catholic Reporter,* June 17, 1983, pp. 5–28.

52. David Lewis, "Devil's Bargains and the Real World," in *The Security Gamble,* p. 147. Lewis directs his argument partly against David Gauthier, "Deterrence, Maximization, and Rationality" (ibid., pp. 100–122) and in support of Gregory Kavka, "Some Paradoxes of Deterrence," *Journal of Philosophy,* 75 (1978), pp. 285–302. Kavka's contribution to *The Security Gamble* ("Nuclear Deterrence: Some Moral Perplexities," pp. 123–140), which Lewis also cites, focuses on other aspects of the problem.

53. Lewis, pp. 149, 151.

54. Many strategists as well as policy makers now stress the importance of existential deterrence: see Robert Jervis, *The Illogic of American Nuclear Strategy* (Ithaca: Cornell University Press, 1984), pp. 137–140, 155; and McGeorge Bundy, "Existential Deterrence and Its Consequences," in *The Security Gamble,* pp. 3–13.

55. Existential deterrence, however, does have significant moral implications. Since it suggests that deterrence can be maintained even with unequal levels of force between adversaries, it would, for example, discourage some aspects of the arms race. More generally, it would also support moves toward denuclearization, which is (as argued later in the text) one plausible response to the moral problem.

56. Cf. Lackey: "The key question . . . is whether making a nuclear threat pushes the probability of carrying it out over a morally acceptable 'threshold

level' " (p. 176). Lackey does not precisely define the threshold level he has in mind, but plainly he thinks much of U.S. nuclear planning goes beyond that level.

57. Lewis, p. 152.

58. Mutual assured destruction may not be an explicit threat, but if it exists, as strategists suggest, "as fact, irrespective of policy" (Jervis, pp. 146, 150), it is no less morally wrong.

59. John Steinbrunner, "Nuclear Decapitation," *Foreign Policy,* 45 (1981–82), pp. 21–23.

60. See H. A. Feiveson, "Can We Decide about Nuclear Weapons?" *Dissent* (Spring 1982), pp. 183–194.

61. See Robert Dahl, *Controlling Nuclear Weapons: Democracy versus Guardianship* (Syracuse, N.Y.: Syracuse University Press, 1985), pp. 69–89.

62. *The Challenge of Peace,* pp. 17–19.

63. Richard H. Ullman, "Denuclearizing International Politics," *Ethics,* 95 (April 1985), pp. 567–588. Also see Joseph Nye, Jr., *Nuclear Ethics* (New York: Free Press, 1986), pp. 120–131.

2. The Moral Responsibililty of Many Hands

1. Even among those scholars who have contributed the most to the recent ethical turn in the study of public policy, the paradigm of the lonely leader still prevails, sometimes explicitly as in the discussions of "dirty hands," more often implicitly as in the analyses of public policy, which normally proceed without references to any agents at all. See, for example, Charles W. Anderson, "The Place of Principles in Policy Analysis," *American Political Science Review,* 73 (September 1979), pp. 711–723; Brian Barry and Douglas Rae, "Political Evaluation," in *Handbook of Political Science,* ed. Fred Greenstein and Nelson Polsby (Reading, Mass.: Addison Wesley, 1975), pp. 337–401; Sissela Bok, *Lying* (New York: Random House, 1979); Joel Fleishman and Bruce Payne, *Ethical Dilemmas and the Education of Policy Makers* (Hastings-on-Hudson, N.Y.: Hastings Center, 1980); Stuart Hampshire et al., *Public and Private Morality* (Cambridge: Cambridge University Press, 1978); David E. Price, "Assessing Policy: Conceptual Points of Departure," in *Public Duties,* ed. Joel Fleishman et al. (Cambridge, Mass; Harvard University Press, 1981), pp. 142–172; John Rohr, *Ethics for Bureaucrats* (New York: Dekker, 1978); and Michael Walzer, "Political Action: The Problem of Dirty Hands," *Philosophy and Public Affairs,* 2 (Winter 1973), pp. 160–180.

2. H. L. A. Hart, *Punishment and Responsibility* (New York: Oxford University Press, 1968), pp. 211–230; and Joel Feinberg, *Doing and Deserving* (Princeton, N.J.: Princeton University Press), pp. 24–54.

3. J. L. Austin's classic essay ("A Plea for Excuses," *Proceedings of the Aristotelian Society,* 57 [1956–57], pp. 1–30) is a valuable source on this topic, but more directly relevant are Feinberg; and H. L. A. Hart and A. M. Honoré, *Causation in the Law* (Oxford: Clarendon Press, 1959).

4. For the analogue in the legislative process, see pp. 107–111.

5. Political responsibility involves a judgment that someone is answerable to an authority according to procedures of a political system. Like moral but unlike legal responsibility, political responsibility may appeal to principles that are often unwritten and too indeterminate to be specified in a system of rules. Like legal but unlike moral responsibility, political responsibility may hold someone responsible for an outcome even though the person did not actually bring it about, or could not have done anything to prevent it from occurring. One aim of this chapter is to suggest that we should make political responsibility more like moral responsibility, though another equally important aim is to suggest that we should revise some of our usual notions of moral responsibility when using it in political contexts.

6. Max Weber, "Bureaucracy," in *From Max Weber,* trans. H. H. Gerth and C. Wright Mills (New York: Oxford University Press, 1958), pp. 196–197.

7. Weber, "Politics as a Vocation," ibid., p. 95; and "Bureaucracy," pp. 214–216.

8. Weber, "Politics as a Vocation," p. 95. This distinction does not depend on accepting Weber's further claim that the political leader should act on an "ethic of responsibility," rather than on an "ethic of ultimate ends" (pp. 120–121).

9. Hugh Heclo, "Issue Networks and the Executive Establishment," in *The New American Political System,* ed. Anthony King (Washington, D.C.: American Enterprise Institute, 1978), pp. 87–124.

10. Graham Allison, *Essence of Decision* (Boston: Little, Brown, 1971), pp. 144–184.

11. Alan A. Altshuler, "The Study of American Public Administration," in *The Politics of the Federal Bureaucracy,* ed. Alan A. Altshuler and Norman C. Thomas (New York: Harper and Row, 1977), pp. 2–17; Theodore J. Lowi, *The End of Liberalism,* 2d ed. (New York: W. W. Norton, 1979), pp. 92–126; and Francis E. Rourke, *Bureaucratic Power in National Politics,* 3d ed. (Boston: Little, Brown, 1978), p. 253.

12. Weber, "Bureaucracy," pp. 232–233.

13. E.g. Lowi, pp. 295–313.

14. Victor Thompson, *Modern Organizations* (New York: Random House, 1961), pp. 129–137; Murray Edelman, *The Symbolic Uses of Politics* (Urbana: University of Illinois Press, 1964), p. 79.

15. Arthur M. Schlesinger, Jr., *A Thousand Days* (Boston: Houghton Mifflin, 1965), pp. 289–290.

16. Transcribed from a tape of the CBS broadcast of Nixon's address to the nation, April 30, 1973.

17. Herbert Kaufman, *Red Tape* (Washington, D.C.: Brookings, 1977), pp. 27–28. For discussion of similar arguments in the context of war crimes, see Peter A. French, ed., *Individual and Collective Responsibility* (Cambridge, Mass: Schenkman, 1972).

18. W. H. Walsh, "Pride, Shame and Responsibility," *Philosophical Quarterly,* 20 (January 1970), p. 4.

19. Ibid., p. 5.

20. Feinberg, p. 248. Since the publication of the original version of this chapter, more defenses of the collective model have appeared. See Peter A. French, *Collective and Corporate Responsibility* (New York: Columbia University Press, 1982); and Ronald Dworkin, *Law's Empire* (Cambridge, Mass.: Harvard University Press, 1986), pp. 167–175, 187.

21. It does not necessarily follow that we should ascribe moral responsibility to the group in such circumstances. Furthermore, even if it makes sense to hold a collectivity morally responsible, individual responsibility for collective faults is not necessarily or usually extinguished. See pp. 67–78.

22. Richard J. Stillman, ed., *Public Administration: Concepts and Cases,* 2d ed. (Boston: Houghton Mifflin, 1976), p. 34. For some other examples, see Edward Weisband and Thomas Franck, *Resignation in Protest* (New York: Penguin, 1976), pp. 79–80.

23. These criteria raise notoriously difficult philosophical issues, only a few of which are mentioned here. In addition to the recent works cited in the notes that follow, see the classic source, which is still the most suggestive: Aristotle, *Ethica Nicomachea, The Works of Aristotle,* ed. W. D. Ross (Oxford: Oxford University Press, 1963), bk. III.1–5. Also see Richard Sorabji, *Necessity, Cause and Blame: Perspectives on Aristotle's Theory* (Ithaca: Cornell University Press, 1980).

24. The interpretation of the criterion is not only more complex than can be indicated here, but it is also a chief point of controversy between the two best works in the theory of responsibility. Cf. Hart and Honoré, pp. 61–62, 103–122; and Feinberg, pp. 184, 201–207. My interpretation here more closely follows Feinberg.

25. E.g., John Ladd, "Morality and the Ideal of Rationality in Formal Organizations," *Monist,* 54 (October 1970), pp. 513–515.

26. Ibid., p. 514.

27. Derek Parfit argues for a revision in our moral thinking that could solve some of the problems of ascribing moral responsibility for the consequences of collective actions (*Reasons and Persons* [Oxford: Clarendon Press, 1984], pp. 67–86). He develops a theory in which, even if an individual act will not harm other people, the act may still be wrong if it is one of a set of acts that together will harm other people. An underlying rationale of this theory is that individual actions affect many more people now under modern conditions than they did when mankind lived in small communities (pp. 85–86). A fortiori, Parfit's theory should apply to public officials (though he does not suggest such an application).

28. Hart and Honoré, p. 117.

29. A political theorist has many excuses, some of which might even be valid, for disregarding the relevant but complex metaphysical problems raised by this criterion. Two of the best contemporary discussions are Harry G. Frankfurt, "Freedom of the Will and the Concept of a Person," *Journal of Philosophy,* 68 (Jan. 14, 1971), pp. 5–20; and P. F. Strawson, "Freedom and Resentment,"

in *Studies in the Philosophy of Thought and Action,* ed. P. F. Strawson (Oxford: Oxford University Press, 1968), pp. 71–96.

30. Aristotle, bk. III.1, 1109b–1111b. Cf. Jonathan Glover, *Responsibility* (London: Routledge and Kegan Paul, 1970), esp. pp. 60–61; and Alan Donagan, *The Theory of Morality* (Chicago: University of Chicago Press, 1977), pp. 112–142.

31. See pp. 72–75.

32. Aristotle, bk. III.1, 1110a, 8–15.

33. Stillman, p. 33.

34. Hart and Honoré, pp. 225–226.

35. Feinberg, pp. 196, 207–212. In this form, then, the excuse from alternative cause turns into what is called later the excuse from null cause. Both kinds of excuses should be distinguished from the excuse from additional cause (see Hart and Honoré, pp. 216–225.).

36. Weisband and Franck, pp. 92–93.

37. Saul Friedlander, *Kurt Gerstein* (New York: Knopf, 1969), p. 199.

38. See Thomas E. Hill, "Symbolic Protest and Calculated Silence," *Philosophy and Public Affairs,* 9 (Fall 1979), pp. 83–102.

39. J. Anthony Lukas, *Nightmare* (New York: Bantam, 1977), p. 592.

40. Bernard Williams, "A Critique of Utilitarianism," in *Utilitarianism: for and against,* ed J. J. C. Smart and Bernard Williams (Cambridge: Cambridge University Press, 1973), pp. 97–98.

41. Ibid., p. 116.

42. But see Bernard Williams, *Moral Luck* (Cambridge: Cambridge University Press, 1981), pp. 40–53.

43. See Hart and Honoré, pp. 69–78, 94, 295.

44. Han Fei Tzu, *The Complete Works* (London: Probsthain, 1939), 1:113–133 (cited in Herbert Goldhamer, *The Adviser* [New York: Elsevier, 1978], p. 118).

45. William R. Nelson, ed., *The Politics of Science* (New York: Oxford University Press, 1968), p. 119; and Lyman Bryson, "Notes on a Theory of Advice," in *Reader in Bureaucracy,* ed. Robert K. Merton et al. (New York: The Free Press, 1952), p. 203.

46. Hart and Honoré recognize that "interpersonal transactions" (which include advising) constitute exceptions to their general principle that a subsequent voluntary intervention "negatives" causal connection and responsibility (pp. 48–55, 171–172). But they still want to insist that (at least in legal theory) an adviser is not responsible for an advisee's actions based on the advice. They must therefore find some way to distinguish advising from other forms of influence, such as inducing, which in their view do warrant the ascription of responsibility. To account for such distinctions, they rely on the idea of one person's acting "in consequence" of another's influence (pp. 51, 78, 338–340). But to interpret this idea in any particular instance, they are forced to invoke noncausal factors—specifically, the intention of the adviser, or the kind of advice given.

47. Arthur M. Schlesinger, Jr., *The Coming of the New Deal* (Boston: Houghton Mifflin, 1959), pp. 514–515; and Allison, pp. 203–204.

48. The excuse could not be used in its pure form without rejecting, or at least supplementing, the weaker interpretation of the causal criterion of personal responsibility presented above. To qualify as a cause, an act or omission would have to be more than just one of many causal factors in the chain leading to the outcome. It would also have to be a significant or salient factor—standing out from the other "causes" in its abnormality. The criticism of the excuse in the text is meant to suggest that this more demanding criterion has fatal limitations in ascribing responsibility to officials in organizations. But the criterion also suffers from more general problems (such as circularity) when used for ascribing responsibility for almost any kind of human action (see Feinberg, pp. 206–207).

49. Cf. Feinberg, pp. 201–205.

50. Thomas Hobbes, *Leviathan*, ed. Michael Oakeshott (New York: Macmillan, 1962), pp. 191–197. Before defining the proper kind of counsel, Hobbes distinguishes counsel from command. Command is directed to the benefit of the commander, while counsel is directed only to the benefit of the person to whom it is given. No one may be "obliged to do as he is counselled, because the hurt of not following it, is his own," and therefore no one should be blamed (accused or punished) for the counsel he gives. Since this distinction thus yields the same results as does the doctrine of *novus actus interveniens*, it would support only the first version of the excuse from null cause. Hobbes's further distinction between types of counsel underlies the second version of the excuse.

51. Hobbes, pp. 192–193. Machiavelli also wants advisers not to "advocate any enterprise with too much zeal," and to give their advice "calmly and modestly." But he does so because he sees this as the only way counselors can hope to cope with a common dilemma in their role: if they "do not advise what seems to them for the good of the republic or the prince . . . then they fail of their duty; and if they do advise it, then it is at the risk of their position and their lives" (Niccolò Machiavelli, *The Discourses*, in *The Prince and The Discourses*, trans. Christian Detmold [New York: Random House, 1950], bk. III, chap. 35, p. 514).

52. Operations Research Society of America, "Guidelines for the Practice of Operations Research," *Operations Research*, 19 (September 1971), pp. 1134–1135, 1144–1148. Also see "Reactions to the Guidelines," *Operations Research*, 20 (January/February 1972), pp. 205–244.

53. Paul Doty, "Can Investigations Improve Scientific Advice? The Case of the ABM," *Minerva*, 10 (April 1972), pp. 282–287. For another example, see Robert Gilpin, *American Scientists and Nuclear Weapons Policy* (Princeton: Princeton University Press, 1962), pp. 262–298.

54. See, e.g., Edward S. Flash, Jr., *Economic Advice and Presidential Leadership* (New York: Columbia University Press, 1965), pp. 276–325; T. E. Cronin and S. D. Greenberg, eds., *The Presidential Advisory System* (New York: Harper and Row, 1969); and Morton H. Halperin, *Bureaucratic Politics and Foreign Policy* (Washington: Brookings, 1974), pp. 158–172.

55. Doty, p. 281.

56. U.S. Atomic Energy Commission, *In the Matter of J. Robert Oppenheimer* (Cambridge, Mass.: MIT Press, 1971), p. 236.

57. Robert J. Donovan, *Conflict and Crisis* (New York: Norton, 1977), p. 97.

58. Alexander George, "The Case for Multiple Advocacy in Making Foreign Policy," *American Political Science Review,* 66 (September 1972), pp. 751–785; and Aaron Wildavsky, *The Politics of the Budgetary Process,* 2d ed. (Boston: Little, Brown, 1974), pp. 166–167.

59. The most influential design proposed by a political scientist in recent years specifies an elaborate set of structural conditions that would be necessary to make it function properly. See George, pp. 784–785.

60. It might be objected that to permit (or require) an adviser to transcend his role in this way is to create an advisory system that is self-defeating. One adviser decides that other advisers collectively are not providing balanced advice at a particular time, and that adviser corrects his or her advice to restore a proper balance. But in the meantime each of the other advisers, seeing the same original imbalance, acts to try to restore the balance. The result will be at best a return to the original imbalance, or at worst, chaos. This objection must assume a system in which advisers act independently and simultaneously, and in which none can inform the advisees that the advice takes into account certain faults in the system. Since these assumptions do not usually hold in real systems, advisers cannot readily appeal to the objection to excuse their failures to compensate for defects in an actual system, even if their usual role would dictate that they ignore such defects.

61. Weisband and Franck, p. 139.

62. Ball's reference to the Honduras desk officer may suggest a somewhat different defense—one based more on the directness than on the scope of the decision that the role requires. The idea seems to be that distance from the harmful decisions decreases responsibility for them: among all the officials who dealt with Vietnam, those who approved and carried out military action bear more responsibility than those who helped sustain diplomatic support for it. But in politics, organization amplifies the effect of individual action, and makes distance (in its various senses) less relevant than in relations among individuals. See pp. 19–21.

63. Immanuel Kant, "On a Supposed Right to Lie from Altruistic Motives," in *Critique of Practical Reason,* ed. Lewis White Beck (Chicago: University of Chicago Press, 1949), pp. 346–350.

64. Donagan, pp. 206–207.

65. Charles Fried, *Right and Wrong* (Cambridge, Mass.: Harvard University Press, 1978), pp. 1–2, 20–28.

66. Fried, pp. 21–22, 26, 28, 42, 168.

67. Fried, pp. 22n, 160.

68. The standard counterexamples to these theories call into question the distinction between consequences that are means to one's end and those that are merely side effects. (Cf. Fried, pp. 23–24, 202–205.) In these examples the agent achieves the intended end, and the issue is whether the agent is responsible for

certain foreseeable consequences (are they "means" or "side effects"?). Although no doubt there are cases of this sort in government, more common and instructive are instances where advisers do not achieve the ends they intend, and indeed may intend just the opposite end.

69. James C. Thomson, "How Could Vietnam Happen? An Autopsy," *Atlantic Monthly,* April 1968, pp. 47–53; and George Reedy, *The Twilight of the Presidency* (New York: World, 1970), p. 11. Cf. Albert O. Hirschman, *Exit, Voice and Loyalty* (Cambridge, Mass.: Harvard University Press, 1970), pp. 115–119.

70. William Safire recalls the "Rejected Counsel": "the White House staffer whose job it is to go into the Oval Office in times of crisis and say 'Mr. President—do the popular thing! Take the easy way!' The President can then say: 'Some of my advisers have suggested that I do what is politically popular. I have rejected such counsel' " ("Rejected Counsel's Return," *New York Times,* Dec. 31, 1979), p. 15.

71. Fried, pp. 34–35. Donald Regan develops a consequentialist theory that would limit the responsibility of agents more than traditional consequentialism but less than theories such as Fried's. Regan's "cooperative utilitarianism" directs each agent to "cooperate with whoever else is cooperating in the production of the best consequences possible, given the behavior of non-cooperators" (*Utilitarianism and Cooperation* [Oxford: Clarendon Press, 1980], pp. 164–189). Although Regan presents his theory as a general moral theory, it seems especially suited to behavior in structured activities—as in organizations, where agents can more clearly identify cooperators and the conduct necessary for cooperation.

72. Robert J. Muller, *Adlai Stevenson* (New York: Harper and Row, 1967), pp. 283–284.

73. Harry Truman, *Memoirs, Years of Decisions* (New York: Doubleday, 1955), 1:97.

74. John Bartlow Martin, *Overtaken by Events* (Garden City, N.Y.: Doubleday, 1966), p. 659.

75. Charles Peters, "The Culture of Bureaucracy," *Washington Monthly,* 5 (September 1973), pp. 22–24. For a different account, see Brent Ashabranner, *A Moment in History* (Garden City, N.Y.: Doubleday, 1971), pp. 19–42.

76. Henry Kissinger, "Letters," *Economist,* 272 (September 8–14, 1979), pp. 6–7; and *White House Years* (Boston: Little, Brown, 1979), pp. 239–254.

77. Its implications have also been more extensively discussed, most notably in the literature on war crimes (see Michael Walzer, *Just and Unjust Wars* [New York: Basic Books, 1977], pp. 287–327). Also, see discussion of organizational dissent (e.g., Sissela Bok, "Blowing the Whistle," in *Public Duties,* ed. Joel Fleishman et al. [Cambridge, Mass.: Harvard University Press, 1981], pp. 204–220).

78. Congressional Quarterly, *Watergate* (Washington, D.C.: Congressional Quarterly, 1975), p. 226.

79. Dennis F. Thompson, "Excuses Officials Use: Moral Responsibility and the New York City Fiscal Crisis," in Fleishman et al., pp. 266–285.

80. Michael Lipsky, *Street-Level Bureaucracy* (New York: Russell Sage, 1980), pp. 81–156.

81. Gideon Sjorberg et al., "Bureaucracy and the Lower Class," in *Bureaucratic Power in National Politics,* ed. Francis E. Rourke (Boston: Little, Brown, 1978), pp. 42–43.

82. For a recent example of a governmental report that adopts criteria resembling those of personal responsibility, see the Commission of Inquiry into the Events at the Refugee Camps in Beirut, 1983, *Final Report,* authorized translation reprinted in the *Jerusalem Post,* Feb. 9, 1983, pp. 3–50.

3. Official Crime and Punishment

1. John Locke, *Second Treatise,* in *Two Treatises of Government,* ed. Peter Laslett (New York: Cambridge University Press, 1963), secs. 240–243.

2. The argument here is compatible with a wide range of theories of punishment. It makes only two assumptions about the nature of justifiable punishment. First, it assumes that a legitimate practice of punishment must grant certain rights to persons who are subject to its sanctions; we should not, for example, punish anyone who had not voluntarily committed an offense. Second, it assumes that punishment characteristically has an expressive function, signifying social attitudes of resentment and judgments of reprobation. No doubt a pure deterrence theory of punishment could not accept these assumptions, but more sophisticated theories, including those of some utilitarians, can accommodate them. The assumptions follow, respectively, H. L. A. Hart, *Punishment and Responsibility* (Oxford: Oxford University Press, 1968), pp. 1–27; and Joel Feinberg, *Doing and Deserving* (Princeton: Princeton University Press, 1970), pp. 95–118.

3. The best discussion is Christopher D. Stone, *Where the Law Ends: The Social Control of Corporate Behavior* (New York: Harper and Row, 1975).

4. E.g. "Developments in the Law—Corporate Crime," *Harvard Law Review,* 92 (April 1979), pp. 1241–1243; Note, "Structural Crime and Institutional Rehabilitation," *Yale Law Journal,* 89 (December 1979), pp. 357–360; Peter French, "The Corporation as Moral Person," *American Philosophical Quarterly,* 16 (July 1979), pp. 207–215; David T. Ozar, "The Moral Responsibility of Corporations," in *Ethical Issues in Business,* ed. Thomas Donaldson and Patricia H. Werhane (Englewood Cliffs, N.J.: Prentice-Hall, 1979), pp. 294–300; Thomas Donaldson, *Corporations and Morality* (Englewood Cliffs, N.J.: Prentice-Hall, 1982), pp. 18–34; and Albert J. Reiss, Jr., "Organizational Deviance," in *Corporate and Governmental Deviance,* ed. M. David Ermann and Richard J. Lundman (New York: Oxford University Press, 1978), esp. pp. 33–35. Christopher Stone defends aspects of the structuralist thesis, but ultimately emphasizes an approach that would punish violations of "standards" ("The Place of Enterprise Liability in the Control of Corporate Conduct," *Yale Law Journal,* 90 [November 1980], pp. 28–55). This latter approach seems consistent with

the notion of personal responsibility as developed here. In a later article, Stone continues to defend aspects of the structuralist position ("A comment on 'Criminal Responsibility in Government'," in *Criminal Justice,* Nomos XXVII, ed. J. Roland Pennock and John W. Chapman (New York and London: New York University Press, 1985], pp. 241–266). Stone's article is a comment on my essay in the same volume, which is substantively identical to this chapter. For some recent contributions to the structuralist position, see Peter A. French, *Collective and Corporate Responsibility* (New York: Columbia University Press, 1982), pp. 173–202; and Ronald Dworkin, *Law's Empire* (Cambridge, Mass.: Harvard University Press, 1986), pp. 167–175, 187.

5. See, e.g., John C. Coffee, Jr., " 'No Soul to Damn: No Body to Kick': An Unscandalized Inquiry into the Problem of Corporate Punishment," *Michigan Law Review,* 79 (January 1981), pp. 386–459.

6. Glanville Williams, *Criminal Law* (London: Stevens and Sons, 1961), p. 31. Also, cf. Hart, pp. 19–22, 143–146, 193–195; George P. Fletcher, *Rethinking Criminal Law* (Boston: Little, Brown, 1978), pp. 439–449; and Hyman Gross, *A Theory of Criminal Justice* (New York: Oxford University Press, 1979), pp. 22–23, 155–156, 167–169.

7. Edouard L. J. Laferrière, *Traité de la jurisdiction administrative* (Paris: Berger Levrault, 1887), p. 648. A survey of interpretations of the distinction is in H. Street, *Governmental Liability* (Cambridge: Cambridge University Press, 1953), pp. 58–62.

8. Cf. Edward D. Banfield, "Corruption as a Feature of Governmental Organization," *Journal of Law and Economics,* 18 (December 1975), pp. 587–588.

9. "Developments in the Law," p. 1259, n. 80.

10. U.S. v. Ehrlichman, 376 F. Supp. 29 (1974) at 35. For a critical discussion of the rationale of the court decisions reversing the conviction of the individuals who carried out Ehrlichman's orders, see Fletcher, pp. 756–758.

11. Williams, pp. 346–427; and Gross, pp. 160–161, 423–436.

12. Paul Finn, "Official Misconduct," *Criminal Law Journal,* 2 (December 1978), p. 315.

13. Testimony to the Knapp Commission investigating police corruption in New York City showed that officials at each level of the hierarchy up to the Mayor's assistant ignored or minimized reports of corruption for a long time before acting on them (*New York City Commission to Investigate Allegations of Police Corruption . . . Commission Report, December 26, 1972* [New York: George Braziller, 1973], pp. 5–7, 210–213).

14. A survey of some eight thousand federal employees indicated that 53 percent of those who observed corruption did not report it because they believed nothing would be done. See U.S. Merit Systems Protection Board, *Whistleblowing and the Federal Employee* (Washington, D.C.: Government Printing Office, 1981), pp. 27–31.

15. William J. Chambliss, "Vice, Corruption, Bureaucracy and Power," in

Official Deviance, ed. Jack Douglas and John Johnson (New York: Lippincott, 1977), pp. 316–325.

16. For an example, see Peter M. Blau, *The Dynamics of Bureaucracy,* rev. ed. (Chicago: University of Chicago Press, 1963), pp. 187–193.

17. Inspectors General Act (1978), 92 Stat. 1101 (Public Law 95–452); Civil Service Reform Act (1978), 92 Stat. 1111 (Public Law 95–454); Bernard Schwartz and H. W. R. Wade, *Legal Control of Government* (Oxford: Clarendon Press, 1972), pp. 64–75; U.S. Department of Labor, Office of the Inspector General, *Semiannual Report of the Inspector-General* (March 31, 1981), pp. 28–29, 35–36, 72, 94; and Jameson W. Doig et al., "Deterring Illegal Behavior in Complex Organizations" *Criminal Justice Ethics,* 3 (Winter/Spring, 1984), pp. 31–34, 44–45. On the difficulties of the use of the common law offense of misprision, see Williams, pp. 422–427.

18. George P. Fletcher, "The Theory of Criminal Negligence: A Comparative Analysis," *University of Pennsylvania Law Review,* 119 (January 1971), pp. 401–402.

19. Note, "Negligence and the General Problem of Criminal Responsibility," *Yale Law Journal,* 81 (April 1972), p. 979.

20. See *Model Penal Code,* sec. 2.02 in *Uniform Laws Annotated* (St. Paul, Minn.: West Publishing, 1974), pp. 464–467. The Supreme Court recently drew a similar boundary in the area of a constitutional right to compensation from negligent state officials: see Davidson v. Cannon 88 L. Ed. 2d 677 (1986).

21. Hart, pp. 136–157.

22. Hart, p. 152. Also see Gross, pp. 419–423. For criticism of Hart, see Richard A. Wasserstrom, "H. L. A. Hart and the Doctrines of *Mens Rea* and Criminal Responsibilty," *University of Chicago Law Review,* 35 (Autumn 1967), pp. 102–104.

23. Hart, pp. 148–149; Note, "Negligence . . ." p. 979; and *Model Penal Code,* sec. 2.02.

24. The definition of "gross" negligence is from William Prosser, *Handbook of the Law of Torts,* 4th ed. (St. Paul, Minn.: West Publishing, 1971), p. 183. The examples are discussed in Jethro K. Lieberman, *How the Government Breaks the Law* (New York: Stein and Day, 1972), pp. 194–195.

25. U.S. National Commission on Reform of Federal Criminal Laws, *Working Papers,* July 1970 (Washington, D.C.: Government Printing Office, 1970), vol. I, pp. 166, 186–187. But cf. U.S. v. Park, 421 U.S. 658 (1975).

26. Prosser, p. 180.

27. Finn, p. 317.

28. This psychological distance, as chapter 1 showed, should not be identified with moral distance (see pp. 19–21). The purpose of the stricter sanctions proposed in the text is in part to counter the false sense that psychological distance makes a moral difference.

29. Anthony Kenny, "Intention and Purpose in the Law," in *Essays in Legal Philosophy,* ed. R. S. Summers (Oxford: Blackwell, 1970), p. 158.

30. *Memoirs of the Prince de Talleyrand* (New York: Putnam, 1891), 3:216–217.

31. French, "The Corporation as Moral Person," p. 207; Donaldson, pp. 30, 124–126; Stone, "The Place of Enterprise Liability," p. 31, but cf. 21–28; "Developments in the Law," pp. 1247–1248. The so-called Chicago School favors corporate sanctions on efficiency grounds: see Richard Posner, *Economic Analysis of Law*, 2d ed. (Boston: Little, Brown, 1977), pp. 165–167.

32. U.S. federal courts have held that any employee may make a corporation liable, but most state law, the Model Penal Code, and British law usually require the involvement of a high-level official. See U.S. Senate, Judiciary Committee, *Criminal Code Reform Act of 1977*, 95th Cong., 1st sess. (Washington, D.C.: Government Printing Office, 1977), pp. 74–78; *Working Papers*, pp. 176–181; and W. Friedman, *Law in a Changing Society*, 2d ed. (New York: Columbia University Press, 1972), pp. 207–210.

33. Coffee, " 'No Soul to Damn'," pp. 390, 407–408; and Coffee, "Corporate Crime and Punishment," *American Criminal Law Review*, 17 (Spring 1980), pp. 419–476.

34. For a perceptive analysis of the meaning and implications of regarding organizations as moral agents, see Susan Wolf, "The Legal and Moral Responsibility of Organizations," in *Criminal Justice*, Nomos XXVII, ed. J. Roland Pennock and John W. Chapman (New York: New York University Press, 1985), pp. 267–286. Also, see French, *Collective and Corporate Responsibility*, pp. 94–111, 164–172.

35. "Developments in the Law," p. 1241; *Working Papers*, pp. 184–185; and Williams, pp. 856–857.

36. Gerhard O. W. Mueller, "Mens Rea and the Corporation," *University of Pittsburgh Law Review*, 19 (Fall 1957), pp. 28–35.

37. An example of such an effort is Donaldson, pp. 125–126.

38. Cf. French, "The Corporation as Moral Person," pp. 207–215; Feinberg, pp. 222–251; and D. E. Cooper, "Collective Responsibility," *Philosophy*, 43 (July 1968), pp. 258–268.

39. U.S. House, Committee on Interstate and Foreign Commerce, Subcommittee on Oversight and Investigations, *Hazardous Waste Disposal*, September 1979, 96th Cong., 1st sess. (Washington, D.C.: Government Printing Office, 1979), esp. p. 18.

40. Stone, "The Place of Enterprise Liability," pp. 26–27; and Coffee, " 'No Soul to Damn'," pp. 401–402. But see French, *Collective and Corporate Responsibility*, pp. 188–190.

41. "Structural Crime," p. 364; and Coffee, " 'No Soul to Damn'," pp. 413–424, 448–457.

42. Donaldson, pp. 18, 26, 209.

43. Cf. Robert Dahl, *Dilemmas of Pluralist Democracy* (New Haven: Yale University Press, 1982), pp. 194–202.

44. For recent views of the distinction between utility and rights, see Ronald Dworkin, *Taking Rights Seriously* (Cambridge, Mass.: Harvard University Press,

1978), pp. 184–205; T. M. Scanlon, "Rights, Goals, and Fairness," in *Public and Private Morality*, ed. Stuart Hampshire et al. (Cambridge: Cambridge University Press, 1978), pp. 93–111; and Samuel Scheffler, *The Rejection of Consequentialism* (Oxford: Clarendon Press, 1984).

45. Howard M. Friedman, "Some Reflections on the Corporation as Criminal Defendant," *Notre Dame Lawyer*, 55 (December 1979), pp. 188–201. More generally, see Arthur S. Miller, *The Modern Corporate State* (Westport, Conn.: Greenwood Press, 1976).

46. A helpful judicial discussion of the First Amendment rights of corporations is: First National Bank of Boston v. Bellotti, 55 L Ed 2nd 707 (1978).

47. Kawananakoa v. Polybank, 205 U.S. 834 at 836 (1907). This was a civil case involving a controversy over a foreclosure of a mortgage on a property, part of which had been conveyed to the territory of Hawaii, which claimed immunity from suit.

48. Thomas Hobbes, *Leviathan*, ed. M. Oakeshott (Oxford: Blackwell, 1946), p. 173, and generally chap. 26, pp. 172–189. Holmes also cited Jean Bodin's famous defense of absolute sovereignty (*Six Books of the Commonwealth*, trans. M. J. Tooley [New York: Barnes and Noble, 1967], chap. 8): "One may be subject to laws made by another, but it is impossible to bind oneself" (p. 28). For good measure, Holmes threw in two more absolutists— Sir John Eliot (1592–1632) and Baldus [presumably Baldo degli Ubaldi] (1327?–1400).

49. Hobbes, p. 121, and generally chap. 19, pp. 121–129.

50. On the problems of overdeterrence from *civil* liability, see Ronald Cass, "Damage Suits Against Public Officers," *University of Pennsylvania Law Review*, 129 (May 1981), pp. 1153–1160.

51. Nixon v. Fitzgerald, 50 LW 4797 at 4806, 4810 (1982). Cf. the treatment of judges: Stump v. Sparkman, 98 S. Ct. 1099 (1979).

52. Congressional Quarterly, *Congressional Ethics*, 2d ed. (Washington, D.C.: Congressional Quarterly, Inc., 1980), pp. 169–175.

53. Association of the Bar of the City of New York, Committee on Federal Legislation, *Remedies for Deprivation of Constitutional Rights by Federal Officers and Employees* (New York: Association of the Bar, 1979), p. 28; and Cass, p. 1167.

54. Cf. *U.S. Code*, Title 18, chaps. 11, 29, 93.

55. Virtually all the recent literature on civil liability warning of the danger of overdeterrence relies on analytic arguments (such as economic models) that are not subjected to empirical test. See Cass, pp. 1153–1160.

56. Peter H. Schuck, *Suing Government* (New Haven: Yale University Press, 1983), pp. 59–81.

57. J. Jackson Walter, "The Ethics in Government Act, Conflict of Interest Laws and Presidential Recruiting," *Public Administration Review*, 41 (November/December 1981), pp. 663–665.

58. Jeremy Bentham, *The Rationale of Reward* (London: Robert Heward, 1830), p. 59n.

59. U.S. v. Musto, U.S. District Court for New Jersey, No. 81–144, May 10, 1982 [court transcript]. Musto eventually lost both his Senate seat and the mayorship under a state statute that requires officials convicted of a crime to forfeit their office, though his wife was elected to serve on the city commission in his place, and his former legislative aide won his Senate seat.

60. Raoul Berger, *Impeachment: The Constitutional Problems* (Cambridge, Mass.: Harvard University Press, 1973), pp. 59–61, 63.

61. Institute for Social Research, *Organizational Assessments of the Effects of Civil Service Reform,* Second Year Report for U.S. Office of Personnel Management (Ann Arbor: University of Michigan, Institute for Social Research, 1981), pp. 22–23.

62. Locke, secs. 135–136, 139, 142, 153, 156, 160, 164, 210, 221–222, 239–240. Although recent scholars have neglected the idea of trusteeship in their interpretations of Locke, earlier commentators recognized its significance. See C. E. Vaughan, *Studies in the History of Political Philosophy* (Manchester: University of Manchester Press, 1939), pp. 143–157, and J. W. Gough, *John Locke's Political Philosophy* (Oxford: Clarendon Press, 1950), pp. 136–171.

63. Locke himself rejects the latter implication, holding that the executive's trust can be revoked only if the trustee violates terms of the trust. Locke, secs. 100, 149, 156, 164; but see sec. 153.

64. Meinhard v. Salmon, 249 N.Y. 458 at 464, 164 N.E. 545 at 546 (1928).

65. R. v. Bembridge, 22 State Tr. 1 (1783). See Finn, pp. 308–309.

66. R. v. Bembridge at 155–156.

67. John C. Coffee, Jr., "From Tort to Crime: Some Reflections on the Criminalization of Fiduciary Breaches and the Problematic Line between Law and Ethics," *American Criminal Law Review,* 19 (Fall 1981), pp. 117–172; and W. Robert Gray, "The Intangible Rights Doctrine and Political Corruption Prosecutions Under the Federal Mail Fraud Statute," *University of Chicago Law Review,* 47 (Spring 1980), pp. 562–587.

68. U.S. v. Isaacs, 493 F. 2d 1124 (7th Cir.), cert. denied, 417 U.S. 976 (1974) (Otto Kerner, Illinois); and U.S. v. Mandel, 591 F. 2d 1347 (4th Cir.), cert. denied, 100 S.C. + 1647 (1980) (Marvin Mandel, Maryland). Governor Blanton of Tennessee was convicted of mail fraud and other charges in June of 1981 (see the *New York Times,* June 10, 1981, A19). Federal bribery statutes could not be applied to the state officials in these cases.

69. U.S. v. Mandel, 1359–1360.

70. Ibid.

71. Coffee, "From Tort to Crime," pp. 132, 141, 142–148; and Gray, pp. 566, 587.

72. Coffee, "From Tort to Crime," pp. 64, 144.

73. Ibid., p. 143.

74. See U.S. v. Dotterweich, 320 U.S. 277 (1943); and U.S. v. Park, 421 U.S. 658 (1975).

75. Cf. Rule on "manipulative and deceptive devices" issued by the Securities and Exchange Commission in accord with the Securities and Exchange Act

of 1934 (17 *C.F.R.* 240.10b–5). The Freedom of Information Act does not penalize officials who fail to release requested information: see *J.U.S.C.*, sec. 552.

76. See, e.g., *U.S. Code,* secs. 1902–1908.

77. Note, "Constitutional Law—Equal Protection—Defendant Permitted to Prove Discriminatory Enforcement . . ." *Harvard Law Review,* 78 (February 1965), pp. 884–887.

78. Nixon v. Fitzgerald, at 4798–4799; and Harlow and Butterfield v. Fitzgerald, 50 LW 4815 at 4819 (1982).

79. U.S. Environmental Protection Agency, Office of Inspector General, Office of Investigations, Report of Investigation, *Thriftway Company* (File #1–82–045, April 5, 1982). My request, under the Freedom of Information Act, for a copy of this report was denied on the grounds that "the production of such records would interfere with enforcement proceedings" (letter to author from Richard M. Campbell, Assistant Inspector General, E.P.A., July 19, 1982). I obtained a copy from another source.

80. American Law Institute, *Model Penal Code,* Proposed official draft, July 30, 1962 (Philadelphia: American Law Institute, 1962), sec. 2.07, comment, p. 38.

81. *Working Papers,* p. 165.

82. Cain v. Doyle, 72 Commonwealth Law Reports 409 (1946). Friedman (*Law in a Changing Society,* pp. 210–212) gives the case a somewhat different interpretation by emphasizing that only one justice dismissed in principle the idea that the Crown can be liable for a criminal offense.

83. Cain v. Doyle at 424.

84. Ibid. at 433–434.

85. U.S. Senate, Committee on Judiciary, Subcommittee on Citizens and Shareholders Rights and Remedies, and Subcommittee on Administrative Practice and Procedure, *Joint Hearing on the Federal Tort Claims Act,* 95th Cong., 2d sess., 1978, p. 358.

86. Coffee, " 'No Soul to Damn'," pp. 448–457; and "Structural Crime and Institutional Rehabilitation," pp. 364–374.

87. On the importance of the stigma of conviction in organizational crime, see Association of the Bar, pp. 20–21; and Friedman, p. 211.

88. See, e.g., U.S. House, Committee on the Judiciary, *New Directions for Federal Involvement in Crime Control* (Washington, D.C.: Government Printing Office, 1977), pp. 62–67.

89. Emile Durkheim, *The Division of Labor in Society* (Glencoe, Ill.: Free Press, 1964), pp. 68–132.

90. A principled distinction between crime and tort, difficult enough to draw for ordinary offenses, becomes even more problematic for governmental crime. Most serious wrongs by officials could very well be seen as offenses against the whole society, and offenses that should be prosecuted by the government and deterred by penalties—traditionally some of the distinguishing characteristics of crimes. For a thoughtful recent analysis of the distinction, see Richard A. Epstein, "Crime and Tort: Old Wine in New Bottles," in *Assessing the Criminal,* ed.

Randy Barnett and John Hagel III (Cambridge, Mass.: Ballinger, 1977), pp. 231–257.

91. See Schuck, pp. 59–121; Cass, pp. 1110–1188; and Jerry L. Mashaw, "Civil Liability of Government Officers," *Law and Contemporary Problems*, 42 (Winter 1978), pp. 8–34.

92. Michael Walzer, *Regicide and Revolution* (Cambridge: Cambridge University Press, 1974), p. 77.

93. Otto Kirchheimer, *Political Justice* (Princeton: Princeton University Press, 1961), pp. 3–118, 419–431.

94. See, e.g., U.S. Senate, Select Committee on Ethics, *Investigation of Senator Harrison A. Williams, Jr.,* September 3, 1981 (Washington, D.C.: Government Printing Office, 1981). More generally, see *Congressional Ethics,* pp. 5–13. On the distinct question of whether the investigation should have been initiated at all, see pp. 26–27.

95. Nicholas D. Kristoff, "The Success of the 'President's Men'," *New York Times,* July 13, 1986, sec. 3, pp. 1, 8.

96. E.g., President Reagan nominated Maurice Stans to a position on the board of the Overseas Private Investment Corporation. Although acquitted of obstructing justice, Stans pleaded guilty to five misdemeanor charges of campaign contribution violations in the 1972 Nixon campaign (*New York Times,* Dec. 10, 1981, p. A30).

97. Kristoff, p. 8.

98. Thomas Powers, *The Man Who Kept Secrets: Richard Helms and the C.I.A.* (New York: Simon and Schuster, 1979), pp. 382–395. On the use of *nolo contendere,* see Marshall Clinard et al., *Illegal Corporate Behavior* (Washington, D.C.: Dept. of Justice, National Institute of Law Enforcement and Criminal Justice), pp. 207–208.

99. Powers, p. 391.

100. Samuel P. Huntington, *American Politics: The Promise of Disharmony* (Cambridge, Mass.: Harvard University Press, 1981), pp. 141–142, 188–189; Bruce Jennings, "The Institutionalization of Ethics in the U.S. Senate," *Hastings Center Report,* special supplement, 11 (February 1981), pp. 5–9; and John T. Elliff, *The Reform of F.B.I. Intelligence Operations* (Princeton: Princeton University Press, 1979), pp. 3–13.

101. Huntington, p. 189.

102. Bentham, pp. 21, 43.

103. Jean Jacques Rousseau, *Gouvernement de Pologne,* chap. 13 in *Political Writings,* ed. C. E. Vaughan (Oxford: Blackwell, 1962), 2:498n (my translation).

104. See Daniel Mornet, *Les origines intellectuelles de la Révolution Française, 1715–1787* (Paris: Collins, 1933), p. 263. More generally, see William J. Goode, *The Celebration of Heroes* (Berkeley: University of California Press, 1978), pp. 151–180, 313, 394.

105. Doig et al., p. 32.

106. Walter, p. 662.

4. Legislative Ethics

1. The problem of legislative ethics also differs in important respects from that of the other major kind of role-oriented ethics—the ethics of the professions, especially medicine and law. One difference is analogous to the difference between legislators and most public officials. Legislators do not control who will become legislators; they do not regulate the education and licensing of would-be members of their profession. A second difference is that the legislator's clients constitute a determinate class of individuals (constituents or voters) who have the power to prevent the legislator from practicing his or her calling.

2. See, e.g., U.S. Senate, Select Committee on Ethics, 96th Cong., 2d sess., *Revising the Senate Code of Official Conduct* (Washington, D.C.: Government Printing Office, 1981); U.S. House, Committee on Standards of Official Conduct, *Code of Official Conduct*, 96th Cong., 1st sess. (Washington, D.C.: Government Printing Office, 1976); and U.S. Senate, Special Committee on Official Conduct, Hearings, *Senate of Code of Official Conduct* (Washington, D.C.: Government Printing Office, 1977). More generally, see the Hastings Center, *The Ethics of Legislative Life* (Hastings-on-Hudson, N.Y., 1985), pp. 24–28.

3. Cf. Senator Howell Heflin's comments about the "chilling effect on the legislative function" that he believes results from broader codes of ethics (Select Committee on Ethics, *Revising the Senate Code of Official Conduct*, p. 86).

4. *The Federalist*, ed. Jacob Cooke (Middletown, Conn.: Wesleyan Univeristy Press, 1961), no. 57, pp. 586–587. Cf. Senator Robert S. Kerr's statement: "I represent the farmers of Oklahoma, although I have large farm interests. I represent the oil business in Oklahoma, because it is Oklahoma's second largest business, and I am in the oil business. I represent the financial institutions in Oklahoma, and I am interested in them, . . . and that is the reason they elect me. They don't want to send a man here who has no community of interest with them, because he wouldn't be worth a nickel to them" (*U.S. News and World Report*, Sept. 3, 1962, p. 86).

5. Robert S. Getz, *Congressional Ethics: The Conflict of Interest Issue* (Princeton, N.J.: Van Nostrand, 1966), pp. 57–58.

6. U.S. Senate Committee on Rules and Administrations, *Standing Rules of the Senate*, 96th Cong., 2d sess. (Washington, D.C.: Government Printing Office, 1980), Rule XXXVII, pp. 46–49.

7. For classic examples of trustee, delegate, and mixed theories, see respectively: Edmund Burke, *Burke's Politics*, ed. Ross Hoffman and Paul Levack (New York: Knopf, 1959), pp. 114–120; Jean Jacques Rousseau, *Gouvernement de Pologne*, chap. 7 in *Political Writings*, ed. C. E. Vaughan (Oxford: Blackwell, 1962), 2; and John Stuart Mill, *Considerations on Representative Government*, in *Collected Works*, ed. John M. Robson (Toronto: University of Toronto Press, 1977), 19, esp. chap. 12.

8. Richard F. Fenno, *Home Style: House Members in Their Districts* (Boston: Little, Brown, 1978), pp. 160–161. Broadly, it seems that citizens are more likely to view representatives as delegates while the representatives are more

likely to see themselves as trustees: see Roger H. Davidson, *The Role of the Congressman* (Indianapolis: Pegasus, 1969), p. 190.

9. At least half of the representatives in most studies are classified as "politicos," which combine both of the traditional roles and seem to include some other roles as well. See, e.g., Davidson, pp. 110–142; and John C. Wahlke et al., *The Legislative System* (New York: John Wiley, 1962), pp. 267–286.

10. Thomas E. Cavanaugh, "Role Orientations of House Members: The Process of Representation," paper prepared for the 1979 Annual Meetings of the American Political Science Association (Washington, D.C., 1979), p. 25. When members are asked more concrete questions about their roles, they are more likely to give informative responses: see, e.g., Kingdon, pp. 29–71, 110–176.

11. See pp. 161–165.

12. Neither is it adequate to suggest, as Hanna Pitkin does, that the choice of the role varies according to the substantive political theory held by the representative or the theorist of representation. According to Pitkin, the concepts of the delegate (who is completely bound by constituents) and the trustee (who acts consistently contrary to constituents) set the "limits of representation" (*The Concept of Representation* [Berkeley: University of California Press, 1967], p. 166). Within those limits, "there is room for a variety of views on what a good representative should and should not do." The views are chosen according to a "metapolitics," which embodies conceptions of human nature, human society, and political life. Contrary to what Pitkin seems to imply, however, the "variety of views" cannot supply the basis for a modified or mixed theory of the role of the representative. While maintaining the same metapolitical view, a representative sometimes acts as a delegate and sometimes as a trustee, and sometimes as both at the same time. A representative can—and, as will be argued later, should—adopt different roles depending not only on the issues under consideration, but, more importantly, on the state of the legislative process at any particular time.

13. Mill, chap. 12, p. 510.

14. John Rawls, *A Theory of Justice* (Cambridge, Mass.: Harvard University Press, 1971), p. 361. Cf. p. 227.

15. Ibid., p. 199.

16. Ibid.

17. In Rawls's ideal political process, the principles are embodied in a constitution, prior to any legislative deliberation (pp. 195–201). But since no actual constitution has yet enacted the principles, a society's choice of the principles must come later. Apart from a constitutional convention, the legislature seems to be the natural—perhaps in practice the only democratic—forum for making that choice.

18. As Rawls has interpreted and developed his theory, he has emphasized its political more than its philosophical foundations, and it has accordingly become less vulnerable to this objection. He argues that a satisfactory conception of justice "should be, so far as possible, independent of controversial philosoph-

ical and religious doctrines . . . we must apply the principle of toleration to philosophy itself" ("Justice as Fairness: Political, Not Metaphysical," *Philosophy and Public Affairs*, 14 [Summer 1985], pp. 223–251). Also see "The Idea of an Overlapping Consensus," *Oxford Journal of Legal Studies* 7 (Spring 1987), pp. 1–25. However, Rawls's theory still appears to exclude from the political agenda many widely accepted conceptions of justice (such as utilitarianism) and therefore still prevents legislators from acting on such conceptions in deliberations on public policy.

19. For an example, see Alan H. Goldman, *The Moral Foundations of Professional Ethics* (Totowa, N.J.: Rowman and Littlefield, 1980), pp. 24, 76, 88–89. Cf. Rawls's alternative description of the duty of representatives: "they must seek first to pass just and effective legislation . . . , and secondly, they must further their constituents' other interests insofar as these are consistent with justice" (p. 227).

20. Richard Fenno is one of the few political scientists who emphasizes the idea of representation as process: "Traditionally, representation has been treated mostly as a structural relationship in which the congruence between the policy preferences of the represented and the policy decisions of the representative is the measure of good representation . . . But we . . . shall have to consider a broader range of House member behavior" (p. 240). Yet Fenno concentrates on what occurs in the constituency more than on what happens in the legislature. Among recent political theorists, Hanna Pitkin is one of the few to notice the significance of process. In the last chapter of her book, Pitkin finally and then only briefly suggests that "perhaps it is a mistake to approach political representation too directly from the various individual-representation analogies" (pp. 221–222). Even so, she never specifies any standards by which we assess those patterns, and scarcely discusses the legislative process itself.

21. Rawls, pp. 130–136; and Kurt Baier, *The Moral Point of View* (Ithaca: Cornell University Press, 1958), pp. 187–213. For further references, see W. K. Frankena, "Recent Conceptions of Morality," in *Morality and the Language of Conduct*, ed. H. N. Castañeda and George Nakhnikian (Detroit: Wayne State University Press, 1965), pp. 1–24. For some doubts about the conception of morality implied by these requirements, see Bernard Williams, *Ethics and the Limits of Philosophy* (Cambridge, Mass.: Harvard University Press, 1985), pp. 71–119.

22. Although the requirements serve a purpose that runs partly contrary to the aim of Rawls's theory, their formulation is significantly indebted to his discussion of the "formal constraints of the concept of right" (pp. 131–135). The use of "generality" here may be understood as combining and simplifying Rawls's conditions of generality and universality. "Publicity" follows his condition of the same name, and "autonomy" is meant to capture the most relevant political elements in his requirement of "ordering" (namely, that the ordering of conflicting claims be independent of the capacity to intimidate and coerce). His condition of finality does not seem necessary or appropriate at the legislative

stage. Despite doubts about other aspects of this approach, Bernard Williams makes publicity, at least in the form of what he calls "transparency," an important ethical ideal (pp. 101–102, 108–110, 199–200).

23. For a lucid discussion and some references to the vast literature on the subject, see J. L. Mackie, *Ethics: Inventing Right and Wrong* (New York: Penguin, 1977), pp. 83–102.

24. Kant, *Critique of Practical Reason*, in *The Philosophy of Kant*, ed. C. J. Friedrich (New York: Random House, 1949), chap. 2, p. 259.

25. See, e.g., R. M. Hare, *Freedom and Reason* (Oxford: Clarendon Press, 1963), pp. 7–50.

26. Even at-large representatives elected nationally, as Mill imagined, stand in a special relationship to those who voted for them. See *Considerations on Representative Government*, chap. 7.

27. "Speech on the State of the Representation," in *Burke's Politics*, p. 229. But Burke also assumes that a representative owes some special obligation to those districts such as Birmingham, which do not yet have members but which share some of the same "interests" with the citizens of Bristol.

28. Jeremy Bentham, *Constitutional Code*, ed. Frederick Rosen and J. H. Burns (Oxford: Oxford University Press, 1983), 1:VI.1.A11, p. 44.

29. Ibid.

30. Fenno, p. 235.

31. E.g., Senator Lowell Weicker's resolution (S. Res. 109) (See Congressional Quarterly, *Congressional Ethics*, 2d ed. [Washington, D.C.: Congressional Quarterly, 1980], p. 57).

32. Edmund Burke, *Burke's Politics*, p. 116.

33. *Congressional Quarterly Weekly*, April 2, 1977, p. 592.

34. Compare Hobbes, *Leviathan*, ed. Michael Oakeshott (Oxford: Blackwell, 1946), pt. I, chap. 15, p. 103; and Kant, *The Metaphysical Elements of Justice*, ed. John Ladd (Indianapolis: Bobbs-Merrill, 1965), sec. 42, p. 71.

35. Fenno, pp. 167–168.

36. Ibid.

37. David Mayhew, *Congress: The Electoral Connection* (New Haven: Yale University Press, 1974), pp. 61–73.

38. Ibid., p. 53.

39. R. Douglas Arnold, *Congress and the Bureaucracy* (New Haven: Yale University Press, 1979), esp. pp. 207–215.

40. For the recent work, see Fenno, pp. 164–168; Morris Fiorina, *Retrospective Voting in American National Elections* (New Haven: Yale University Press, 1981), pp. 210–211; "The Decline of Collective Responsibility," *Daedalus*, 109 (Summer 1980), pp. 26, 39, 40; Kingdon, pp. 51–53; Mayhew, pp. 114–122; and James L. Sundquist, *The Decline and Resurgence of Congress* (Washington, D.C.: Brookings, 1981), pp. 451, 455. For earlier statements of the view, see Woodrow Wilson, *Congressional Government* (Boston: Houghton Mifflin, 1885), p. 318; and James Bryce, *Modern Democracies* (New York: Macmillan, 1921), 2:494–495.

41. Fiorina, "Decline of Collective Responsibility," pp. 39–44.

42. Ibid., pp. 28–39; and David E. Price, *Bringing Back the Parties* (Washington, D.C.: Congressional Quarterly Press, 1984), pp. 104–116.

43. More discussion of the kind of system of political parties that would be necessary to satisfy the requirements is in the article from which this essay is partly drawn: see Dennis F. Thompson, "Representatives in the Welfare State," in *Democracy and the Welfare State,* ed. Amy Gutmann (Princeton: Princeton University Press, forthcoming).

44. Kingdon, pp. 266–267.

45. Ibid., p. 267.

46. Immanuel Kant, *The Metaphysical Elements of Justice,* trans. John Ladd (Indianapolis: Bobbs-Merrill, 1965), pp. 15–16.

47. Rawls, p. 516.

48. Even Burke recognizes a special duty to party. He condemns any representative who "abandons the party in which he has long acted, and tells you it is because he proceeds upon his own judgment; and that he acts on the merits of the several measures as they arise; and that he is obliged to follow his own conscience" (*Burke's Politics,* p. 42). To accomplish anything in politics, Burke reminds us, representatives must act in concert, and that means that they must be open to influence from members of their party.

49. Except in a few specific areas (e.g., banking), the financial holdings of congressmen do not seem to incline them to cast roll-call votes that favor those interests. Indeed, in some areas the pattern is the opposite: congressmen who have large holdings in military industries vote for smaller defense budgets and less military construction. See Susan Welch and John G. Peters, "Private Interests and Public Interests: An Analysis of Congressional Voting and Personal Finance," paper prepared for the Annual Meeting of the American Political Science Association, Washington, D.C., August, 1980. As with campaign contributions, however, the distortions may not show up in roll-call votes but in the access that representatives grant to lobbyists or the response representatives give to information from various sources.

50. W. P. Welch, "Campaign Contribution and Legislative Voting: Milk Money and Dairy Price Supports," *Western Political Quarterly,* 35 (December 1982), pp. 478–495; and Henry Chappell, "Campaign Contributions and Voting on the Cargo Preference Bill," *Public Choice,* 36 (1981), pp. 310–312.

51. Ralph K. Winter, *Campaign Finance and Political Freedom* (Washington, D.C.: American Enterprise Institute, 1973), p. 5.

52. James F. Herndon, "Access, Record, and Competition as Influence on Interest Group Contributions to Congressional Campaigns," *Journal of Politics,* 44 (November 1982), pp. 996–1019. Also see Michael J. Malbin, "Of Mountains and Molehills: PACs, Campaigns, and Public Policy," in *Parties, Interest Groups and Campaign Finance Laws,* ed. Michael Malbin (Washington, D.C.: American Enterprise Institute, 1980), pp. 152–184.

53. E. E. Schattschneider, *The Semi-Sovereign People* (New York: Holt, Rinehart and Winston, 1960), p. 35.

54. Federal Election Commission, *Federal Election Campaign Finance Laws* (Washington, D.C.: Government Printing Office, 1980). Generally on the reform movement, see Gary Jacobson, *Money in Congressional Elections* (New Haven: Yale University Press, 1980), pp. 163–200.

55. Jacobson, pp. 193, 196.

56. Ibid., p. 194.

57. Morris Fiorina, *Congress—Keystone of the Washington Establishment* (New Haven: Yale University Press, 1977), pp. 12–13.

58. There is some evidence that a majority of citizens favor public funding of Congressional campaigns (Jacobson, p. 225).

59. For some detailed proposals, see Joel Fleishman and Pope McCorkle, "Level-Up Rather Than Level-Down: Toward a New Theory of Campaign Finance Reform," *Journal of Law and Politics,* 1 (Spring 1984), pp. 275–298; and Jacobson, pp. 201–226, 239–243.

60. Elizabeth Drew, *Politics and Money* (New York: Macmillan, 1983), p. 156.

61. Ibid.

62. Immanuel Kant, *Eternal Peace,* in *The Philosophy of Kant,* ed. Carl J. Friedrich (New York: Random House, 1949), p. 470. Also see Rawls, *Theory of Justice,* pp. 133, 177–182; and "Kantian Constructivism in Moral Theory," *Journal of Philosophy,* 77 (September 1980), pp. 535–543, 553–554.

63. Kant, *Eternal Peace,* p. 470. Rawls's interpretation of the condition of publicity is also hypothetical in the sense that it is meant to constrain choices in an "original position," in which the agents do not know their particular circumstances. But part of his rationale for the condition refers to its consequences for actual political life: publicly known principles "support the stability of social cooperation" (p. 133).

64. Cf. Mill, *Consideration on Representative Government,* p. 493. Sissela Bok emphasizes the importance of actual publicity as a criterion of morality: see *Lying* (New York: Random House, 1979), pp. 99–108; and *Secrets* (New York: Pantheon, 1982), pp. 112–115.

65. See pp. 127–129.

66. Arthur Maass, *Congress and the Common Good* (New York: Basic Books, 1983), pp. 62–66.

67. It was probably considerations such as these that led the framers of the Constitution to keep the proceedings of the Convention secret. Madison claimed that "no Constitution would ever have been adopted by the Convention if the debates had been public" (*The Records of the Federal Convention of 1787,* ed. Max Farrand [New Haven: Yale University Press, 1966], 2:33n; 3:28, 73, 368). But none of the delegates seriously proposed that the new Congress be granted the right to close its proceedings. In any case, many contemporaries condemned the Convention for its secrecy. At the same time that Jefferson called the Convention an "assembly of demi-gods," he criticized its secrecy: "I am sorry that they began their deliberations by so abominable a precedent as that of tying up

the tongues of their members. Nothing can justify this example but . . . ignorance of the value of public discussions" (*Records,* vol. 3, p. 76).

68. Cf. pp. 29–31.

69. Richard Rettig, "The Policy Debate on Patient Care Financing for Victims of End-State Renal Disease," *Law and Contemporary Problems,* 40 (Autumn 1976), p. 221.

70. Steven E. Rhoads, "How Much Should We Spend to Save a Life?" in *Valuing Life,* ed. Steven E. Rhoads (Boulder, Colo.: Westview Press, 1980), p. 304.

71. Ibid.

72. Robert Goodin, *Political Theory and Public Policy* (Chicago: University of Chicago Press, 1982), pp. 120–121.

73. Fiorina, "Decline of Collective Responsibility," p. 41.

74. Ibid., p. 44. Since Fiorina himself considers this an abuse, he clearly does not favor letting legislators "put the lid on" all controversial issues. Yet he does not indicate how we should distinguish the issues that should be suppressed from those that should not; nor does he suggest that such distinctions should be discussed in the legislature itself.

75. On these structural changes in Congress, see Lawrence Dodd, "Congress and the Quest for Power," in *Congress Reconsidered,* ed. Lawrence Dodd and Bruce Oppenheimer (New York: Praeger, 1977), pp. 269–307; and Dodd, "The Cycles of Legislative Change," in *Political Science,* ed. Herbert Weisberg (New York: Agathon Press, 1986), pp. 82–104.

76. Cf. Daniel Callahan et al., *Congress and the Media* (Hastings-on-Hudson, N.Y.: Hastings Center, 1985), p. 6.

77. Ibid., p. 15.

5. The Private Lives of Public Officials

1. On the expansion of privacy of citizens, see Franklyn S. Haiman, *Speech and Law in a Free Society* (Chicago: University of Chicago Press, 1981) pp. 61–86; "The Privacy Act of 1974," in *Privacy: A Public Concern,* ed. Kent S. Larsen (Washington, D.C.: Government Printing Office, 1975), pp. 162–178; David W. Ewing, *Freedom Inside the Organization* (New York: Dutton, 1977) pp. 133–138; and Alan F. Westin, *Privacy and Freedom* (New York: Atheneum, 1970), pp. 349–364, 367.

2. Congressional Quarterly, *Congressional Ethics,* 2d ed. (Washington, D.C.: Congressional Quarterly, Inc., 1980), pp. 48–57, 75–88, 182–203; and Brit Hume, "Now It Can Be Told . . . Or Can It?" *More,* April 1975, p. 6. On financial disclosure, see also Sandra Williams, *Conflict of Interest: The Ethical Dilemma in Politics* (Aldershot, Eng.: Gower, 1985), pp. 113–129.

3. Cf. Alfred Hill, "Defamation and the First Amendment," *Columbia Law Review,* 76 (December 1976), esp. pp. 1211–1218; Clifton O. Lawhorne, *Defamation and Public Officials* (Carbondale, Ill.: Southern Illinois University

Press, 1971), pp. 213–228, 265–283; and "The Supreme Court, 1984 Term: Leading Cases," *Harvard Law Review,* 99 (November 1985), pp. 212–223.

4. It may sometimes be useful to distinguish between permissive, obligatory, and superogatory disclosure by an official whose privacy is in question and by other persons who challenge his or her privacy. But the crucial issue is usually whether the official has an obligation to reveal aspects of what would otherwise be his or her private life, and whether other people have an obligation not to disclose or to consider these aspects.

5. Westin argues that organizations may claim confidentiality on the same grounds that individuals claim privacy (pp. 42–51). Although parallels exist (for example, privacy protects the liberty of both individuals and organizations), we would generally accept a claim of confidentiality by a governmental organization only if we accept the ends it is pursuing and if we regard confidentiality as a necessary means. A claim of individual privacy may be warranted whether or not we accept the ends the individual is pursuing.

6. One of the few general surveys of existing legal doctrine relating to the privacy of public officials is still Robert M. O'Neil, "The Private Lives of Public Employees," *Oregon Law Review,* 51 (Fall 1971), pp. 70–112. The most developed aspect of the law concerns the relation between libel of public figures and the First Amendment (see Hill, "Defamation," pp. 1206–1313), but since most cases have involved matters of public controversy, the question of how far the private life of a public official is protected has not been resolved. "Some aspects of the lives of even the most public men fall outside the area of matters of public or general concern" (Rosenbloom v. Metromedia, Inc., 402 U.S. at 48 [1971], but the court has not determined what those aspects are. Whatever they are, they would evidently be more protected than public aspects: see Gertz v. Robert Welch, Inc., 418 U.S. at 347 (1974).

7. See Note, "Application of the Constitutional Privacy Right to Exclusion and Dismissals from Public Employment," *Duke Law Journal,* 1973 (December 1973), pp. 1054–1055, 1062.

8. "Private" is often used in a broader way than "privacy," so that almost any activity can be private with respect to some wider group or with respect to the government (for example, a private club, a private company, the private sector). This broader notion of private, however, raises the question of the legitimate scope of intervention by the government and other members of society in the whole range of economic, social, and political activities. The distinctive claims made in behalf of a private life, though related to this general question, are better conceived as based specifically on individual privacy. For a careful analysis of the concept of the private, see W. L. Weinstein, "The Private and the Free: A Conceptual Inquiry," in *Privacy,* Nomos XIII, ed. Roland Pennock and John W. Chapman (New York: Atherton Press, 1971), pp. 27–55.

9. See Stanley I. Benn, "Privacy, Freedom, and Respect for Persons," in Pennock and Chapman, pp. 1–3; and Charles Fried, *An Anatomy of Values* (Cambridge, Mass.: Harvard University Press, 1970), p. 141.

10. Plato, *The Republic,* trans. Paul Shorey (Cambridge, Mass.: Harvard

University Press, 1963), 1:315, 475–483; 2:141 (419a, 464b–466d, 519e–520a).

11. See Hannah Arendt, *The Human Condition* (Chicago: University of Chicago Press, 1959), pp. 23–69.

12. Aristotle, *Politics,* trans. H. Rackham (Cambridge, Mass.: Harvard University Press, 1967), pp. 5–13, 85–89 (1252a–1253b, 1263a–1263b).

13. Jean Jacques Rousseau, *Gouvernement de Pologne,* in *Political Writings,* ed. C. E. Vaughan (Oxford: Blackwell, 1962), 2:491. In other moods, Rousseau celebrated the charms of private life; see, for example, *Emile,* trans. Barbara Foxley (London: Dent, 1963), pp. 438–439; and *Les Reveries du promeneur solitair,* ed. Raymond Bernex (Paris: Bordas, 1966).

14. G. W. F. Hegel, *Philosophy of Right,* trans. T. M. Knox (Oxford: Oxford University Press, 1962), p. 281, addition to paragraph 265; cf. pp. 155–158, paragraph 258. Hegel does not, however, ignore the ethical value of private life—for example, in the family (pp. 110–122, paragraphs 158–181).

15. See, for example, Marx, "On the Jewish Question," in *The Marx-Engels Reader,* ed. Robert Tucker, 2d ed. (New York: Norton, 1978), pp. 33–35.

16. For example, Thomas Hobbes, *Leviathan,* ed. Michael Oakeshott (New York: Macmillan, 1962), chaps. 13–14, 17, 21; and John Locke, *Two Treatises of Government,* ed. Peter Laslett (Cambridge: Cambridge University Pres, 1960) *Second Treatise,* chaps. 2, 7–9.

17. Kant's ideal state, traditionally liberal in many ways, nevertheless already removes from the private sphere the provision of welfare (*The Metaphysical Elements of Justice,* trans. John Ladd [Indianapolis: Bobbs-Merrill, 1965], p. 93). By the mid-nineteenth century, John Stuart Mill is struggling to maintain a private sphere merely for self-regarding action: *On Liberty,* in *Collected Works,* ed. John M. Robson (Toronto: University of Toronto Press, 1977), 18:276–291.

18. Here it is less important what those activities are than that some significant zone of privacy should be generally respected. Our broader interest in privacy, as Thomas Scanlon points out, is in "having a zone of privacy in which we can carry out our activities without . . . being continually alert for possible observers, listeners, etc." ("Thomson on Privacy," *Philosophy and Public Affairs,* 4 [Summer 1975], pp. 317–318).

19. It is important, however, to distinguish the instrumental value of privacy from the value of liberty or fairness, since they do not always coincide. If an activity is private, an official may claim not only that the activity should not be disclosed (a privacy claim), but also that if the activity is somehow disclosed, the official should not be harmed or disadvantaged because of it (a liberty or fairness claim). Generally, if an activity is protected by privacy, it would also be protected by a principle of liberty or fairness, but some activities that are not private (for example, political speech) may still enjoy protection under a principle of liberty or of fairness.

20. Fried, pp. 140–147; James Rachels, "Why Privacy Is Important," *Philosophy and Public Affairs,* 4 (Summer 1975), pp. 323–332; and Jeffrey H. Reiman, "Privacy, Intimacy and Personhood," *Philosophy and Public Affairs,* 6 (Fall 1976), pp. 26–44.

21. Benn, pp. 3–13.

22. Erving Goffman, *Stigma* (Englewood Cliffs, N.J.: Prentice-Hall, 1963), p. 71.

23. See Michael Walzer, "Political Action: The Problem of Dirty Hands," *Philosophy and Public Affairs,* 2 (Winter 1973), pp. 160–180.

24. On the forms and difficulties of symbolic representation, see Hanna Pitkin, *The Concept of Representation* (Berkeley: University of California Press, 1967), pp. 92–111.

25. Edward N. Stirewalt, "Yardsticks for Rulers," *Washington Post,* Aug. 1, 1976, p. C1.

26. J. D. Legge, *Sukarno: A Political Biography* (New York: Praeger, 1972), p. 336.

27. Paul A. Freund, "Privacy: One Concept or Many," in Pennock and Chapman, p. 187; and Westin, p. 375. Cf. Gertz v. Robert Welch, Inc., 418 U.S. at 344–345 (1974): "Public officials . . . have voluntarily exposed themselves to increased risk of injury from defamatory falsehoods concerning them."

28. William W. Van Alstyne, "The Demise of the Right-Privilege Distinction in Constitutional Law," *Harvard Law Review,* 81 (May 1968), pp. 1439–1464. Although more recently the Court has revived the distinction, it has still not used it to deny federal employees constitutional rights. See Rodney A. Smolla, "The Re-emergence of the Right-Privilege Distinction in Constitutional Law: The Price of Protesting Too Much," *Stanford Law Review,* 35 (November 1982), pp. 69–120.

29. For example, William L. Rivers and Wilbur Schramm, *Responsibility in Mass Communications,* rev. ed. (New York: Harper and Row, 1969), p. 164.

30. By issuing a thirty-three page statement on the Sarsfield's incident, the White House may have generated more publicity than would otherwise have occurred. Press Secretary Jody Powell claims, however, that the report was an "in-house memo," given only to reporters on request (letter to author, May 12, 1978).

31. *Washington Post,* Dec. 22, 1976, pp. A1, A5; (Dec. 23, 1976), pp. A1, A17; and (Dec. 24, 1976), pp. A2, A15. Compare the controversy over the relevance of Senator Robert Byrd's earlier association with the Ku Klux Klan to his possible nomination to the Supreme Court: see John L. Hulteng, *The Messenger's Motives* (Englewood Cliffs, N.J.: Prentice-Hall, 1976), p. 68.

32. Bruns v. Pomeyleau, 319 F. Supp. 58 (D. Md. 1970).

33. Benjamin R. Epstein and Arnold Forster, *The Radical Right* (New York: Random House, 1967), pp. 180–181.

34. See Pitkin, pp. 144–167.

35. See pp. 96–105.

36. See Arthur M. Schlesinger, Jr., *The Coming of the New Deal* (Boston: Houghton Mifflin, 1959), pp. 105–110; and Hume, p. 6.

37. Max Weber, "Bureaucracy," in *From Max Weber,* ed. H. H. Gerth and C. Wright Mills (New York: Oxford University Press, 1958), pp. 197, 199.

38. Hugh Heclo, *A Government of Strangers: Executive Politics in Washington* (Washington, D.C.: Brookings, 1977), pp. 34–83, 154–155.

39. Congressional Quarterly, pp. 75–88, 182–188. Also see pp. 97–99, 114–116.

40. *New York Times,* June 21, 1978, p. A18.

41. Ibid., Aug. 2, 1978, pp. A1, A14.

42. Congressional Quarterly, pp. 75–88.

43. David Arnold Anderson, "A Constitutional Right of Privacy Protects Personal Financial Affairs of Public Officials from Overbroad Disclosure Requirements," *Texas Law Review,* 49 (January 1971), pp. 346–356.

44. *Congressional Quarterly Weekly Report,* 32 (June 19, 1976), p. 1565.

45. Ibid., p. 1564; and *Washington Post,* Oct. 24, 1976, p. E1. All won their elections in the fall except Hays, who did not run, and Howe, who ran in a Mormon-dominated district in Utah. For cases involving lower-level officials, see O'Neil, pp. 75–76.

46. *Washington Post,* Oct. 26, 1976, p. A5.

47. U.S. House Committee on Post Office and Civil Service, Subcommittee on Manpower and Civil Service, *Final Report: Violations and Abuses of Merit Principles in Federal Employment* (Washington, D.C.: Government Printing Office, 1976), p. 163.

48. Marriages not on the public record may also be fair game. If President Kennedy had been previously married and the record suppressed, as was widely rumored, the press should have reported these facts. (See Tom Wicker, *On Press* [New York: Viking Press, 1978], p. 111.) Bigamous marriages are also properly a matter of public concern, not merely because they are illegal, but because they may demonstrate an officials' attitude toward a major social question. See "Newspaper Wins Bigamist Case," *The News Media and the Law,* 2 (April 1978), p. 25.

49. Susan Brownmiller, quoted in Deirdre Carmody, "Campaigns Raising Debates on Privacy," *New York Times,* Nov. 18, 1979, p. 31.

50. Hume, p. 8. Also see Rivers and Schramm, pp. 164, 169.

51. Alan L. Otten, "No More Tiptoeing," *Wall Street Journal,* Sept. 4, 1975, p. 10. The Judicial Council of the American Medical Association has held that a "physician may not discuss the patient's health condition with the press or the public without the patient's consent" (American Medical Association, *Opinions and Reports of the Judicial Council* [Chicago, 1977], sec. 6.09). Presumably, proposals for publicizing the results of physical exams would include a requirement that the candidate give his or her consent.

52. Lawrence K. Altman, "A Justice's Health: What Is Private?" *New York Times,* Jan. 4, 1983, p. A20.

53. For an example of such a proposal, see Harold D. Lasswell, *Power and Personality* (New York: Norton, 1948), pp. 186–187.

54. Theodore H. White, *The Making of the President 1972* (New York: Atheneum, 1973), pp. 263–275; and *Congressional Quarterly Weekly Report,* 30 (July 29, 1972), pp. 1851–1852.

55. *New York Times,* July 21, 1978, pp. A1, A8.

56. Even when such practices are against the law, they are not necessarily

removed from the private sphere, since it can be argued that the law should be changed.

57. Gary Wills, *The Kennedy Imprisonment* (Boston: Little, Brown, 1981), p. 37.

58. Theodore White, *The Making of the President 1964* (New York: Atheneum, 1965), pp. 367–372. That the first newspaper editors who learned of the Jenkins incident did not print it, and that Senator Goldwater did not make it an issue in the presidential campaign, suggest that many people believed that homosexual incidents of this sort should not be widely publicized (whether or not they should be grounds for dismissal).

59. Norton v. Macy, U.S. Court of Appeals, D.C. Circuit, 417 F.2d 1161 (1969). That Norton did not "openly flaunt" his homosexuality seemed to be a factor in the court's decision. A later case upheld the dismissal of a homosexual public employee, evidently because he publicly pursued an "activist role in implementing his unconventional beliefs" (McConnell v. Anderson, U.S. Court of Appeals, Eighth Circuit, 451 F.2d 193 [1971], cert. denied, 405 U.S. 1046 [1972]. Generally, the courts have not sufficiently distinguished between the public practice of the homosexual activity itself, and the public advocacy or public knowledge of the activity; the former may sometimes be relevant but the latter seldom should be.

60. John Stuart Mill, *On Liberty,* pp. 223–224, 280–283.

61. For a sample of the controversy since Mill, see Richard Wasserstrom, ed., *Morality and the Law* (Belmont, Calif.: Wadsworth, 1971); Thomas C. Grey, *The Legal Enforcement of Morality* (New York: Knopf, 1983), pp. 3–35; and Joel Feinberg, *Harm to Others* (New York: Oxford University Press, 1984), pp. 65–104.

62. For example, Ronald Dworkin, "Lord Devlin and the Enforcement of Morals," in *Morality and the Law,* ed. Richard Wasserstrom (Belmont, Calif.: Wadsworth, 1971), pp. 55–72.

63. It is therefore too simple to assert, as Tom Wicker does, that "a reporter should write and a newspaper should print what they know" (pp. 111–112). On his view, even if a reporter believes for good reason that, say, an extramarital affair of a politician is not any business of the public, he should still report it. The reporter, Wicker maintains, has no right to impose on readers his moral judgment about what is relevant to public duty; moreover, if one paper declines to report the story, some other paper will publish it anyhow. But on many topics the press already exercise discretion about what is relevant, and in principle they could do so with respect to private lives too. The decision to publish information about private lives is no more morally neutral than the decision not to publish it. If papers that disregard the legitimate rights of privacy thereby gain a significant competitive advantage (a consequence more feared than proved), they could be made subject to some professional or perhaps even legal sanctions.

64. Brooks Jackson, "John Fedders of SEC is Pummeled by Legal and Personal Problems," *Wall Street Journal,* Feb. 25, 1985, p. 1.

65. Stuart Taylor, Jr., "Life in the Spotlight: Agony of Getting Burned," *New York Times,* Feb. 27, 1985, p. 24.

66. See the comments by editors of the *New York Times* and the *Washington Post* (ibid.).

67. J. Anthony Lukas, *Nightmare: The Underside of the Nixon Years* (New York: Viking, 1976), pp. 126–138, 218–219.

68. Rivers and Schramm, p. 166.

69. Lukas, pp. 66–84.

70. "Kissinger's Threat to Resign—June 11, 1974," in *Historic Documents of 1974* (Washington, D.C.: Congressional Quarterly, Inc., 1975), p. 495.

71. But see Rivers and Schramm, pp. 165–166.

72. Ewing, p. 130.

73. See Taylor Branch, "The Odd Couple," in *Blowing the Whistle,* ed. Charles Peters and Taylor Branch (New York: Praeger, 1972), pp. 222–245; and Committee on the Judiciary. Subcommittee to Investigate the Administration of the Internal Security Act and Other Internal Security Laws, *State Department Security, 1963–1965* (Washington, D.C.: Government Printing Office, 1967).

74. For some cases involving seizure of personal effects from employee's lockers and trunks, see O'Neil, p. 97.

75. Alan F. Westin, "Privacy and Personnel Records," *The Civil Liberties Review,* 4 (January/February, 1978), p. 30.

76. Westin, *Privacy and Freedom,* pp. 259–268.

77. U.S. Congress, Senate Committee on the Judiciary, Subcommittee on Constitutional Rights, *Privacy, Polygraphs, and Employment* (Washington, D.C.: Government Printing Office, 1974), p. 5.

78. "Use of Polygraph in Personal Investigation of Competitive Service Applicants and Appointees to Competitive Service Positions," in *Federal Personnel Manual* (Washington, D.C.: Government Printing Office, January 1972), chap. 736, appendix D; U.S. Congress, House Committee on Armed Services, Subcommittee on Investigations, 98th Cong., 2d sess. (1984), *Hearings on H.R. 4681, Relating to the Administration of Polygraph Examinations and Prepublication Review Requirements by Federal Agencies;* Note, "The Presidential Polygraph Order and the Fourth Amendment: Subjecting Federal Employees to Warrantless Searches," *Cornell Law Review,* 69 (April 1984), pp. 896–924.

79. "The Morley Affair" (Cambridge, Mass.: Kennedy School of Government, Harvard University, 1976). The text follows the more widely used version of this case, which was edited and revised by Peter Brown and Paul Vernier at the University of Maryland Center for Philosophy and Public Policy, and distributed by the Intercollegiate Case Clearing House at Boston University. The original versions of this case ("The Deagle Affair") were prepared at the Kennedy School by Diana Gordon and Jan Downing, and used the real names of the participants.

80. An analogous dilemma confronts a candidate for a federal administrative post when he is subject to a "political affiliation check." It may be to his

237

advantage to have investigators go beyond his public party registration and scrutinize his general "political concepts and philosophies." But often this is done without the candidate's knowledge and for supposedly nonpolitical career positions. See House Subcommittee on Manpower and Civil Service, *Final Report: Violations and Abuses of Merit Principles*, pp. 190–192, 201, 204.

81. *New York Times*, Dec. 20, 1985, p. A1; Dec. 21, 1985, p. A1; and Dec. 22, 1985, sec. IV, p.1.

82. See U.S. Executive Order, "Drug-Free Federal Workplace," Sept. 15, 1986; and Capua v. City of Plainfield, Tompkins v. City of Plainfield, U.S. District Court, New Jersey, Civil Action no. 86–2992, Sept. 18, 1986.

83. See Ewing, pp. 136–138; and Westin, "Privacy and Personnel Records," pp. 28–34.

84. Robert G. Vaughan, *The Spoiled System* (New York: Charterhouse, 1975), pp. 308–309.

6. Paternalistic Power

1. So John Locke long ago recognized: There is "reason to ask, Whether [power over children] might not be more properly called *Parental Power*. For whatever obligation Nature and the right of Generation lays on Children, it must certainly bind them equal to both the concurrent Causes of it" (*Two Treatises of Government*, ed. Peter Laslett [New York: Cambridge University Press, 1963], *Second Treatise*, secs. 52–53). But Locke quickly abandoned his effort to change the "names that have obtained in the World" (see secs. 69, 170), just as have most modern liberals, reminding us how much still remains to be done in understanding differences in power between the sexes.

2. John Stuart Mill, *On Liberty*, in *Collected Works*, ed. John Robson (Toronto: University of Toronto Press, 1977), 18:223–224, 280, 282.

3. Ibid., p. 294.

4. This definition is consistent with those proposed by philosophers who regard paternalism as involving a constraint on liberty, though they would disagree with many of the implications drawn in the analysis that follows. See especially Gerald Dworkin, "Paternalism," *Morality and the Law*, ed. Richard Wasserstrom (Belmont, Calif.: Wadsworth, 1971), p. 108; and Joel Feinberg, "Legal Paternalism," *Canadian Journal of Philosophy*, 1 (September 1971), p. 105. Also see Rosemary Carter, "Justifying Paternalism," *Canadian Journal of Philosophy*, 7 (March 1977), p. 133; Jeffrie G. Murphy, "Incompetence and Paternalism," *Archiv fur Rechts- und Sozial-philosophie*, 60 (1974), p. 465; and Albert Weale, "Paternalism and Social Policy," *Journal of Social Policy*, 7 (April 1978), pp. 160, 163. Two recent discussions of paternalism are John Kleinig, *Paternalism* (Totowa, N.J.: Rowman and Allanheld, 1984), pp. 3–17; and Donald VanDeVeer, *Paternalistic Intervention: The Moral Bounds of Benevolence* (Princeton, N.J.: Princeton University Press, 1986), pp. 16–28. Both of these valuable books appeared after the earlier version of this chapter had been published.

5. See Amy Gutmann, "Children, Paternalism and Education," *Philosophy and Public Affairs,* 9 (Summer 1980), pp. 338–358; and Francis Schrag, "The Child in the Moral Order," *Philosophy,* 2 (April 1977), pp. 167–177.

6. Further complications in the locus of paternalism arise when one state acts paternalistically toward another, and especially where each subscribes to fundamentally different ethical and political principles, or stands at different levels of development. Despite Mill's refusal to apply the principle of liberty to persons who live in "those backward states of society in which the race itself may be considered as in its nonage" (*On Liberty,* p. 224), some recent writers on political development argue that many programs in developing nations (such as "consciousness raising") constitute unjustified forms of paternalism. See, for example, Peter L. Berger, *Pyramids of Sacrifice: Political Ethics and Social Change* (New York: Basic Books, 1974), pp. 111–131. More generally on "political paternalism," see Kleinig, pp. 169–174.

7. Cf. Mill, *Principles of Political Economy,* in *Collected Works,* ed. John Robson (Toronto: University of Toronto Press, 1977), 3:956.

8. Bernard Gert and Charles M. Culver, "Paternalistic Behavior," *Philosophy and Public Affairs,* 6 (1976), p. 49. For an even broader definition, see N. Fotion, "Paternalism," *Ethics,* 89 (Fall 1979) pp. 194–198.

9. In a comment on an earlier version of this chapter, Gerald Dworkin, though agreeing that paternalism involves imposing a conception of good on someone who does not want to be so treated, objects that paternalism should not always be regarded as a restriction of liberty. However, to say that you impose something on someone is normally to imply that you restrict or constrain his actions in some way, and that he is therefore less at liberty to do what he wishes to do, or would have wished to do. A similar reply applies to Kleinig's objection to including liberty in the definition of paternalism (see Kleinig, pp. 5–14). VanDeVeer (pp. 26–27) is probably correct—at least in many cases involving only individuals—that it is not crucial to settle this question. But in cases involving collectivities (including individuals acting in professional roles) the broader definition may lead us astray by implying that paternalism does not restrict liberty, and does not therefore involve any constraint or exercise of power.

10. But see Sissela Bok, *Lying* (New York: Random House, 1979), pp. 19–23.

11. Cf. Allen Buchanan, "Medical Paternalism," *Philosophy and Public Affairs,* 8 (Summer 1978), pp. 371–372.

12. Cf. Hillel Steiner, "Liberty," *Journal of Medical Ethics,* 2 (September 1976), pp. 147–148.

13. H. L. A. Hart, *Law, Liberty and Morality* (London: Oxford University Press, 1963), pp. 30–33. See also C. L. Ten, "Paternalism and Morality," *Ratio,* 13 (June 1971), pp. 56–66.

14. See, e.g., Feinberg, p. 106n. Mill defends the distinction in *On Liberty,* pp. 223–224, 276–277, 292, and esp. 280 (where he anticipates the standard objection to the distinction).

15. Some writers argue that much so-called paternalistic legislation can be

justified on grounds of harm to others: e.g., Donald Regan, "Justification for Paternalism," in *The Limits of Law,* Nomos XV, ed. J. Roland Pennock and John W. Chapman (New York: New York University Press, 1974), pp. 189–210. However, when courts have followed this approach, they have often ended up construing "harm to others" so broadly that individual liberty begins to disappear (as when they count any diminution in an individual's economic productivity as a harm to society): see the Comment, "Limiting the State's Police Power: Judicial Reaction to John Stuart Mill," *University of Chicago Law Review,* 37 (Spring 1970), esp. pp. 620–622. Mill himself objects strongly to such an approach (*On Liberty,* p. 280).

16. See Feinberg, pp. 105–106.

17. Michael Bayles, "Criminal Paternalism," in Pennock and Chapman, pp. 179–188; and Tom L. Beauchamp, "Paternalism and Biochemical Control," *Monist,* 60 (January 1977), pp. 62–80.

18. Mill, *On Liberty,* p. 294.

19. For related versions of necessary and sufficient conditions, see Carter, pp. 136–138; Dworkin, pp. 122–126; Feinberg, p. 113; John D. Hodson, "The Principle of Paternalism," *American Philosophical Quarterly,* 14 (January 1977), pp. 62–65; Murphy, p. 479; John Rawls, *A Theory of Justice* (Cambridge, Mass.: Harvard University Press, 1971), pp. 248–250; Ten, p. 65; and Weale, pp. 170–172. For a different approach, see Bernard Gert and Charles M. Culver, "The Justification of Paternalism," *Ethics,* 89 (January 1979), pp. 199–210.

20. For a survey and critique of consent-based arguments, see VanDeVeer, pp. 45–94; also see Kleinig, pp. 55–67. Kleinig believes that the most promising justification is an "argument from personal integrity" (pp. 67–73), but in presenting it he implicitly relies on a form of consent in at least one of his "limiting maxims" (p. 75).

21. An excellent short discussion of the relation between such impairments and paternalism is in Murphy, pp. 468–475.

22. Some theorists distinguish "strong paternalism" (restriction of voluntary choice) from "weak paternalism" (restriction of nonvoluntary choice), and hold that only the latter is justifiable. This view is consistent with the analysis here only if one adopts, as Feinberg does (pp. 110–111, 124), a broad concept of voluntary choice corresponding to the notion of deliberate choice.

23. Notice that even "negative" paternalism, which aims to prevent only bad consequences, has different implications, depending on whether the purpose is prevention of harm, or of suffering; the former might prohibit euthanasia, while the latter would permit or even require it (Christine Pierce, "Hart on Paternalism," *Analysis,* 35 [June 1975], p. 206).

24. Cf. Mill, *On Liberty,* pp. 229–300; and *Principles of Political Economy,* pp. 953–954.

25. These wills are not without problems: see Marc I. Steinberg, "The California Natural Death Act: A Failure to Provide for Adequate Patient Safeguards and Individual Autonomy," *Connecticut Law Review,* 8 (Winter 1977), pp. 203–220.

26. It is difficult to avoid appealing to some kind of theory of the good, as Hodson (pp. 63–68) discovers. After criticizing other theorists for in effect using such a theory, he proposes a concept of a "hypothetical unencumbered decision," which in some cases permits an appeal to a "rational will." See also Dworkin, pp. 121–122; Murphy, pp. 481–483; and Weale, pp. 171–172.

27. Rawls, p. 249.

28. Ibid., pp. 62, 90–93, 395–452.

29. Thomas Nagel, "Rawls on Justice," in *Reading Rawls,* ed. Norman Daniels (New York: Basic Books, 1975), pp. 9–10.

30. George Lukács, *History and Class Consciousness,* trans. Rodney Livingstone (London: Merlin Press, 1971), pp. 51–54, 64–65, 72. The classical sources are Karl Marx and Friedrich Engels, "The German Ideology," in *The Marx-Engels Reader,* ed. Robert Tucker, 2d ed. (New York: W. W. Norton, 1978), pp. 154–155, 163–175.

31. Lukács, p. 52.

32. For the conditions that such institutions should satisfy, see pp. 105–122.

33. Ernest Greenwood, "The Elements of Professionalization," in *Professionalization,* ed. H. M. Vollmer and D. L. Mills (Englewood Cliffs, N.J.: Prentice-Hall, 1966), pp. 12–16; Magali Sarfatti Larson, *The Rise of Professionalism* (Berkeley: University of California Press, 1977), p. x; and Richard Wasserstrom, "Lawyers as Professionals: Some Moral Issues," *Human Rights,* 5 (Fall 1975), p. 1.

34. Greenwood, p. 12; Everett C. Hughes, "Professions," in *The Professions in America,* ed. Kenneth Lynn et al. (Boston: Beacon Press, 1963), pp. 2–3; and Larson, pp. 220–225.

35. Bernard Barber, "Compassion in Medicine: Toward New Definitions and New Institutions," *New England Journal of Medicine,* 295 (Oct. 21, 1976), pp. 939–940; and Note, "Restructuring Informed Consent: Legal Therapy for the Doctor-Patient Relationship," *Yale Law Journal,* 79 (July 1970), pp. 1535–1537.

36. See, e.g., Buchanan, pp. 370–387; VanDeVeer, pp. 197–203; and Edmund Pellegrino, "Medical Ethics, Education, and the Physician's Image," *Journal of the American Medical Association,* 235 (March 6, 1976), pp. 1043–1044.

37. On truth-telling in medicine, see Bok, pp. 220–241, and the essays in Stanley Joel Reiser et al., *Ethics in Medicine* (Cambridge, Mass.: MIT Press, 1977), pp. 201–240.

38. Roger D. Masters, "Is Contract an Adequate Basis for Medical Ethics?" *Hastings Center Report,* 6 (December 1975), pp. 26–28; and William F. May, "Code, Covenant, Contract, or Philanthropy," *Hastings Center Report,* 6 (December 1975), p. 36. Cf. Robert M. Veatch, *A Theory of Medical Ethics* (New York: Basic Books, 1981), pp. 79–107, 193–94.

39. C. L. Peck and N. J. King, "Compliance and the Doctor-Patient Relationship," *Drugs,* 30 (July 1985), pp. 78–84; and Vivian Nagy and Gary Wolfe, "Cognitive Predictors of Compliance in Chronic Disease Patients," *Medical Care,* 22 (October 1984), pp. 912–921. But see Steve Wartman et al., "Patient Un-

derstanding and Satisfaction as Predictors of Compliance," *Medical Care,* 21 (September 1983), pp. 886–891.

40. George J. Annas and Joseph M. Healey, "The Patient Rights Advocate: Redefining the Doctor-Patient Relationship in the Hospital Context," *Vanderbilt Law Review,* 27 (March 1974), pp. 243–269; Joseph Margolis, "Conceptual Aspects of a Patient's Bill of Rights," *Journal of Value Inquiry,* 12 (Summer 1978), pp. 126–135; and Veatch, pp. 193–194, 327–330.

41. Note, "Restructuring Informed Consent," pp. 1555–1556; and Benjamin Freedman, "A Moral Theory of Informed Consent," *Hastings Center Report,* 6 (December 1975), pp. 34–36.

42. David Luban, "Paternalism and the Legal Profession," *Wisconsin Law Review,* 1981 (1981), pp. 454–493; Warren Lehman, "The Pursuit of a Client's Interest," *Michigan Law Review,* 77 (April 1979), pp. 1080–1081; William H. Simon, "Visions of Practice in Legal Thought," *Stanford Law Review,* 36 (January 1984), pp. 469–508; Mark Spiegel, "Lawyering and Client Decisionmaking: Informed Consent and the Legal Profession," *University of Pennsylvania Law Review,* 128 (November 1979), pp. 73–112; and Wasserstrom, pp. 16–22. Cf. Jones v. Barnes 463 U.S. 745 (1983).

43. Douglas Rosenthal, *Lawyer and Client* (New York: Russell Sage Foundation, 1974), p. 162.

44. Mirta T. Mulhare, "How to Handle a New Client," *The Practical Lawyer,* 21 (October 1975), pp. 20, 22.

45. See Marvin E. Frankel, "Experiments in Serving the Indigent," *American Bar Association Journal,* 51 (May 1965), p. 461. A more radical view of the practice of poverty law is Stephen Wexler, "Practicing Law for Poor People," *Yale Law Journal,* 79 (May 1970), pp. 1049–1067.

46. See Wasserstrom, p. 14. Cf. Charles Fried, "The Lawyer as Friend: The Moral Foundations of the Lawyer-Client Relation," *Yale Law Journal,* 85 (July 1976), p. 1066n.

47. Rosenthal, pp. 148–149.

48. Ibid., pp. 153, 156–157; and Wasserstrom, pp. 23–24. On the use of clinical education to combat paternalism in the legal profession, see Robert Condlin, "The Moral Failure of Clinical Legal Education," in *The Good Lawyer: Lawyers' Roles and Lawyers' Ethics,* ed. David Luban (Totowa, N.J.: Rowman and Allanheld, 1983), pp. 319–324.

49. Lester J. Mazor, "Power and Responsibility in the Attorney-Client Relation," *Stanford Law Review,* 20 (June 1968), pp. 1138–1139.

50. Ira Glasser, "Prisoners of Benevolence: Power Versus Liberty in the Welfare State," in *Doing Good: The Limits of Benevolence,* ed. Willard Gaylin et al. (New York: Pantheon Books, 1978), pp. 107–108, 118–119; Marie R. Haug and Marvin B. Sussman, "Professional Autonomy and the Revolt of the Client," *Social Problems,* 71 (Fall 1969), pp. 156–159; and Frederic G. Reamer, "The Concept of Paternalism in Social Work," *Social Services Review,* 57 (June 1983), pp. 254–271.

51. Nina Toren, "The Structure of Social Casework and Behavioral Change," *Journal of Social Policy*, 3 (October 1974), p. 343.

52. Joseph E. Paull, "Recipients Aroused: The New Welfare Rights Movement," *Social Work*, 12 (April 1967), pp. 101–106; Ad Hoc Committee on Advocacy, "The Social Worker as Advocate," *Social Work*, 14 (April 1969), pp. 19–20; and Glasser, pp. 127–145.

53. Alfred H. Katz, "Self-Help Organizations and Volunteer Participation in Social Welfare," *Social Work*, 15 (January 1970), pp. 52–53; and Anthony J. Vattano, "Power to the People: Self-Help Groups," *Social Work*, 17 (July 1972), pp. 13–24.

54. Irving Piliavin, "Restructuring the Provision of Social Services," *Social Work*, 13 (January 1968), pp. 36–37.

55. On social workers, see Willard Gaylin, "In the Beginning: Helpless and Dependent," in Gaylin et al., pp. 32–33; and Donald Feldstein, "Do We Need Professions in our Society? Professionalization versus Consumerism," *Social Work*, 16 (October 1971), pp. 5–11.

56. E.g., the American Bar Association's Code of Professional Responsibility gives the attorney a right to control "certain areas of legal representation not affecting the merits of the cause or substantially prejudicing the rights of a client" (EC 7–7). Also see Spiegel, pp. 77, 82–85.

57. Robert M. Byrn, "Compulsory Lifesaving Treatment for the Competent Adult," *Fordham Law Review*, 44 (October 1975), pp. 1–36; Alan Meisel, "The 'Exceptions' to the Informed Consent Doctrine: Striking a Balance between Competing Values in Medical Decision-Making," *Wisconsin Law Review*, 1979 (1979), pp. 413–488; Note, "Informed Consent and the Dying Patient," *Yale Law Journal*, 83 (July 1974), pp. 1632–1664; and Marjorie Maguire Shultz, "From Informed Consent to Patient Choice: A New Protected Interest," *Yale Law Journal*, 95 (December 1985), pp. 219–299.

58. The question of compulsory sterilization illustrates poignantly some of the difficulties in distinguishing the paternalistic justification for intervention from one based on avoiding harm to others and to society. See "Sterilization of the Retarded: In Whose Interest?" *Hastings Center Report*, 9 (June 1978), pp. 29–41.

59. Byrn, pp. 20–35.

60. On the ethics of administering placebos, see the articles in Reiser et al., pp. 240–252; and Bok, pp. 61–68, 97.

61. VanDeVeer, pp. 248–260. Also see Byrn, p. 8; and Note, "Informed Consent," pp. 1649–1650.

62. See the articles in Bonnie Steinbeck, ed., *Killing and Letting Die* (Englewood Cliffs, N.J.: Prentice-Hall, 1980). Also see Charles Fried, *Right and Wrong* (Cambridge, Mass.: Harvard University Press, 1978), pp. 201–204, 206–207, and citations therein.

63. See Buchanan, pp. 387–388.

64. For some of the difficult theoretical and practical problems in specifying

criteria for noncompetency, see Meisel, pp. 439–453; John Moskop, "Competence, Paternalism, and Public Policy for Mentally Retarded People," *Theoretical Medicine,* 4 (October 1983), pp. 291–302; and Richard Momeyer, "Medical Decisions Concerning Noncompetent Patients," *Theoretical Medicine,* 4 (October 1983), pp. 275–290. For a philosophical analysis, see VanDeVeer, pp. 345–421.

65. Ruth Faden and Alan Faden, "False Belief and the Refusal of Medical Treatment," *Journal of Medical Ethics,* 3 (September 1977), pp. 133–136. Also see Kleinig, pp. 133–134.

66. For a proposal that would establish such a standard in the law, see Note, "Informed Consent," p. 1642.

67. In re Quinlan, 70 N.J. 10, 355 A. 2d 647 at 671 ff. (1976). See also Harold L. Hirsch and Richard E. Donovan, "The Right to Die: Medico-Legal Implications of *In Re Quinlan,*" *Rutgers Law Review,* 30 (Winter 1977), pp. 267–303; and the articles in "The Quinlan Decision: Five Commentaries," *Hastings Center Report,* 7 (February 1976), pp. 8–19.

68. Cf. the cases in Byrn, pp. 10–13; and Reiser et al., pp. 199–200.

69. For a survey and analysis, see the various articles in the special section, "Ethics Committees: How Are They Doing?" *Hastings Center Report,* 16 (June 1986), pp. 19–24.

70. Generally, see Richard C. Allen, Alyce Z. Ferster, and Henry Weihofen, *Mental Impairment and Legal Incompetency* (Englewood Cliffs, N.J.: Prentice-Hall, 1968), pp. 70–112; Richard V. Mackay, *Law of Guardianships,* 3d ed. (Dobbs Ferry, N.Y.: Oceana Publications, 1980), pp. 1–23, 65–69; and Note, "The Disguised Oppression of Involuntary Guardianship: Have the Elderly Freedom to Spend?" *Yale Law Journal,* 73 (March 1964), pp. 676–692. Similar issues arise when governmental agencies (the Social Security Administration or the Veterans Administration) appoint a "representative payee" or "fiduciary" to receive someone's payments (see Allen et al., pp. 114–142). On closely related issues also see Suzanne Williams, "The Role of the Judiciary and the Legislature in Decisionmaking on Behalf of Incompetents: Substituted Judgment in Medical Decisionmaking for Incompetent Persons: *In re Storar,*" *Wisconsin Law Review,* 1982 (1982), pp. 1173–1198; and Donald J. Hermann, "Barriers to Providing Effective Treatment: A Critique of Revision in Procedural, Substantive and Dispositional Criteria in Involuntary Civil Commitment," *Vanderbilt Law Review,* 39 (January 1986), pp. 83–106.

71. Allen et al., pp. 73–74, 236.

72. Note, "Disguised Oppression," pp. 680–681.

73. Allen et al., pp. 89, 92–93, 228–230.

74. Ibid., pp. 99–112.

75. But see Weale, pp. 164–165.

76. Mill, *Principles of Political Economy,* p. 961.

77. See Daniel Moynihan, *The Politics of Guaranteed Income* (New York: Random House, 1973), pp. 141–142, 218–220.

78. Donald V. Fandetti, "Income versus Service Strategies," *Social Work,* 17 (January 1972), pp. 87–93; Moynihan, pp. 116–124; Lester C. Thurow,

"Government Expenditures: Cash or In-Kind Aid?" *Philosophy and Public Affairs,* 6 (Summer 1976), pp. 372–375; and Weale, pp. 166–169.

79. For example, Lewis Coser, "What Do the Poor Need? (Money)," *Dissent,* 18 (October 1971), p. 488.

80. Generally, see Moynihan, pp. 17–59, 113–227; and Martha Ozawa, *Income Maintenance and Work Incentives: Toward a Synthesis* (New York: Praeger, 1982); Larry D. Singell, "A Federally Guaranteed Minimum Income: Pros and Cons," *Current History,* 65 (August 1973), pp. 62–87.

81. Thurow, pp. 372–375.

82. Mill, *On Liberty,* pp. 294–297.

83. Cf. Hess and Clark, Div. of Rhodia, Inc., v. FDA, 495 F.2d 975, 993–994 (D.C. Cir. 1974).

84. See, e.g., Brandenfels v. Heckler, 716 F. 2d 553 (9th Cir., 1983); and U.S. v. Generix Drug Corp., 460 U.S. 453 (1983). More generally, see David Boies and Paul R. Verkuil, *Public Control of Business* (Boston: Little, Brown, 1977), pp. 720–741.

85. 21 U.S.C. 301 et seq. esp. 355(d).

86. Representative Steven D. Symms (interview), "Legalize Laetrile as a Cancer Drug?" *U.S. News and World Report,* June 13, 1977, p. 51. For other evaluations, see Richard Landau, ed., *Regulating New Drugs* (Chicago: Center for Policy Study, University of Chicago, 1973).

87. Boies and Verkuil, pp. 735–736.

88. Generally, see FDA, "Laetrile: Commissioner's Decision on Status," *Federal Register,* Washington, D.C., August 5, 1977, pp. 39768–39805. The FDA case concentrated on the inefficacy of Laetrile, but more recently some evidence suggests that the drug may be harmful also.

89. Daniel B. Moscowitz, "Therapy Choice Increasingly Judged Layman's Domain," *Medical World News,* 19 (Feb. 20, 1978), p. 80.

90. FDA, "Laetrile," pp. 39803–3904.

91. Ibid.

92. Ibid., p. 39805.

93. Cf. "Ethical Dilemmas: The Laetrile Issue," *Medical Economics,* Nov. 28, 1977, pp. 162–169.

94. Without considering the ethics of paternalism, the Supreme Court has upheld the authority of the FDA to ban Laetrile even for terminal patients: see U.S. v. Rutherford, 61 L Ed 2d 68 (1979).

95. See, e.g., U.S. v. General Motors Corp., 574 F. Supp. 1047, 1049 (D.C., 1983). Also see Boies and Verkuil, pp. 719–720.

96. Chrysler Corp. v. DOT, 472 F. 2d 659 (6th Cir. 1972); and 15 U.S.C. 1397 (1974). See Comment, "Limiting the State's Police Power," pp. 605–627.

97. Kleinig (pp. 82–96) clearly distinguishes the two kinds of arguments, and concludes that paternalistic considerations "taken together" with public interest or social harm considerations would justify the laws. But he does not explain how considerations that are problematic alone become any less so in combination.

98. Ben Kelley, "Make Motorcyclists Wear Helmets?" *U.S. News and World Report,* July 18, 1977, pp. 39–40 (interview); and "Motorcycles and Public Apathy," *American Journal of Public Health,* 66 (May 1976), p. 475.

99. The paternalistic benefits of helmets are clearer. Although the claim that helmet *laws* reduce injuries has been challenged, most studies have confirmed that riders who wear helmets are less likely to suffer serious injuries and death. See Nelson S. Hartunian et al., "The Economics of Safety Deregulation: Lives and Dollars Lost Due to Repeal of Motorcycle Helmet Laws," *Journal of Health Politics, Policy and Law,* 8 (Spring 1983), pp. 76–98; and Jess F. Kraus et al., "Some Epidemiologic Features of Motorcycle Collision Injuries," *American Journal of Epidemiology,* 102 (July 1975), pp. 74–109.

100. American Motorcycle Ass'n. v. State Police, 11 Mich. App. 351, 158 N.W. ed 72, 75 (1968). Cf. Nevada v. Eighth Judicial District Court, 101 Nev. Adv. Ops. 133, 708 P. 2d 1022 (1985); Simon v. Sargent, 346 F. Supp. 277 (1972); Kingery v. Chapple, 504 P. 2d 831 (Alas. 1972); People v. Fries, 42 Ill. 2d 446, 250 N.E. 2d 149 (1969); and State ex/rel. Calvin V. Lombardi, 104 R.I. 28, 241A. 2d 625 (1968), aff'd. State v. Lombardi, 110 R.I. 776, 298 A. 2d, 141 (1972).

101. American Motorcycle Ass'n. v. State Police, 75.

102. In an effort to justify helmet laws under a "harm principle," Regan suggests that even motorcyclists who renounce their claim on society's resources still harm other people (pp. 202–205). They put other people in a position where they must undertake some burden or expense to satisfy their general moral obligation to help others in need. But to sustain his argument, Regan is ultimately forced to propose a curious theory of personal identity, according to which a motorcyclist before an accident is literally a different person from the motorcyclist after the accident.

7. The Ethics of Social Experiments

1. U.S. Department of Housing and Urban Development, Office of Policy Development and Research, *Experimental Housing Allowance Program No. A1979, Report of Findings* (Washington, D.C.: H.U.D., April 1979); Edward M. Gramlich and Patricia P. Koshel, *Educational Performance Contracting: An Evaluation of an Experiment* (Washington, D.C.: Brookings, 1975); Joseph Newhouse, *A Design for a Health Insurance Experiment* (Santa Monica, Calif.: RAND Corp., 1972); Joseph Pechman and P. Michael Timpane, eds., *Work Incentives and Income Guarantees* (Washington, D.C.: Brookings, 1975); and Manpower Demonstration Research Corporation, *Summary of Findings of National Supported Work Demonstration* (Cambridge, Mass.: Ballinger, 1980).

2. See Alice M. Rivlin, and P. Michael Timpane, eds., *Ethical and Legal Issues of Social Experimentation* (Washington, D.C.: Brookings, 1975); and Gordon Bermant et al., eds., *The Ethics of Social Intervention* (Washington, D.C.: Hemisphere Publishing, 1978).

3. Generally, see P. H. Rossi et al., "The New Jersey-Pennsylvania Income

Maintenance Experiment," in Bermant et al., pp. 245–266; and Michael Barth et al., "Policy Implications: A Positive View," in Pechman and Timpane, pp. 206–223.

4. Memorandum from William Morrill to Undersecretary of HEW, March 4, 1974. All memoranda cited here are from HEW files; copies are in the possession of the author.

5. Memorandum from Robert Carleson to The Secretary, March 12, 1974.

6. Memorandum from James S. Dwight to Nelson Sabatini, March 20, 1974.

7. Memorandum from William Morrill to the Undersecretary of HEW, April 18, 1974.

8. Memorandum from R. G. Spiegelman to Jacob Shockley, August 7, 1973.

9. Letter from Jacob Shockley to "Dear Family," State of Colorado, Department of Social Services, Denver, Colorado (n.d.).

10. Enrollment Agreement, Council for Grants to Families, Denver, Colorado (n.d.). The full text is reproduced in Amy Gutmann and Dennis Thompson, eds., *Ethics and Politics* (Chicago: Nelson-Hall, 1984), pp. 74–75.

11. Philip K. Robins and Gary L. Stieger, "The Labor Supply Response of Twenty Year Families in the Denver Income Maintenance Experiment," (Menlo Park, Calif.: SRI International, 1978). A more recent review confirms the seriousness of the error in the expansion of the sample, but nevertheless draws some conclusions about the effect of income maintenance and suggests that continuing the experiment might have yielded some useful data about single female heads of families. See Philip K. Robins and Gary L. Stieger, "An Analysis of the Labor Supply Response of Twenty-Year Families in the D.I.M.E." (Menlo Park, Calif.: SRI International, draft, April 1980).

12. Memorandum from R. G. Spiegelman/R. Emmick to Douglas Wolf/Jacob Shockley, March 20, 1979.

13. Memorandum from John Palmer to the Secretary (n.d., not transmitted).

14. Michael Barth, "Denver Income Maintenance Experiment 20-Year Sample: Background Paper" (Washington, D.C.: Department of Health, Education and Welfare, March 25, 1980).

15. Rossi et al., p. 259.

16. Compare the criteria that HEW has established to regulate the use of humans in medical experimentation: U.S. Department of Health, Education and Welfare, *The Institutional Guide to DHEW Policy on Protection of Human Subjects* (Washington, D.C.: DHEW, 1971). Also, see Robert M. Veatch, "Ethical Principles of Medical Experimentation," in Rivlin and Timpane, pp. 21–59.

17. For some recent discussions of utilitarianism, see J. J. C. Smart and Bernard Williams, *Utilitarianism: for and against* (Cambridge: Cambridge University Press, 1973); J. L. Mackie, *Ethics* (New York: Penguin, 1977), pp. 125–148; and Alan Donagan, *The Theory of Morality* (Chicago: University of Chicago Press, 1977), pp. 172–209.

18. Michael Barth et al., pp. 214–215.

19. D. N. Kershaw, "Comments," in Rivlin and Timpane, p. 63.

20. Thomas C. Schelling, "General Comments," in Rivlin and Timpane, p. 168.

21. Generally, see Peter G. Brown, "Informed Consent in Social Experimentation," in Rivlin and Timpane, pp. 79–100.

22. Memorandum from Joseph Corbett to R. G. Spiegelman, August 8, 1973, p. 2.

23. Veatch, p. 64. This incident occurred in New Jersey in an earlier phase of the income maintenance experiments.

24. Brown, p. 91.

25. Cf. Rossi et al., p. 257; and Veatch, p. 65.

26. Schelling p. 174. Paternalism also arises at another point in this case: HEW's decision to have the transition payments to the families decline gradually so that the families would appreciate the fact that the program would end soon. Thus allegedly "for their own good" the families received even less than they otherwise would have. More generally, on the justifiability of paternalism, see pp. 154–161, 170–172.

27. This seems clear in the series of memoranda from R. G. Spiegelman and Joseph Corbett at MPR, Robert Williams at Mathematica, and Shockley during July 1974.

28. Cf. Brown, p. 99; and Joseph Newhouse, "Comments," in Rivlin and Timpane, p. 103.

29. On the moral foundations of promises, see David Hume, *Treatise of Human Nature,* ed. L. A. Selby-Bigge (Oxford: Oxford University Press, 1960), bk. III, pt. II, sec. v; Immanuel Kant, *Foundations of the Metaphysics of Morals,* trans. Lewis Beck White (Indianapolis: Bobbs-Merrill, 1959), esp. pp. 40–41; Henry Sidgwick, *The Methods of Ethics* (London: Macmillan, 1962), pp. 303–311; H. A. Prichard, *Moral Obligation* (Oxford: Oxford University Press, 1949), pp. 169–179; John Rawls, *A Theory of Justice* (Cambridge, Mass.: Harvard University Press, 1971), pp. 344–348; and Charles Fried, *Contract as Promise* (Cambridge, Mass.: Harvard University Press, 1981).

30. Fried challenges the view that the moral foundation of promising is reliance (pp. 4–5, 7–27). Fried's own view, which founds the promise on the expectations it creates, might seem to establish a stonger basis for the claim of the families. They would not have to show that they suffered harm from relying on the promise. But when circumstances change as much as in this case, Fried's view seems to imply that no promise exists because the parties could not have intended it to apply in the new circumstances (cf. pp. 59–60, 67). For the view that Fried criticizes and which would better support the analysis of DIME given here, see Patrick Atiyah, *The Rise and Fall of Freedom of Contract* (Oxford: Oxford University Press, 1979).

31. Neil MacCormick, "Voluntary Obligations and Normative Powers," *Proceedings of the Aristotelian Society,* supp. vol. 46 (July 1972), pp. 64, 73.

32. Letter from Thomas Harper to DIME families, January 31, 1979 (letterhead: Council for Grants to Families).

33. See Sidgwick, pp. 306–307.

34. Cf. Immanuel Kant, "On the Supposed Right to Lie from Altruistic Motives," in *Critique of Practical Reason,* ed. Lewis White Beck (Chicago: University of Chicago Press, 1949), pp. 346–350.

Credits

Permission to use in revised form some of my own previously published work has been kindly granted by:

The American Political Science Association, publisher of the *American Political Science Review*, in which most of chapter 2 appeared as the "Moral Responsibility of Public Officials: The Problem of Many Hands," 74 (December 1980), pp. 905–916;

Harvard University Press, publisher of *Public Duties: The Moral Obligations of Government Officials*, edited by Joel Fleishman et al. (Cambridge, Mass., 1981), in which most of chapter 5 appeared as "The Private Lives of Public Officials," pp. 221–247;

The John F. Kennedy School of Government, Harvard University, publisher of *Public Policy*, in which chapter 7 appeared as "The Ethics of Social Experimentation: The Case of the DIME," 29 (Summer 1981), pp. 369–398;

The Hastings Center—Institute of Society, Ethics and the Life Sciences, owner of the copyright of *Representation and Responsibility*, edited by Daniel Callahan and Bruce Jennings (New York: Plenum Press, 1985), in which parts of chapter 4 appeared as "The Theory of Legislative Ethics," pp. 167–195; and *Ethics Teaching in Higher Education*, edited by Daniel Callahan and Sissela Bok (New York: Plenum Press, 1980), in which a different version of chapter 6 appeared as "Paternalism in Medicine, Law and Public Policy," pp. 245–301;

New York University Press, publisher of *Criminal Justice*, Nomos XXVII, edited by J. Roland Pennock and John Chapman (New York, 1984), in which chapter 3 appeared as "Criminal Responsibility of Government," pp. 201–240;

Princeton University Press, publisher of *Philosophy and Public Affairs*, in which several paragraphs of chapter 1 appeared in "Philosophy and Policy," 14 (Spring 1985), pp. 205–218; and also the publisher of *Democracy and the Welfare State*, edited by Amy Gutmann (Princeton, forthcoming), in which part of chapter 4 appears as "Representatives in the Welfare State";

The University of Chicago Press, publisher of *Ethics*, in which part of chapter 2 appeared as "Ascribing Responsibility to Advisers in Government," 93 (April 1983), pp. 546–560.

Index

English law, 83–84
Entrapment, 27
Environmental Protection Agency (EPA), 86, 144–145
Epstein, Benjamin R., 234n33
Epstein, Richard A., 223n90
Equality, 26, 91–92, 115, 125, 126, 130, 150, 162. *See also* Democracy; Justice; Representation
Ethics, 1, 2, 3, 11, 15, 58, 96, 124, 163, 167, 180. *See also* Moral philosophy; Moral responsibility; Political ethics; Public morality
Ethics committees, 169
Ethics in Government Act, 82, 94
Excuses: of officials, 48–50, 52, 53, 56–57. *See also* Compulsion; Ignorance
Executives, 29, 41, 82, 85, 87, 131–132. *See also* Administrators; Officials

Faden, Alan and Ruth, 244n65
Family life: of officials, 134–135, 139–140
Fandetti, Donald V., 244n78
FBI. *See* Federal Bureau of Investigation
FDA. *See* Food and Drug Administration
Federal Bureau of Investigation (FBI), 27, 62, 92, 93
Federal Election Campaign Act (1971), 115
Feinberg, Joel, 210nn2, 3, 212nn20, 24, 213n35, 214n49, 217n2, 220n38, 238n4, 239n14, 240nn16, 19, 22
Feiveson, H. A., 210n60
Feldstein, Donald, 243n55
Fenno, Richard F., 110, 225n8, 227n20, 228nn30, 35, 36, 40
Ferster, Alyce Z., 244n70
Fielding, Henry, 69, 140
Financial disclosure. *See* Disclosure, of finances
Finn, Paul, 218n12, 219n27
Fiorina, Morris, 228n40, 229n41, 230n57, 231nn73, 74
Flash, Edward S., Jr., 214n54
Fleishman, Joel, 210n1, 230n59
Fletcher, George P., 218n6, 219n18
Food and Drug Administration (FDA), 50, 72, 81, 173–174
Forster, Arnold, 234n33

Franck, Thomas, 212n22, 213n36, 215n61
Frankel, Charles, 50–51
Frankel, Marvin E., 242n45
Frankena, W. K., 227n21
Frankfurt, Harry G., 212n29
Freedman, Benjamin, 242n41
French law, 69
French, Peter A., 212n20, 218n4, 220nn31, 34, 38
Freund, Paul A., 234n27
Fried, Charles, 215nn65, 66, 67, 216n71, 232n9, 233n20, 242n46, 243n62, 248nn29, 30
Friedlander, Saul, 213n37
Friedman, Howard M., 221n45, 223n87
Functionalist ethics, 99–102, 104

Gauthier, David, 209n52
Gaylin, Wilard, 243n55
Generality, 26–29, 31, 32, 105–111, 117–118
George, Alexander, 215n58
Gerstein, Kurt, 51
Gert, Bernard, 239n8, 240n19
Getz, Robert S., 225n5
Gilpin, Robert, 214n53
Glasser, Ira, 242n50
Glover, Jonathan, 207n22, 213n30
Goffman, Erving, 126, 234n22
Goldman, Alan H., 206n12, 227n19
Goodin, Robert, 231n72
Gough, J. W., 222n62
Governmental advisers: responsibility of, 52–57
Governmental crime. *See* Official crime
Gramlich, Edward M., 246n1
Gravel, Mike, 31
Gray, L. Patrick, 62
Gray, W. Robert, 222n67
Greenwood, Ernest, 241nn33, 34
Gross, Hyman, 218nn6, 11, 219n22
Guardianship law, 169–170
Guilt: of officials, 13, 16, 68, 140, 199. *See also* Responsibility
Gutmann, Amy, 239n5

Haiman, Franklyn S., 231n1
Halberstam, David, 207nn28, 30
Halperin, Morton H., 141, 214n54

Harvard University Press is a member of Green Press Initiative (greenpressinitiative.org), a nonprofit organization working to help publishers and printers increase their use of recycled paper and decrease their use of fiber derived from endangered forests. This book was printed on recycled paper containing 30% post-consumer waste and processed chlorine free.